Math

Lesson Guide

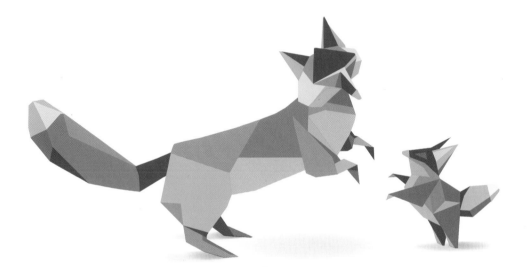

Book Staff and Contributors

Lisa White *Lead Content Specialist*
Megan Simmons *Content Specialist*
Lauralyn Vaughn *Manager, Instructional Design*
Maureen Steddin *Text Editor*
Tricia Battipede *Senior Creative Manager*
Jayoung Cho *Senior Visual Designer*
Caitlin Gildrien *Visual Designer*
Sheila Smith *Cover Designer*
Deborah Benton, Dana Crisafulli, Alisa Steel *Writers*
Amy Eward *Senior Manager, Writing and Editing*
Abhilasha Parakh *Senior Project Manager*

Doug McCollum *Senior Vice President, Product Development*
Kristin Morrison *Vice President, Design, Creative, and UX*
Kelly Engel *Senior Director, Curriculum*
Christopher Frescholtz *Senior Director, Program Management*
Erica Castle *Director, Creative Services*
Lisa Dimaio Iekel *Senior Production Manager*

Illustrations Credits

All illustrations © Stride, Inc. unless otherwise noted.
Characters: Tommy DiGiovanni, Matt Fedor, Ben Gamache, Shannon Palmer
Cover: Fox. © cavemanboon/Getty Images; Fox pup. © DenisProduction.com/Shutterstock; Pastel wallpaper patterns. © mxtama/iStock.
Interior Pattern: Pastel wallpaper patterns. © mxtama/iStock.

At Stride, Inc. (NYSE: LRN)—formerly K12 Inc.—we are reimagining lifelong learning as a rich, deeply personal experience that prepares learners for tomorrow. Since its inception, Stride has been committed to removing barriers that impact academic equity and to providing high-quality education for anyone—particularly those in underserved communities. The company has transformed the teaching and learning experience for millions of people by providing innovative, high-quality, tech-enabled education solutions, curriculum, and programs directly to students, schools, the military, and enterprises in primary, secondary, and post-secondary settings. Stride is a premier provider of K-12 education for students, schools, and districts, including career learning services through middle and high school curriculum. Providing a solution to the widening skills gap in the workplace and student loan crisis, Stride equips students with real world skills for in-demand jobs with career learning. For adult learners, Stride delivers professional skills training in healthcare and technology, as well as staffing and talent development for Fortune 500 companies. Stride has delivered millions of courses over the past decade and serves learners in all 50 states and more than 100 countries. The company is a proud sponsor of the Future of School, a nonprofit organization dedicated to closing the gap between the pace of technology and the pace of change in education. More information can be found at stridelearning.com, K12.com, destinationsacademy.com, galvanize.com, techelevator.com, and medcerts.com.

ISBN: 978-1-60153-602-0

Printed by Walsworth, Marceline, MO, USA, April 2022.

Table of Contents

K12 Summit Math 3 Overview x

How to Use This Guide xxiii

Patterns and Number Sense

Number Sense (A) 2

Number Sense (B) 5

Number Sense (C) 8

Number Sense (D) 10

Compare and Order Numbers (A) 12

Compare and Order Numbers (B) 15

Compare and Order Numbers (C) 18

Compare and Order Numbers (D) 20

Rounding Numbers (A) 22

Rounding Numbers (B) 25

Rounding Numbers (C) 28

Rounding Numbers (D) 31

Rounding Numbers (E) 33

Big Ideas: Mini-Project 35

Addition and Subtraction Strategies

Estimation (A) 38

Estimation (B) 41

Estimation (C) 44

Strategies for Exact Sums and Differences (A) 46

Strategies for Exact Sums and Differences (B) 49

Strategies for Exact Sums and Differences (C) 52

Strategies for Exact Sums and Differences (D) 54

Using a Standard Addition Algorithm (A) 56

Using a Standard Addition Algorithm (B) 59

Using a Standard Addition Algorithm (C) 62

Using a Standard Addition Algorithm (D) 65

Using a Standard Subtraction Algorithm (A) 67

Using a Standard Subtraction Algorithm (B) 69

Using a Standard Subtraction Algorithm (C) 71

Using a Standard Subtraction Algorithm (D) 73

Using a Standard Subtraction Algorithm (E) 76

Perimeter (A) 78

Perimeter (B) 81

Perimeter (C) 83

Perimeter (D) 85

Big Ideas: Extended Problems 87

Exploring Multiplication

Skip Counting Patterns (A) 90

Skip Counting Patterns (B) 93

Skip Counting Patterns (C) 96

Skip Counting Patterns (D) 98

Equal Groups (A) 100

Equal Groups (B) 103

Equal Groups (C) 106

Equal Groups (D) 109

Multiples of 10 and 5 (A) 111

Multiples of 10 and 5 (B) 113

Multiples of 10 and 5 (C) 115

Big Ideas: Mini-Project 117

Multiplication Properties and Strategies

Multiplication Patterns (A) 120

Multiplication Patterns (B) 123

Multiplication Patterns (C) 126

Multiplication Patterns (D) 128

Multiplication Patterns (E) 130

Strategies for Multiplying (A) 132

Strategies for Multiplying (B) **134**

Strategies for Multiplying (C) **137**

Strategies for Multiplying (D) **139**

Strategies for Multiplying (E) **142**

Problem Solving with Multiplication (A) **144**

Problem Solving with Multiplication (B) **146**

Problem Solving with Multiplication (C) **148**

Problem Solving with Multiplication (D) **151**

Big Ideas: Extended Problems **153**

Exploring Division

Division Concepts (A) **156**

Division Concepts (B) **159**

Division Concepts (C) **161**

Division Concepts (D) **164**

Division Concepts (E) **167**

Division Patterns (A) **169**

Division Patterns (B) **172**

Division Patterns (C) **174**

Division Patterns (D) **176**

Big Ideas: Mini-Project **178**

Division Equations and Strategies

Division Equations (A) **180**

Division Equations (B) **183**

Division Equations (C) **186**

Division Equations (D) **189**

Division Equations (E) **191**

Problem Solving with Division (A) **193**

Problem Solving with Division (B) **195**

Problem Solving with Division (C) **197**

Problem Solving with Division (D) **200**

Big Ideas: Extended Problems **202**

Shapes

Exploring Shapes and Shared Attributes (A) 204

Exploring Shapes and Shared Attributes (B) 206

Exploring Shapes and Shared Attributes (C) 209

Exploring Shapes and Shared Attributes (D) 211

Exploring Shapes and Shared Attributes (E) 213

Polygons (A) 215

Polygons (B) 217

Polygons (C) 219

Quadrilaterals (A) 221

Quadrilaterals (B) 224

Quadrilaterals (C) 226

Quadrilaterals (D) 228

Big Ideas: Challenge Problems 230

Geometric Measurement: Area

Area Concepts (A) 232

Area Concepts (B) 234

Area Concepts (C) 236

Measuring and Calculating Area (A) 238

Measuring and Calculating Area (B) 240

Measuring and Calculating Area (C) 243

Measuring and Calculating Area (D) 246

Applying Formulas and Properties (A) 248

Applying Formulas and Properties (B) 250

Applying Formulas and Properties (C) 252

Applying Formulas and Properties (D) 254

Applying Formulas and Properties (E) 257

Applying Formulas and Properties (F) 260

Big Ideas: Extended Problems 262

Fractions

Unit Fractions (A)...264

Unit Fractions (B)...267

Unit Fractions (C)...269

Unit Fractions (D)...271

Non-Unit Fractions (A)...273

Non-Unit Fractions (B)...276

Non-Unit Fractions (C)...278

Non-Unit Fractions (D)...280

Non-Unit Fractions (E)...282

Reasoning with Fractions (A).....................................284

Reasoning with Fractions (B).....................................286

Reasoning with Fractions (C).....................................288

Reasoning with Fractions (D).....................................291

Big Ideas: Challenge Problems....................................293

Equivalent Fractions and Comparisons

Fraction Equivalence (A)...296

Fraction Equivalence (B)...299

Fraction Equivalence (C)...301

Fraction Equivalence (D)...304

Fraction Equivalence (E)...306

Fractions and Whole Numbers (A)..................................308

Fractions and Whole Numbers (B)..................................311

Fractions and Whole Numbers (C)..................................314

Compare Fractions (A)..316

Compare Fractions (B)..319

Compare Fractions (C)..322

Big Ideas: Extended Problems.....................................324

Measurement: Time and Length

Clock Time and Units of Time (A) 326

Clock Time and Units of Time (B) 329

Clock Time and Units of Time (C) 332

Clock Time and Units of Time (D) 334

Clock Time and Units of Time (E) 336

Measuring Length (A) 338

Measuring Length (B) 341

Measuring Length (C) 343

Measuring Length (D) 345

Big Ideas: Mini-Project 347

Measurement: Liquid Volume and Mass

Liquid Volume (A) 350

Liquid Volume (B) 353

Liquid Volume (C) 355

Liquid Volume (D) 358

Mass (A) 360

Mass (B) 363

Mass (C) 365

Mass (D) 367

Big Ideas: Mini-Project 368

Data Displays

Picture and Bar Graphs (A) 370

Picture and Bar Graphs (B) 373

Picture and Bar Graphs (C) 376

Picture and Bar Graphs (D) 379

Picture and Bar Graphs (E) 381

Line Plots (A) **383**

Line Plots (B) **385**

Line Plots (C) **387**

Line Plots (D) **389**

Big Ideas: Extended Problems **390**

End-of-Year Project

End-of-Year Project **392**

K12 Summit Math 3 Overview

Welcome to Summit Math 3! We're grateful for this opportunity to play a role in your students' math education. We've provided the following overview of the content and structure of the course so that you can best support your students. At any time, if you have questions or would like further clarification, never hesitate to reach out to us. Let's get started!

Summit Math 3 encourages students to learn independently. As a Learning Coach, your role is to support and enhance the learning experience. Each lesson includes rich interactivity to ensure students build the depth of understanding they need to succeed on state assessments. Online interactions provide a wealth of data, so teachers know exactly where students are struggling. Additionally, the offline practice, during which students write directly in an Activity Book, offers variety. With rich content designed to engage and motivate students, and enough practice to reinforce each concept, Summit Math 3 includes the tools and technology that students need to succeed in math.

Course Components

Online Lessons

The online lessons provide the core instruction and multiple opportunities for practice in Summit Math 3. The online lessons include

- A predictable lesson structure
- Interactive **problems** and assessments that challenge students to use higher-order thinking skills
- A carefully thought-out progression from guided to independent practice
- Computer-scored practice with instant and meaningful feedback
- Learning experiences that support struggling students

- Explanations and exploratory interactions that support deep understanding, coupled with enough practice to build speed and accuracy
- Frequent practice with math facts, including games to engage and motivate students
- Student-friendly learning goals

In addition to the online lessons, rich print materials support learning.

Lesson Guide

Each course is accompanied by a Lesson Guide that makes it quick and easy for Learning Coaches to understand each lesson at a glance—without logging in. The Lesson Guide provides an overview of a lesson's content, activities, and materials; answer keys for Activity Book pages; alerts when special Learning Coach attention is needed; and other features to aid the Learning Coach in supporting students.

Activity Book

Summit Math 3 includes an Activity Book where students can put pencil to paper every instructional day. Key features include

- Full color pages with adequate space for answers
- Problems that require students to draw sketches, show problem-solving steps, evaluate answers, and write explanations
- Step-by-step problems that prepare students for the independent practice problems

Additional Supplied Materials

K12 supplies a base-10 blocks set, which is valuable for modeling place value and basic operations, and a set of dimension tiles that students can use to explore shapes.

Also Needed

Students should obtain a binder or spiral notebook to use as their Math Notebook, in which they can work problems, make sketches, and take notes as they work through a lesson. Students should always have paper and a pencil handy.

Other common items that may be useful for some lessons include a ruler and scissors.

Course Structure

Summit Math 3 is designed to lead students through a logical sequence of concepts based on current state and national academic standards. The material is structured to fit a typical, 180-day school year, but it can also be easily adapted to fit individual needs.

Summit Math 3 is divided into **units**. A typical unit is divided into a series of related **concepts**, which are in turn divided into **daily lessons**. The final lesson in each concept includes a review of the concept and a **Concept Quiz**. A separate, **Big Ideas lesson** synthesizes the course content and appears at the end of the unit.

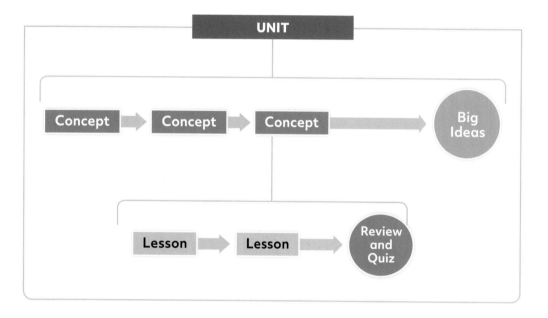

Lesson Model Overview

Concepts in Summit Math 3 follow a multiday learning cycle consisting of an initial lesson, one or more middle lessons, and a final lesson, each of which follows a consistent, predictable instructional formula.

INITIAL AND MIDDLE DAYS

During the initial and middle days, students learn and practice the core content. As students work through these lessons, they are asked to work more and more independently. They progress from concrete explorations and explicit instruction, through guided practice, to independent practice and application.

FINAL DAY

The final day of each concept includes practice problems that prepare students for the Concept Quiz. The Concept Quiz is computer graded and is based on the concept's key objectives. Students will also have an opportunity to practice in Stride on final days. Stride is a dynamic teaching tool that guides students to practice where they need it most.

		Initial Day	Middle Days	Final Day
GET READY				
	Get Ready activities introduce and orient students to the lesson content.	Lesson Introduction/ Hook	Lesson Introduction	Lesson Introduction
		Look Back	Math Facts	
LEARN AND TRY IT				
	Learn and **Try It** activities include multiple cycles of bite-sized instruction coupled with guided practice. The multiple cycles are followed by independent practice problems.	**LEARN**	**LEARN**	**TRY IT** Review
		TRY IT Guided	**TRY IT** Guided	
		TRY IT Independent	**TRY IT** Independent	
QUIZ				
				Concept Quiz
WRAP-UP				
	Wrap-Up activities include one or two ungraded questions that gauge student understanding as they exit the lesson or a graded quiz on the final day of each concept.	**WRAP-UP** Formative Assessment	**WRAP-UP** Formative Assessment	**STRIDE**

Activity Descriptions

This table briefly describes specific activity types in Summit Math 3.

GET READY	Description
Lesson Introduction	The Lesson Introduction introduces the content of the lesson within an engaging context. It also presents the objectives as student-friendly goals, defines any new keywords that students will encounter in the lesson, and lists the relevant state academic standards covered in the lesson.
Look Back	The Look Back is a quick review of prerequisite skills that are essential to understanding the new concept. Students who struggle with the Look Back should seek additional help before proceeding.
Math Facts	A Math Facts practice provides independent practice of math facts. Students build speed and accuracy through interactive online questions and games.
LEARN AND TRY IT	**Description**
Learn	All initial and middle days include one or more bite-sized Learn and Try It cycles. These activities include a variety of approaches, including guided explorations and explicit instruction. Some particularly difficult concepts are explained in a video that features an expert teacher.
Try It (Guided)	Each Learn activity is followed by a short, guided Try It that allows students to immediately apply the concepts they have just learned. All problems include feedback based on student answers as well as complete solutions. The guided Try Its prepare students for the independent practice.

LEARN AND TRY IT	Description
Try It (Guided with Remediation)	Lessons with particularly important concepts include Try Its with branching pathways for struggling students. The questions in this activity are designed to uncover and correct misconceptions and common errors. As students work through the problem set, they receive targeted feedback depending on how they answer the questions. Struggling students are then guided through a reteaching activity to dispel the misconception or correct the common error.
Try It (Independent)	All initial and middle days include an independent Try It. The independent practice has two parts: an online part and an offline part. The independent online practice problems are like the types of problems students will encounter in the Concept Quiz. The offline problems are found in the student Activity Book.
Try It (Review)	The final day of each concept includes a Try It that is designed to prepare students for the Concept Quiz. The review includes online interactive problems, which are sometimes in the form of a game.
WRAP-UP	**Description**
Formative Assessment	Initial and middle days end with a short check-in that includes one or two ungraded questions that gauge students' understanding at the end of the lesson. Although the questions are ungraded, the results are available to teachers.
Stride	Final days end with independent practice in Stride.

A Balance of Online and Offline Time

Summit Math 3 online activities make up about 75 percent of core lesson time. However, equally critical to learning is that students practice working out math calculations by hand. Summit Math 3 incorporates a daily offline activity in a predictable place within each lesson sequence. In the last Try It activity of each lesson day, after completing online practice in which instant feedback can help address any misunderstandings, students work out related problems in their Activity Book.

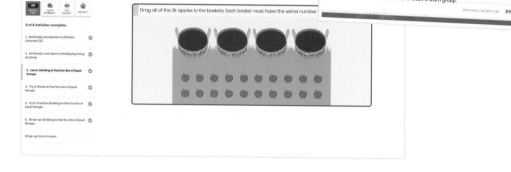

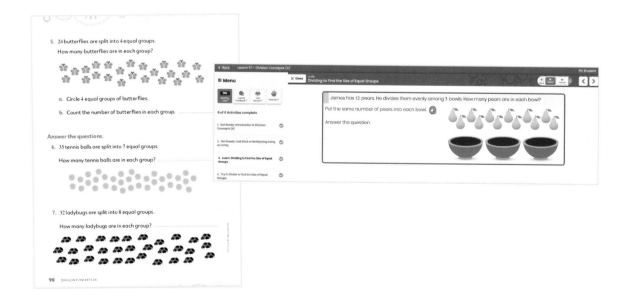

Special Features

In addition to the standard units and lessons, Summit Math 3 has these special features.

Big Ideas Lessons

Big Ideas lessons occur at the end of most units. In these lessons, students complete an assignment that gauges their ability to synthesize content and use higher-order thinking skills, such as analysis, evaluation, complex problem solving, and creativity. These assignments prepare students for the types of questions they will encounter on state assessments.

There are three types of Big Ideas lessons, which vary in the type of assignment students complete:

- Extended Problems
- Mini-Project
- Challenge Problems

Note: The Extended Problems are intended to be used as graded assessments that should contribute a significant number of points toward students' grades.

Instant Recall: Facts Fluency

Students need to be able to recall addition, subtraction, multiplication, and division facts quickly and accurately. Summit Math 3 includes cycles of practice that look at specific sets of facts. There are three types of Math Facts practice:

1. Matching problems to provide scaffolding as students build familiarity
2. A set of fill-in-the-blank problems for the student to build mastery
3. A game for students to continue to practice automatic recall of facts in a fun way

Game-Like Embedded Practice

Repetition is an important part of building speed and accuracy. However, students must be motivated to practice in a variety of ways. Built-in games engage students to spend sufficient time practicing until key math tasks become natural and automatic.

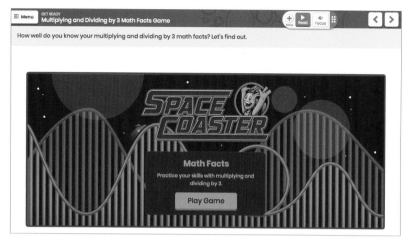

Virtual Manipulatives

Virtual manipulatives are digital versions of physical objects you might typically see in a math classroom. These highly interactive experiences allow students to play with and explore mathematical concepts. Virtual manipulatives provided in Summit Math 3 include

- Fraction Strips
- Pattern Blocks
- Base-10 Blocks

All explorations with virtual manipulatives are followed by direct explanations to ensure that students grasp the critical concepts. A version of these activities using printable or tactile manipulatives is available for students who need or prefer an offline version.

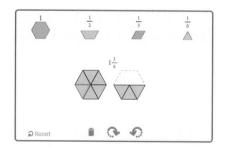

Pattern Blocks

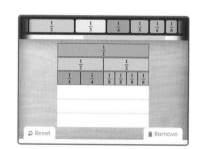

Fraction Strips

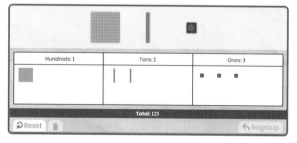

Base-10 Blocks

End-of-Year Project

The end-of-year project is an extended, inquiry-based activity that is designed to build a deeper understanding of mathematics. Students use critical thinking skills and creativity as they explore an authentic, real-world problem. The project cuts across curricular areas, showing the impact and relevance of math while building twenty-first-century skills.

The project is structured around a question that is both engaging and relevant to students and their community. To find answers to the question, students will apply the mathematics they already know and then expand their knowledge to fill in the gaps. Students create and submit a final product that demonstrates what they have learned.

Assessment Overview

To ensure students can show what they have learned and to support high academic outcomes, students need exposure to the types questions they will see on state assessments.

Online Interactive Questions

Online interactive questions, similar in style and format to today's digital state assessments, provide powerful opportunities for students to demonstrate deep understanding. For this reason, a variety of online question types, including drag and drop and fill in the blank, are used throughout Summit Math 3.

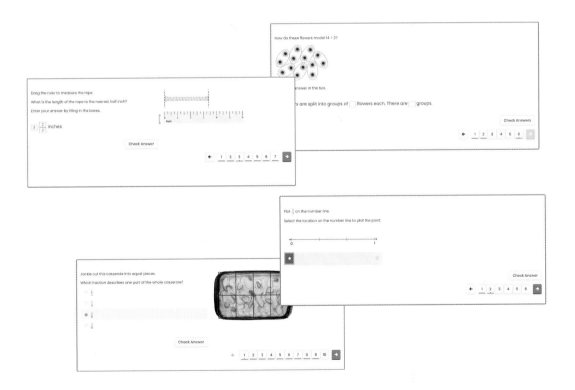

Graded Assessments

Summit Math 3 includes quizzes at the end of each concept, as well as teacher-graded assignments within Big Ideas lessons. Students are also asked to complete an in-depth project at the end of the year.

Assessment Type	How Many?
Concept Quiz	36
Big Ideas: Extended Problems	6
Big Ideas: Mini-Project	5
Mid-Year Assessment	1
End-of-Year Project	1
End-of-Year Assessment	1

Instructional Approach

Building Balanced Understanding and Efficiency

For a long period of time, most math instruction focused strictly on how—not why—to perform calculations. Summit Math 3 balances conceptual instruction and exploration to explain the why, with procedural practice designed to move students toward speed and accuracy. As you look across a lesson, a concept, and even a unit, you will see a careful progression in which students first use models to grasp why the math works, and then move toward more efficient methods of solving problems.

Conceptual Explorations

Conceptual Explanations

Procedural Explanations

Making Math Relevant with Real-World, Concrete Examples

Summit Math 3 intentionally progresses from concrete, real-world scenarios and models, to visual models, and finally to abstracted math to build a depth of knowledge.

From Concrete

To Abstract

Content Focus

- Students develop speed and accuracy with addition and subtraction by using estimation, number lines, compatible numbers, and basic number properties. Students also use standard algorithms to add and subtract vertically to 1,000 with and without regrouping.

- Students develop a greater understanding of single-digit multiplication and division with single-digit divisors through equal-sized groups, arrays, skip counting patterns, repeated subtraction, and the relationship between multiplication and division. Students develop fluency by practicing multiplication and division facts throughout the course.

- Students are introduced to fractions by exploring parts of shapes and sets and locations on number lines. Students reason with fractions and understand that the size of a fractional part is relative to the size of the whole. They learn to compare fractions with the same denominator and same numerator, and represent equivalent fractions with and without visual models. Students are also introduced to improper fractions and mixed numbers.

- Students explore the concept of area in rectangles and in figures that can be divided into more than one rectangle. They find the area of rectangles by tiling with unit squares and by using formulas.

Individualized Learning

Summit Math 3 is designed to help all students succeed.

Branching Pathways are practice problems for particularly difficult concepts to support struggling students. These problems are designed to uncover misconceptions and common errors. Students receive feedback targeted to their individual responses and are then led through a reteaching activity that corrects the misconception or common error, only if needed. Branching Pathways create a "tighter net" that catches struggling students at the point of instruction.

Stride is an engaging teaching tool that motivates students toward mastery and rewards learning with games. Following each Concept Quiz, students will practice related concepts based on their specific needs. Time to use Stride is integrated right into the course to ensure sufficient independent practice time.

Stride's adaptive technology guides students to practice where they need it most— and then serves a variety of content that's lively and engaging. Stride's vast database of questions, problems, video lessons, and printable resources deliver grade-level appropriate content aligned to the rigor of the Common Core and individual state standards. Stride's assessments identify where students are performing on specific grade-level standards throughout the year and help identify critical foundational gaps missed in prior grade levels. Test prep capabilities pinpoint student strengths and weaknesses for improved student outcomes on end-of-year assessments.

The Help Me button, which is located on the lesson menu, is an additional personalization feature that lets students opt into activities that are dynamically chosen based on the concept they are studying. Recommendations are powered by a sophisticated engine designed to serve up the activities most likely to be effective for individual students.

How to Use This Guide

The Lesson Guide contains information that will be helpful to you as you begin Summit Math 3 and daily as you work through the program. Here is what the Lesson Guide contains and how to use it.

Lesson Title

The title indicates the lesson topic and matches the title you will see in the online course.

Lesson Overview Table

This table has an overview of the lesson's activities, their approximate times, and whether they take place offline or online.

Content Background

This information will help you better understand the content students will be learning.

Materials

This box lists all materials needed for the lesson and indicates whether they are Supplied or Also Needed.

Keywords

The definitions of key terminology specific to the lesson are here.

Lesson Goals

The goals indicate what students will do in the lesson.

Activities

Each lesson is broken down into two or more main sections: Get Ready, Learn and Try It, Concept Quiz (final days only), and Wrap-Up. Each section is broken down into individual activities. A brief explanation of each activity is included.

Answer Keys

The Lesson Guide includes answer keys for Activity Book pages.

Lessons with Graded Assessments

Check in with students when a lesson has a graded assessment.

- The final lesson of every concept has a computer-scored quiz. Check to make sure students have completed and submitted the Concept Quiz.

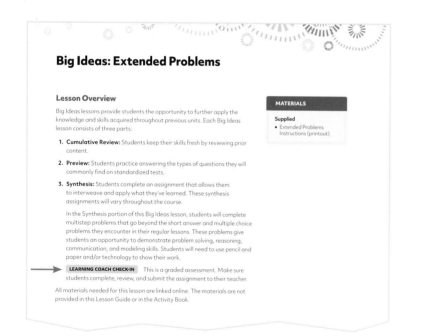

- Big Ideas lessons and the end-of-year project lesson have teacher-graded assignments. Students will complete and turn in the Extended Problems and Mini-Projects in the Big Ideas lessons, plus a project in the last lesson of the course. Teachers will grade these based on a standard rubric. Learning Coaches may need to help students submit their assignments to their teachers. Discuss the best method of turning in work with your students' teachers.

Remember

Academic support at home is critical to student success. While Summit Math 3 empowers students to work independently, this guide is designed help you support your students each day to help them maximize learning.

Patterns
and
Number Sense

Number Sense (A)

Lesson Overview

ACTIVITY	ACTIVITY TITLE	TIME	ONLINE/OFFLINE
GET READY	Introduction to Number Sense (A)	**2** minutes	🖥️
	Look Back at Place Value	**8** minutes	🖥️
LEARN AND **TRY IT**	Writing Number Names from Standard Form	**7** minutes	🖥️
	Write Number Names from Standard Form	**7** minutes	🖥️
	Writing Numbers in Standard Form from Number Names	**7** minutes	🖥️
	Write Numbers in Standard Form from Number Names	**7** minutes	🖥️
	Practice Writing Number Names and Numbers in Standard Form	**20** minutes	🖥️ and 📄
WRAP-UP	Writing Number Names and Numbers in Standard Form	**2** minutes	🖥️

Content Background

Students will write numbers with words and with digits. The math term *digit* refers to any of the numbers 0 through 9 when they appear within another number. A number represented by digits is in standard form. A number represented by words is in word form, which is also called a number name.

Students often struggle to understand the value of each digit in a number. They may incorrectly say that the greatest digit in a number has the greatest value. The place where a digit is located is its place value. A place-value chart can help students understand the value of each digit in a number. Write the number name for 472 using the place-value chart.

Ones		
hundreds	tens	ones
4	7	2

The digit 4 has a value of four hundred. The digit 7 has a value of seventy. The digit 2 has a value of 2 ones, or two. Combine the values of all the digits to write the number name: 472 is four hundred seventy-two.

MATERIALS

Supplied
- *Summit Math 3 Activity Book:* Practice Writing Number Names and Numbers in Standard Form

KEYWORDS

standard form – the usual way of writing a number by using digits

Lesson Goals

- Write a number using words.
- Write a number word using digits.

GET READY

Introduction to Number Sense (A)

After a quick introductory activity, students will read the lesson goals and keywords. Have students select each keyword and preview its definition.

Look Back at Place Value

Students will practice the prerequisite skill of understanding place value.

LEARN AND TRY IT

LEARN   Writing Number Names from Standard Form

Students will learn to write number names from numbers in standard form.

TIP   Remind students not to use the word *and* in their number names. Eventually students will learn that *and* indicates the fraction or decimal part of a number.

TRY IT   Write Number Names from Standard Form

Students will practice writing number names from numbers in standard form. Support will be provided to help students overcome misconceptions.

LEARN   Writing Numbers in Standard Form from Number Names

Students will learn to write numbers in standard form from number names.

TRY IT   Write Numbers in Standard Form from Number Names

Students will practice writing numbers in standard form from number names. Support will be provided to help students overcome misconceptions.

TRY IT   Practice Writing Number Names and Numbers in Standard Form

Students will complete online practice problems. Then they will complete Practice Writing Number Names and Numbers in Standard Form from *Summit Math 3 Activity Book.*

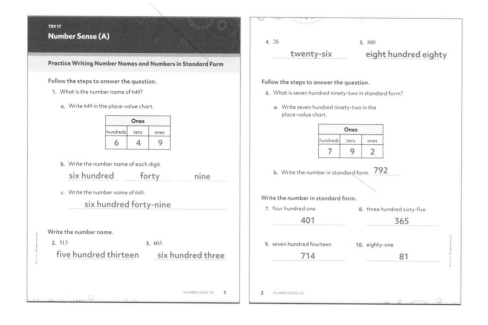

WRAP-UP

Writing Number Names and Numbers in Standard Form

Students will solve a problem to show that they understand how to write number names and numbers in standard form.

Number Sense (B)

Lesson Overview

ACTIVITY	ACTIVITY TITLE	TIME	ONLINE/OFFLINE
GET READY	Introduction to Number Sense (B)	**2** minutes	🖥️
	Adding and Subtracting 1, 2, and 3 Math Facts	**8** minutes	🖥️
LEARN AND **TRY IT**	Writing Numbers in Expanded Form from Standard Form	**7** minutes	🖥️
	Write Numbers in Expanded Form from Standard Form	**7** minutes	🖥️
	Writing Numbers in Standard Form from Expanded Form	**7** minutes	🖥️
	Write Numbers in Standard Form from Expanded Form	**7** minutes	🖥️
	Practice Writing Numbers in Standard Form and Expanded Form	**20** minutes	🖥️ and 📄
WRAP-UP	Writing Numbers in Standard Form and Expanded Form	**2** minutes	🖥️

Content Background

Students will learn to write numbers in expanded form from standard form. The expanded form of a number is the sum of the values of each digit. Students can use base-10 blocks or a place-value chart to write the expanded form of a number.

You can use a place-value chart to find the expanded form of the number 507.

Ones		
hundreds	tens	ones
5	0	7

The number 507 has 5 hundreds and 7 ones, so the expanded form of 507 is 500 + 7. Notice that 0 tens are not included in the expanded form of 507. A place value of 0 need not be included in the expanded form of a number. To go from expanded form to standard form, simply add the values in the expression.

MATERIALS

Supplied
- *Summit Math 3 Activity Book:* Practice Writing Numbers in Standard Form and Expanded Form

KEYWORDS

expanded form – a way to write a number that shows the place value of each of its digits; for example, 543 = 500 + 40 + 3, or 5 hundreds + 4 tens + 3 ones

standard form – the usual way of writing a number by using digits

Lesson Goals

- Write numbers in standard form.
- Write numbers in expanded form.

Introduction to Number Sense (B)

Students will get a glimpse of what they will learn about in the lesson. They will also read the lesson goals and keywords. Have students select each keyword and preview its definition.

Adding and Subtracting 1, 2, and 3 Math Facts

Students will practice adding and subtracting 1, 2, and 3.

LEARN AND TRY IT

LEARN Writing Numbers in Expanded Form from Standard Form

Students will learn to write numbers in expanded form from standard form.

TRY IT Write Numbers in Expanded Form from Standard Form

Students will practice writing numbers in expanded form from standard form. Support will be provided to help students overcome misconceptions.

LEARN Writing Numbers in Standard Form from Expanded Form

Students will learn to write numbers in standard form from expanded form.

TRY IT Write Numbers in Standard Form from Expanded Form

Students will practice writing numbers in standard form from expanded form. Support will be provided to help students overcome misconceptions.

TRY IT Practice Writing Numbers in Standard Form and Expanded Form

Students will complete online practice problems. Then they will complete Practice Writing Numbers in Standard Form and Expanded Form from *Summit Math 3 Activity Book*.

TRY IT
Number Sense (B)

Practice Writing Numbers in Standard Form and Expanded Form

Follow the steps to answer the question.

1. What is 388 in expanded form?

   a. Write 388 in the place-value chart.

Ones		
hundreds	tens	ones
3	8	8

   b. Write the value of each digit in standard form.

   300   80   8

   c. Write the expanded form of 388. $300 + 80 + 8$

Write the number in expanded form.

2. 903   3. 678

   $900 + 3$ $600 + 70 + 8$

NUMBER SENSE (B)   **3**

---

4. 24   5. 414

   $20 + 4$ $400 + 10 + 4$

Follow the steps to answer the question.

6. $400 + 90 + 4$

   a. Write $400 + 90 + 4$ in the place-value chart.

Ones		
hundreds	tens	ones
4	9	4

   b. Write the standard form of $400 + 90 + 4$.   494

Write the number in standard form.

7. $600 + 1$ 8. $500 + 90$

   601   590

9. $300 + 20 + 8$ 10. $300 + 40 + 9$

   328   349

4   NUMBER SENSE (B)

WRAP-UP

Writing Numbers in Standard Form and Expanded Form

Students will solve a problem to show that they understand how to write numbers in standard form and expanded form.

Number Sense (C)

Lesson Overview

ACTIVITY	ACTIVITY TITLE	TIME	ONLINE/OFFLINE
GET READY	Introduction to Number Sense (C)	**2** minutes	🖥️
	Adding and Subtracting 1, 2, and 3 with Instant Recall	**8** minutes	🖥️
LEARN AND **TRY IT**	Solving Problems with Numbers in Different Forms	**15** minutes	🖥️
	Solve Problems with Numbers in Different Forms	**10** minutes	🖥️
	Practice Solving Problems with Numbers in Different Forms	**20** minutes	🖥️ and 📄
WRAP-UP	Solving Problems with Numbers in Different Forms	**5** minutes	🖥️

Content Background

Students will learn to solve problems with numbers in different forms. Encourage students to continue to use a place-value chart to understand the value of each digit in a number. The place-value chart can be used to write numbers in standard form, expanded form, or in words.

MATERIALS

Supplied

- *Summit Math 3 Activity Book:* Practice Solving Problems with Numbers in Different Forms

Lesson Goals

- Solve problems with numbers in standard form, word form, or expanded form.

GET READY

Introduction to Number Sense (C)

Students will get a glimpse of what they will learn about in the lesson. They will also read the lesson goals.

Adding and Subtracting 1, 2, and 3 with Instant Recall

Students will practice adding and subtracting 1, 2, and 3.

LEARN   Solving Problems with Numbers in Different Forms

Students will learn to solve problems with numbers in different forms.

TRY IT   Solve Problems with Numbers in Different Forms

Students will practice solving problems with numbers in different forms. Support will be provided to help students overcome misconceptions.

TRY IT   Practice Solving Problems with Numbers in Different Forms

Students will complete online practice problems. Then they will complete Practice Solving Problems with Numbers in Different Forms from *Summit Math 3 Activity Book*.

TRY IT
Number Sense (C)

Practice Solving Problems with Numbers in Different Forms

Three friends play a beanbag game. Each beanbag scores 1, 10, or 100 points depending on where it lands.

Follow the steps to answer the questions.

1. James lands 3 beanbags in the 100-point area, 4 beanbags in the 10-point area, and 1 beanbag in the 1-point area.

   How many points does James score in all?

   a. Write James's score in expanded form. $300 + 40 + 1$

   b. Write James's score in standard form.   341

   c. James tells his friends his score.

      Write the number name that James says.

      three hundred forty-one

NUMBER SENSE (C)   **5**

---

2. Jessica lands 5 beanbags in the 100-point area, 1 beanbag in the 10-point area, and 2 beanbags in the 1-point area.

   How many points does Jessica score in all?

   a. Write Jessica's score in expanded form. $500 + 10 + 2$

   b. Write Jessica's score in standard form.   512

   c. Jessica tells her friends her score.

      Write the number name that Jessica says.

      five hundred twelve

3. Juan lands 3 beanbags in the 100-point area, 0 beanbags in the 10-point area, and 5 beanbags in the 1-point area.

   How many points does Juan score in all?

   a. Write Juan's score in expanded form. $300 + 5$

   b. Write Juan's score in standard form.   305

   c. Juan tells his friends his score.

      Write the number name that Juan says.

      three hundred five

6   NUMBER SENSE (C)

Solving Problems with Numbers in Different Forms

Students will solve a problem to show that they understand how to solve problems with numbers in different forms.

Number Sense (D)

Lesson Overview

ACTIVITY	ACTIVITY TITLE	TIME	ONLINE/OFFLINE
GET READY	Introduction to Number Sense (D)	**2** minutes	🖥️
TRY IT	Review Number Sense	**18** minutes	🖥️
QUIZ	Number Sense	**25** minutes	🖥️
WRAP-UP	More Math Practice	**15** minutes	🖥️

Lesson Goals

- Review the word form, standard form, and expanded form of a number.
- Take a quiz.

MATERIALS

There are no materials to gather for this lesson.

GET READY

Introduction to Number Sense (D)

Students will read the lesson goals.

TRY IT

Review Number Sense

Students will answer questions to review what they have learned about number sense.

QUIZ

Number Sense

Students will complete the Number Sense quiz.

More Math Practice

Students will practice skills according to their individual needs.

Compare and Order Numbers (A)

Lesson Overview

ACTIVITY	ACTIVITY TITLE	TIME	ONLINE/OFFLINE
GET READY	Introduction to Compare and Order Numbers (A)	**2** minutes	🖥️
	Look Back at Counting to 1,000	**8** minutes	🖥️
LEARN AND **TRY IT**	Using Number Lines to Compare Numbers	**7** minutes	🖥️
	Use Number Lines to Compare Numbers	**7** minutes	🖥️
	Using Place-Value Chart to Compare Numbers	**7** minutes	🖥️
	Use Place-Value Chart to Compare Numbers	**7** minutes	🖥️
	Practice Comparing Numbers	**20** minutes	🖥️ and 📄
WRAP-UP	Comparing Numbers	**2** minutes	🖥️

Content Background

Students will learn to use a number line and a place-value chart to compare two numbers. They will use the symbols >, <, and = to write comparison statements.

On a number line, points to the left model numbers that are lesser and points to the right model numbers that are greater. This number line shows that 241 is greater than 234, 241 > 234. You could also say that 234 is less than 241, 234 < 241.

To compare numbers using a place-value chart, compare each place from left to right. Focus on the first place value where the digits are different and compare those digits.

Ones		
hundreds	tens	ones
2	4	7
2	4	3

This place-value chart shows that 247 and 243 have the same number of hundreds and tens. Compare the digits in the ones place: 7 > 3, so 247 > 243, or 243 < 247.

TIP Every two-digit number is less than any three-digit number.

Lesson Goals

- Use a number line to compare two numbers.
- Use a place-value chart to compare two numbers.

GET READY

Introduction to Compare and Order Numbers (A)

Students will get a glimpse of what they will learn about in the lesson. They will also read the lesson goals.

Look Back at Counting to 1,000

Students will practice the prerequisite skill of counting to 1,000.

LEARN AND TRY IT

LEARN   Using Number Lines to Compare Numbers

Students will learn to use number lines to compare numbers.

TRY IT   Use Number Lines to Compare Numbers

Students will practice using number lines to compare numbers. Support will be provided to help students overcome misconceptions.

LEARN   Using Place-Value Chart to Compare Numbers

Students will learn to use a place-value chart to compare numbers.

TRY IT   Use Place-Value Chart to Compare Numbers

Students will practice using a place-value chart to compare numbers. Support will be provided to help students overcome misconceptions.

TRY IT   Practice Comparing Numbers

Students will complete online practice problems. Then they will complete Practice Comparing Numbers from *Summit Math 3 Activity Book*.

Practice Comparing Numbers

Follow the steps to compare the numbers.

1. 82 and 79

   a. Plot 82 and 79 on the number line.

   75 76 77 78 79 80 81 82 83 84 85

   b. Fill in the blanks to make the sentence true.

   82 is to the __right__ of 79, so 82 is __greater__ than 79.

   c. Write <, >, or = in each box.

   82 [>] 79   79 [<] 82

2. 43 and 46

   a. Plot 43 and 46 on the number line.

   40 41 42 43 44 45 46 47 48 49 50

   b. Write <, >, or = in each box.

   43 [<] 46   46 [>] 43

COMPARE AND ORDER NUMBERS (A)   7

---

3. 851 and 874

   a. Write both numbers in the place-value chart.

Ones		
hundreds	tens	ones
8	5	1
8	7	4

   b. Write <, >, or = in each box.

   8 hundreds [=] 8 hundreds   5 tens [<] 7 tens

   c. Write <, >, or = in each box.

   851 [<] 874   874 [>] 851

Compare the numbers. Write <, >, or = in the box.

4. 315 [>] 92   5. 508 [<] 512

6. 963 [=] 963   7. 794 [>] 791

8. 400 [>] 379   9. 672 [>] 627

10. 456 [=] 456   11. 334 [>] 332

8   COMPARE AND ORDER NUMBERS (A)

WRAP-UP

Comparing Numbers

Students will solve a problem to show that they understand how to compare numbers.

Compare and Order Numbers (B)

Lesson Overview

ACTIVITY	ACTIVITY TITLE	TIME	ONLINE/OFFLINE
GET READY	Introduction to Compare and Order Numbers (B)	**2** minutes	🖥️
	Adding and Subtracting 1, 2, and 3 Math Facts Game	**8** minutes	🖥️
LEARN AND **TRY IT**	Using Number Lines to Order Numbers	**7** minutes	🖥️
	Use Number Lines to Order Numbers	**7** minutes	🖥️
	Using Place-Value Chart to Order Numbers	**7** minutes	🖥️
	Use Place-Value Chart to Order Numbers	**7** minutes	🖥️
	Practice Ordering Numbers	**20** minutes	🖥️ and 📄
WRAP-UP	Ordering Numbers	**2** minutes	🖥️

Content Background

Students will learn to use number lines and place-value charts to order numbers.

On a number line, values to the left are lesser and values to the right are greater. This number line shows that 22 is the least value and 29 is the greatest value. The numbers on this number line, in order from greatest to least, are 29, 26, 22.

Order 102, 92, and 109 from least to greatest using a place-value chart.

Ones		
hundreds	tens	ones
1	0	2
	9	2
1	0	9

Every two-digit number is less than any three-digit number, so 92 is the least value. Both 102 and 109 have the same number of hundreds and tens. Compare the digits in the ones places of 102 and 109: 2 < 9, so 102 < 109. The numbers in order from least to greatest are 92 < 102 < 109.

MATERIALS

Supplied
- *Summit Math 3 Activity Book:* Practice Ordering Numbers

Lesson Goals

- Use a number line to order three or more numbers.

- Use a place-value chart to order three or more numbers.

Introduction to Compare and Order Numbers (B)

Students will get a glimpse of what they will learn about in the lesson. They will also read the lesson goals.

Adding and Subtracting 1, 2, and 3 Math Facts Game

Students will play a game to practice adding and subtracting 1, 2, and 3.

LEARN   Using Number Lines to Order Numbers

Students will learn to use number lines to order numbers.

TRY IT   Use Number Lines to Order Numbers

Students will practice using number lines to order numbers. Support will be provided to help students overcome misconceptions.

LEARN   Using Place-Value Chart to Order Numbers

Students will learn to use a place-value chart to order numbers.

TRY IT   Use Place-Value Chart to Order Numbers

Students will practice using a place-value chart to order numbers. Support will be provided to help students overcome misconceptions.

TRY IT   Practice Ordering Numbers

Students will complete online practice problems. Then they will complete Practice Ordering Numbers from *Summit Math 3 Activity Book*.

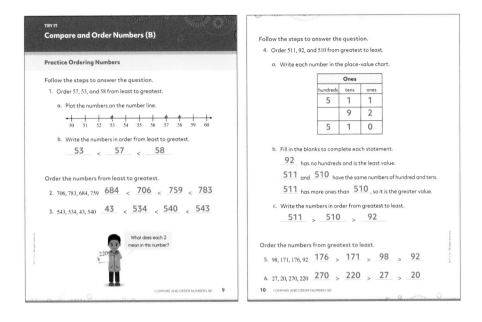

WRAP-UP

Ordering Numbers

Students will solve a problem to show that they understand how to order numbers.

Compare and Order Numbers (C)

Lesson Overview

ACTIVITY	ACTIVITY TITLE	TIME	ONLINE/OFFLINE
GET READY	Introduction to Compare and Order Numbers (C)	**2** minutes	🖥️
	Adding and Subtracting 5 and 10 Math Facts	**8** minutes	🖥️
LEARN AND **TRY IT**	Comparing and Ordering Numbers in Real-World Problems	**15** minutes	🖥️
	Compare and Order Numbers in Real-World Problems	**10** minutes	🖥️
	Practice Comparing and Ordering Numbers in Real-World Problems	**20** minutes	🖥️ and 📄
WRAP-UP	Comparing and Ordering Numbers in Real-World Problems	**5** minutes	🖥️

Content Background

Students will learn to solve real-world problems by comparing and ordering numbers. Encourage students to use a number line or a place-value chart to compare and order numbers.

Lesson Goals

- Solve real-world problems by comparing or ordering numbers.

MATERIALS

Supplied

- *Summit Math 3 Activity Book:* Practice Comparing and Ordering Numbers in Real-World Problems

GET READY

Introduction to Compare and Order Numbers (C)

Students will get a glimpse of what they will learn about in the lesson. They will also read the lesson goals.

Adding and Subtracting 5 and 10 Math Facts

Students will practice adding and subtracting 5 and 10.

LEARN AND TRY IT

LEARN   Comparing and Ordering Numbers in Real-World Problems

Students will learn to compare and order numbers in real-world problems.

TRY IT   Compare and Order Numbers in Real-World Problems

Students will practice comparing and ordering numbers in real-world problems. Support will be provided to help students overcome misconceptions.

TRY IT   Practice Comparing and Ordering Numbers in Real-World Problems

Students will complete online practice problems. Then they will complete Practice Comparing and Ordering Numbers in Real-World Problems from *Summit Math 3 Activity Book*.

TRY IT
Compare and Order Numbers (C)

Practice Comparing and Ordering Numbers in Real-World Problems

A fruit stand has these items.

Item	Amount
apricots	167
bananas	281
apples	285
peaches	164
watermelons	61

Use the table and follow the steps to answer the questions.

1. Does the fruit stand have more apricots or peaches?

    a. Plot the number of apricots and the number of peaches on the number line.

    160 161 162 163 164 165 166 167 168 169 170

    b. Compare the numbers. Write <, >, or = in the box.

    167 > 164

    c. Fill in the blank.

    The fruit stand has more **apricots**.

COMPARE AND ORDER NUMBERS (C)   11

---

2. Order the amounts of fruit from least to greatest.

    a. Write each amount of fruit in the place-value charts.

Ones		
hundreds	tens	ones
1	6	7
2	8	1

Ones		
hundreds	tens	ones
2	8	5
1	6	4

Ones		
hundreds	tens	ones
	6	1

    b. Fill in the blanks to compare the hundreds.

    ___61___ has no hundreds and is the least value.

    ___167___ and ___164___ both have ___1___ hundred.

    ___281___ and ___285___ both have ___2___ hundreds.

    c. Fill in the blanks to compare the tens.

    ___167___ and ___164___ both have ___6___ tens.

    ___281___ and ___285___ both have ___8___ tens.

    d. Fill in the blanks to compare the ones.

    ___167___ has more ones than ___164___, so it is the greater value.

    ___285___ has more ones than ___281___, so it is the greater value.

    e. Order the numbers from least to greatest.

    ___61___ < ___164___ < ___167___ < ___281___ < ___285___

12   COMPARE AND ORDER NUMBERS (C)

WRAP-UP

Comparing and Ordering Numbers in Real-World Problems

Students will solve a problem to show that they understand how to compare and order numbers in real-world problems.

Compare and Order Numbers (D)

Lesson Overview

ACTIVITY	ACTIVITY TITLE	TIME	ONLINE/OFFLINE
GET READY	Introduction to Compare and Order Numbers (D)	**2** minutes	🖥
TRY IT	Review Compare and Order Numbers	**18** minutes	🖥
QUIZ	Compare and Order Numbers	**25** minutes	🖥
WRAP-UP	More Math Practice	**15** minutes	🖥

Lesson Goals

- Review using number lines and place-value charts to compare numbers, order three or more numbers, and solve real-world problems.

- Take a quiz.

MATERIALS

There are no materials to gather for this lesson.

GET READY

Introduction to Compare and Order Numbers (D)
Students will read the lesson goals.

TRY IT

Review Compare and Order Numbers
Students will answer questions to review what they have learned about comparing and ordering numbers.

QUIZ

Compare and Order Numbers
Students will complete the Compare and Order Numbers quiz.

More Math Practice

Students will practice skills according to their individual needs.

Rounding Numbers (A)

Lesson Overview

ACTIVITY	ACTIVITY TITLE	TIME	ONLINE/OFFLINE
GET READY	Introduction to Rounding Numbers (A)	**2** minutes	🖥️
	Look Back at Place Value in 3-Digit Numbers	**8** minutes	🖥️
LEARN AND **TRY IT**	Using a Number Line to Round a 2-Digit Number to Nearest 10	**7** minutes	🖥️
	Use a Number Line to Round a 2-Digit Number to Nearest 10	**7** minutes	🖥️
	Using Place Value to Round a 2-Digit Number to Nearest 10	**7** minutes	🖥️
	Use Place Value to Round a 2-Digit Number to Nearest 10	**7** minutes	🖥️
	Practice Rounding a 2-Digit Number to Nearest 10	**20** minutes	🖥️ and 📄
WRAP-UP	Rounding a 2-Digit Number to Nearest 10	**2** minutes	🖥️

Content Background

Students will learn to round a two-digit number to the nearest ten. Rounding is a way to estimate a number. To round to the nearest ten means to give the ten that is the *closest* to a number. Students will use number lines and place-value charts to build an understanding of the rules of rounding. Every number falls between two tens. One is lower than the number while the other is higher. For example, 72 is between 70 and 80. Encourage students to identify the two closest tens.

Students will learn that the digit in the ones place is used to determine whether to round up or down to the nearest ten. Digits less than 5 round down. Digits 5 or greater round up. For example, the ones place of 72 is 2, which is less than 5, so 72 rounds down to 70.

Lesson Goals
- Round a two-digit number to the nearest ten.

MATERIALS

Supplied
- *Summit Math 3 Activity Book:* Practice Rounding a 2-Digit Number to Nearest 10

KEYWORDS

round (v.) – to change a number to the nearest place value asked in a problem; for example, rounding 532 to the nearest ten would be 530

Introduction to Rounding Numbers (A)

Students will get a glimpse of what they will learn about in the lesson. They will also read the lesson goals and keywords. Have students select each keyword and preview its definition.

Look Back at Place Value in 3-Digit Numbers

Students will practice the prerequisite skill of understanding place value in three-digit numbers.

LEARN AND TRY IT

LEARN   Using a Number Line to Round a 2-Digit Number to Nearest 10

Students will learn to use a number line to round a two-digit number to the nearest ten.

TRY IT   Use a Number Line to Round a 2-Digit Number to Nearest 10

Students will practice using a number line to round a two-digit number to the nearest ten. Support will be provided to help students overcome misconceptions.

LEARN   Using Place Value to Round a 2-Digit Number to Nearest 10

Students will learn to use place value to round a two-digit number to the nearest ten.

TRY IT   Use Place Value to Round a 2-Digit Number to Nearest 10

Students will practice using place value to round a two-digit number to the nearest ten. Support will be provided to help students overcome misconceptions.

TRY IT   Practice Rounding a 2-Digit Number to Nearest 10

Students will complete online practice problems. Then they will complete Practice Rounding a 2-Digit Number to Nearest 10 from *Summit Math 3 Activity Book.*

WRAP-UP

Rounding a 2-Digit Number to Nearest 10

Students will solve a problem to show that they understand how to round a two-digit number to the nearest ten.

Rounding Numbers (B)

Lesson Overview

ACTIVITY	ACTIVITY TITLE	TIME	ONLINE/OFFLINE
GET READY	Introduction to Rounding Numbers (B)	**2** minutes	🖥️
	Adding and Subtracting 5 and 10 with Instant Recall	**8** minutes	🖥️
LEARN AND **TRY IT**	Using a Number Line to Round a 3-Digit Number to Nearest 100	**7** minutes	🖥️
	Use a Number Line to Round a 3-Digit Number to Nearest 100	**7** minutes	🖥️
	Using Place Value to Round a 3-Digit Number to Nearest 100	**7** minutes	🖥️
	Use Place Value to Round a 3-Digit Number to Nearest 100	**7** minutes	🖥️
	Practice Rounding a 3-Digit Number to Nearest 100	**20** minutes	🖥️ and 📄
WRAP-UP	Rounding a 3-Digit Number to Nearest 100	**2** minutes	🖥️

Content Background

Students will learn to round a three-digit number to the nearest hundred. To round to the nearest hundred means to give the hundred that is the *closest* to a number. Every number on a number line falls between two hundreds. One is lower than the number while the other is higher. For example, 582 is between 500 and 600. Encourage students to identify the two closest hundreds.

Students will learn that the digit in the tens place is used to round up or down to the nearest hundred. The same rounding rules apply. Digits less than 5 round down. Digits 5 or greater round up. For example, the tens place of 582 is 8, which is greater than 5, so 582 rounds up to 600.

Lesson Goals
- Round a three-digit number to the nearest hundred.

MATERIALS

Supplied
- *Summit Math 3 Activity Book:* Practice Rounding a 3-Digit Number to Nearest 100

KEYWORDS

round (v.) – to change a number to the nearest place value asked in a problem; for example, rounding 532 to the nearest ten would be 530

Introduction to Rounding Numbers (B)

Students will get a glimpse of what they will learn about in the lesson. They will also read the lesson goals and keywords. Have students select each keyword and preview its definition.

Adding and Subtracting 5 and 10 with Instant Recall

Students will practice adding and subtracting 5 and 10.

LEARN AND TRY IT

LEARN   Using a Number Line to Round a 3-Digit Number to Nearest 100

Students will learn to use a number line to round a three-digit number to the nearest hundred.

TRY IT   Use a Number Line to Round a 3-Digit Number to Nearest 100

Students will practice using a number line to round a three-digit number to the nearest hundred. Support will be provided to help students overcome misconceptions.

LEARN   Using Place Value to Round a 3-Digit Number to Nearest 100

Students will learn to use place value to round a three-digit number to the nearest hundred.

TRY IT   Use Place Value to Round a 3-Digit Number to Nearest 100

Students will practice using place value to round a three-digit number to the nearest hundred. Support will be provided to help students overcome misconceptions.

TRY IT   Practice Rounding a 3-Digit Number to Nearest 100

Students will complete online practice problems. Then they will complete Practice Rounding a 3-Digit Number to Nearest 100 from *Summit Math 3 Activity Book*.

TRY IT
Rounding Numbers (B)

Practice Rounding a 3-Digit Number to Nearest 100

Follow the steps to answer the questions.

1. What is 143 rounded to the nearest hundred?

   a. Plot 143 on the number line.

   b. Fill in the blanks.

   143 is between __100__ and __200__.

   143 is closer to __100__, so 143 rounds to __100__.

2. What is 850 rounded to the nearest hundred?

   a. Write 850 in the place-value chart.

Ones		
hundreds	tens	ones
8	5	0

ROUNDING NUMBERS (B)   **15**

b. Fill in the blanks.

850 is between __800__ and __900__.

Use the __tens__ place to round to the nearest hundred.

The digit __5__ rounds __up__.

850 rounds to __900__.

Round to the nearest hundred.

3. 652 __700__   4. 719 __700__

5. 949 __900__   6. 150 __200__

7. 406 __400__   8. 245 __200__

9. 350 __400__   10. 117 __100__

16   ROUNDING NUMBERS (B)

WRAP-UP

Rounding a 3-Digit Number to Nearest 100

Students will solve a problem to show that they understand how to round a three-digit number to the nearest hundred.

Rounding Numbers (C)

Lesson Overview

ACTIVITY	ACTIVITY TITLE	TIME	ONLINE/OFFLINE
GET READY	Introduction to Rounding Numbers (C)	**2** minutes	🖥️
	Adding and Subtracting 5 and 10 Math Facts Game	**8** minutes	🖥️
LEARN AND **TRY IT**	Using a Number Line to Round a 3-Digit Number to Nearest 10	**7** minutes	🖥️
	Use a Number Line to Round a 3-Digit Number to Nearest 10	**7** minutes	🖥️
	Using Place Value to Round a 3-Digit Number to Nearest 10	**7** minutes	🖥️
	Use Place Value to Round a 3-Digit Number to Nearest 10	**7** minutes	🖥️
	Practice Rounding a 3-Digit Number to Nearest 10	**20** minutes	🖥️ and 📄
WRAP-UP	Rounding a 3-Digit Number to Nearest 10	**2** minutes	🖥️

Content Background

Students will round a three-digit number to the nearest ten. The rules for rounding a number to the nearest ten are the same regardless of how many digits a number has. However, some students find it difficult to identify which tens a number falls between when the number goes to the hundreds place. For example, a student might incorrectly say that 697 is between 690 and 710. Although this is a true statement, 700 is the ten that is closest to 697. Remind students that a hundred is also a ten.

Lesson Goals

- Round a three-digit number to the nearest ten.

MATERIALS

Supplied

- *Summit Math 3 Activity Book:* Practice Rounding a 3-Digit Number to Nearest 10

KEYWORDS

round (v.) – to change a number to the nearest place value asked in a problem; for example, rounding 532 to the nearest ten would be 530

GET READY

Introduction to Rounding Numbers (C)

Students will get a glimpse of what they will learn about in the lesson. They will also read the lesson goals and keywords. Have students select each keyword and preview its definition.

Adding and Subtracting 5 and 10 Math Facts Game

Students will play a game to practice adding and subtracting 5 and 10.

LEARN AND TRY IT

LEARN Using a Number Line to Round a 3-Digit Number to Nearest 10

Students will learn to use a number line to round a three-digit number to the nearest ten.

TRY IT Use a Number Line to Round a 3-Digit Number to Nearest 10

Students will practice using a number line to round a three-digit number to the nearest ten. Support will be provided to help students overcome misconceptions.

LEARN Using Place Value to Round a 3-Digit Number to Nearest 10

Students will learn to use place value to round a three-digit number to the nearest ten.

TRY IT Use Place Value to Round a 3-Digit Number to Nearest 10

Students will practice using place value to round a three-digit number to the nearest ten. Support will be provided to help students overcome misconceptions.

TRY IT Practice Rounding a 3-Digit Number to Nearest 10

Students will complete online practice problems. Then they will complete Practice Rounding a 3-Digit Number to Nearest 10 from *Summit Math 3 Activity Book*.

Rounding a 3-Digit Number to Nearest 10

Students will solve a problem to show that they understand how to round a three-digit number to the nearest ten.

Rounding Numbers (D)

Lesson Overview

ACTIVITY	ACTIVITY TITLE	TIME	ONLINE/OFFLINE
GET READY	Introduction to Rounding Numbers (D)	**2** minutes	🖥️
	Adding and Subtracting 4 and 6 Math Facts	**8** minutes	🖥️
LEARN AND **TRY IT**	Rounding in Real-World Problems	**15** minutes	🖥️
	Round in Real-World Problems	**10** minutes	🖥️
	Practice Rounding in Real-World Problems	**20** minutes	🖥️ and 📄
WRAP-UP	Rounding in Real-World Problems	**5** minutes	🖥️

Content Background

Students will learn to round numbers in real-world problems. If needed, use a number line or a place-value chart to determine whether to round to the ten or hundred before the number or the ten or hundred after the number.

TIP   If the digit to the right of the rounding place is less than 5, round down. If the digit to the right of the rounding place is greater than or equal to 5, round up.

Lesson Goals

- Solve real-world problems using rounding.

MATERIALS

Supplied
- *Summit Math 3 Activity Book:* Practice Rounding in Real-World Problems

KEYWORDS

round (v.) – to change a number to the nearest place value asked in a problem; for example, rounding 532 to the nearest ten would be 530

GET READY

Introduction to Rounding Numbers (D)
Students will get a glimpse of what they will learn about in the lesson. They will also read the lesson goals and keywords. Have students select each keyword and preview its definition.

Adding and Subtracting 4 and 6 Math Facts
Students will practice adding and subtracting 4 and 6.

LEARN   Rounding in Real-World Problems

Students will learn to round in real-world problems.

TRY IT   Round in Real-World Problems

Students will practice rounding in real-world problems. Support will be provided to help students overcome misconceptions.

TRY IT   Practice Rounding in Real-World Problems

Students will complete online practice problems. Then they will complete Practice Rounding in Real-World Problems from *Summit Math 3 Activity Book*.

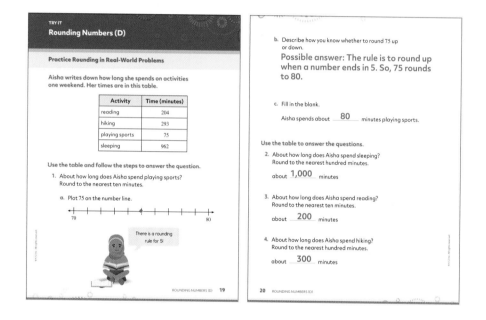

Rounding in Real-World Problems

Students will solve a problem to show that they understand how to round in real-world problems.

Rounding Numbers (E)

Lesson Overview

ACTIVITY	ACTIVITY TITLE	TIME	ONLINE/OFFLINE
GET READY	Introduction to Rounding Numbers (E)	**2** minutes	🖥️
TRY IT	Review Rounding Numbers	**18** minutes	🖥️
QUIZ	Rounding Numbers	**25** minutes	🖥️
WRAP-UP	More Math Practice	**15** minutes	🖥️

Lesson Goals

- Review rounding to the nearest ten or hundred, and rounding to solve real-world problems.

- Take a quiz.

MATERIALS

There are no materials to gather for this lesson.

GET READY

Introduction to Rounding Numbers (E)

Students will read the lesson goals.

TRY IT

Review Rounding Numbers

Students will answer questions to review what they have learned about rounding numbers.

QUIZ

Rounding Numbers

Students will complete the Rounding Numbers quiz.

More Math Practice

Students will practice skills according to their individual needs.

Big Ideas: Mini-Project

Lesson Overview

Big Ideas lessons provide students the opportunity to further apply the knowledge and skills acquired throughout previous units. Each Big Ideas lesson consists of two types of activities:

1. **Cumulative Review:** Students keep their skills fresh by reviewing prior content.

2. **Synthesis:** Students complete an assignment that allows them to interweave and apply what they've learned. These synthesis assignments will vary throughout the course.

   In the Synthesis portion of this Big Ideas lesson, students will complete a small, creative project designed to tie together concepts and skills that students have encountered across units. These small projects are designed to emphasize a real-world application that connects mathematics to other subjects, including science, technology, engineering, art, and history. Students will need to use pencil and paper and/or technology to show their work.

   LEARNING COACH CHECK-IN Make sure students complete, review, and submit the assignment to their teacher.

All materials needed for this lesson are linked online. The materials are not provided in this Lesson Guide or in the Activity Book.

Supplied
- Mini-Project Instructions (printout)

Addition and
Subtraction
Strategies

Estimation (A)

Lesson Overview

ACTIVITY	ACTIVITY TITLE	TIME	ONLINE/OFFLINE
GET READY	Introduction to Estimation (A)	**2** minutes	🖥️
	Look Back at Rounding Numbers	**8** minutes	🖥️
LEARN AND **TRY IT**	Estimating Sums by Rounding	**7** minutes	🖥️
	Estimate Sums by Rounding	**7** minutes	🖥️
	Estimating Sums Using Compatible Numbers	**7** minutes	🖥️
	Estimate Sums Using Compatible Numbers	**7** minutes	🖥️
	Practice Estimating Sums	**20** minutes	🖥️ and 📄
WRAP-UP	Estimating Sums	**2** minutes	🖥️

Content Background

Students will learn to estimate a sum by rounding and by using compatible numbers. Usually, students must round or find compatible numbers for both addends to estimate a sum. A common mistake is to automatically round both numbers up or both numbers down regardless of the rounding rules. Encourage students to apply the rounding rules to each number individually.

TIP Remind students that when the digit to the right of the rounding digit is less than 5, round down; when it is 5 or greater, round up.

Compatible numbers are also known as friendly numbers. They are numbers that usually end in a 5 or 0, so they are easy to add mentally. There are often different compatible numbers for the same addends. For example, consider estimating the sum of 127 and 271. You could use 130 and 270 to get a sum of 400. You could also use multiples of 25: 125 is close to 127 and 275 is close to 271, for a sum of 400. Another estimate uses 125 and 270 for a sum of 395. Since an estimate is simply a rough calculation, there can be more than one correct answer.

MATERIALS

Supplied

- *Summit Math 3 Activity Book:* Practice Estimating Sums

Lesson Goals

- Estimate a sum using rounding.
- Estimate a sum using compatible numbers.

GET READY

Introduction to Estimation (A)

After a quick introductory activity, students will read the lesson goals and keywords. Have students select each keyword and preview its definition.

Look Back at Rounding Numbers

Students will practice the prerequisite skill of rounding two-digit numbers.

LEARN AND TRY IT

LEARN   Estimating Sums by Rounding

Students will learn to estimate sums by rounding.

TRY IT   Estimate Sums by Rounding

Students will practice estimating sums by rounding. Support will be provided to help students overcome misconceptions.

LEARN   Estimating Sums Using Compatible Numbers

Students will learn to estimate sums using compatible numbers.

TRY IT   Estimate Sums Using Compatible Numbers

Students will practice estimating sums using compatible numbers. Support will be provided to help students overcome misconceptions.

TRY IT Practice Estimating Sums

Students will complete online practice problems. Then they will complete Practice Estimating Sums from *Summit Math 3 Activity Book*.

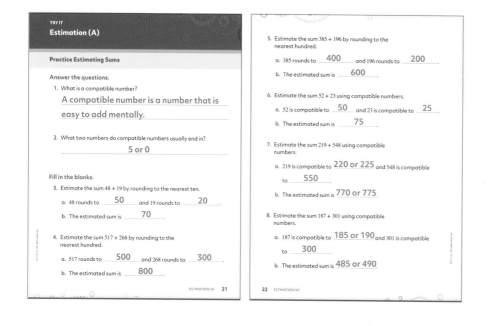

WRAP-UP

Estimating Sums

Students will solve problems to show that they understand how to estimate sums.

Estimation (B)

Lesson Overview

ACTIVITY	ACTIVITY TITLE	TIME	ONLINE/OFFLINE
GET READY	Introduction to Estimation (B)	**2** minutes	🖥️
	Adding and Subtracting 4 and 6 with Instant Recall	**8** minutes	🖥️
LEARN AND TRY IT	Estimating Differences by Rounding	**7** minutes	🖥️
	Estimate Differences by Rounding	**7** minutes	🖥️
	Estimating Differences Using Compatible Numbers	**7** minutes	🖥️
	Estimate Differences Using Compatible Numbers	**7** minutes	🖥️
	Practice Estimating Differences	**20** minutes	🖥️ and 📄
WRAP-UP	Estimating Differences	**2** minutes	🖥️

Content Background

Students will learn to estimate a difference by rounding and by using compatible numbers. An estimate is more accurate the closer a rounded or compatible number is to the original number. Sometimes compatible numbers give a better estimate, and other times rounded numbers do. Whether you round to the nearest hundred or ten can also affect an estimate's accuracy. Consider the difference of 569 and 147. Rounding to the nearest hundred gives the estimate $600 - 100 = 500$. Using compatible numbers gives the estimate $575 - 150 = 425$. And rounding to the nearest ten gives the estimate $570 - 150 = 420$. The actual difference is 422, so using compatible numbers or rounding to the nearest ten both give good estimates.

TIP Encourage students to think about which numbers will give a *good* estimate of a difference. Although they have not yet learned how to find exact sums and differences, making predictions will help them build number sense.

> ### Lesson Goals
> - Estimate a difference using rounding.
> - Estimate a difference using compatible numbers.

MATERIALS

Supplied
- *Summit Math 3 Activity Book:* Practice Estimating Differences

Introduction to Estimation (B)

Students will get a glimpse of what they will learn about in the lesson. They will also read the lesson goals and keywords. Have students select each keyword and preview its definition.

Adding and Subtracting 4 and 6 with Instant Recall

Students will practice adding and subtracting 4 and 6.

LEARN AND TRY IT

LEARN Estimating Differences by Rounding

Students will learn to estimate differences by rounding.

TRY IT Estimate Differences by Rounding

Students will practice estimating differences by rounding. Support will be provided to help students overcome misconceptions.

LEARN Estimating Differences Using Compatible Numbers

Students will learn to estimate differences using compatible numbers.

TRY IT Estimate Differences Using Compatible Numbers

Students will practice estimating differences using compatible numbers. Support will be provided to help students overcome misconceptions.

KEYWORDS

compatible numbers – numbers that are easy to compute using mental math

difference – the answer to a subtraction problem

estimate (n.) – a very good guess or rough calculation of an answer, when the exact answer is not necessary

estimate (v.) – to make a very good guess or rough calculation of an answer when the exact answer is not necessary

round (v.) – to change a number to the nearest place value asked in a problem; for example, rounding 532 to the nearest ten would be 530

TRY IT   Practice Estimating Differences

Students will complete online practice problems. Then they will complete Practice Estimating Differences from *Summit Math 3 Activity Book.*

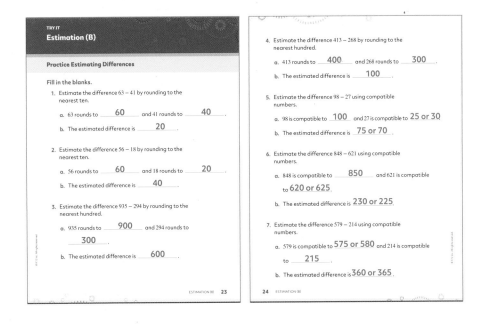

WRAP-UP

Estimating Differences

Students will solve problems to show that they understand how to estimate differences.

Estimation (C)

Lesson Overview

ACTIVITY	ACTIVITY TITLE	TIME	ONLINE/OFFLINE
GET READY	Introduction to Estimation (C)	**2** minutes	🖥️
TRY IT	Review Estimation	**18** minutes	🖥️
QUIZ	Estimation	**25** minutes	🖥️
WRAP-UP	More Math Practice	**15** minutes	🖥️

Lesson Goals

- Review estimating a sum or difference using rounding and compatible numbers.
- Take a quiz.

MATERIALS

There are no materials to gather for this lesson.

GET READY

Introduction to Estimation (C)

Students will read the lesson goals.

TRY IT

Review Estimation

Students will answer questions to review what they have learned about estimation.

QUIZ

Estimation

Students will complete the Estimation quiz.

More Math Practice

Students will practice skills according to their individual needs.

Strategies for Exact Sums and Differences (A)

Lesson Overview

ACTIVITY	ACTIVITY TITLE	TIME	ONLINE/OFFLINE
GET READY	Introduction to Strategies for Exact Sums and Differences (A)	**2** minutes	🖥️
	Look Back at Adding and Subtracting	**8** minutes	🖥️
LEARN AND **TRY IT**	Using a Number Line to Add or Subtract	**7** minutes	🖥️
	Use a Number Line to Add or Subtract	**7** minutes	🖥️
	Using Compatible Numbers to Add or Subtract	**7** minutes	🖥️
	Use Compatible Numbers to Add or Subtract	**7** minutes	🖥️
	Practice Using Strategies to Add or Subtract	**20** minutes	🖥️ and 📄
WRAP-UP	Using Strategies to Add or Subtract	**2** minutes	🖥️

Content Background

Students will learn to use a number line and compatible numbers to add and subtract. To add on a number line, plot one addend, then make a jump for each place value in the other addend. The place where you land is the sum. There are different ways to subtract on a number line. One way is to plot the minuend, then make jumps backwards for each place value in the subtrahend. The place where you land is the difference. The other method is to plot both the minuend and the subtrahend, then use jumps to find the distance between them. The distance between the numbers is the difference.

The goal of adding or subtracting with compatible numbers is to change how the numbers look, without changing the overall value, so that it is easier to add mentally. This can be a difficult concept for students because the method is slightly different depending on whether you are finding a sum or a difference. To add, value is transferred from one addend to another. For example, to add $117 + 372$, transfer 2 from 372 to 117. The result is the expression $119 + 370$, which is easier to add mentally. To subtract, value is either added to or removed from both the minuend and subtrahend. For example, to subtract $372 - 117$, add 3 to both numbers. The result is the expression $375 - 120$, which is easier to subtract mentally.

MATERIALS

Supplied

- *Summit Math 3 Activity Book:* Practice Using Strategies to Add or Subtract

Lesson Goals

- Use a number line to add or subtract.

- Use compatible, or friendly, numbers to add or subtract.

GET READY

Introduction to Strategies for Exact Sums and Differences (A)

Students will get a glimpse of what they will learn about in the lesson. They will also read the lesson goals and keywords. Have students select each keyword and preview its definition.

Look Back at Adding and Subtracting

Students will practice the prerequisite skill of adding and subtracting.

LEARN AND TRY IT

LEARN   Using a Number Line to Add or Subtract

Students will learn to use a number line to add or subtract.

TRY IT   Use a Number Line to Add or Subtract

Students will practice using a number line to add or subtract. Support will be provided to help students overcome misconceptions.

LEARN   Using Compatible Numbers to Add or Subtract

Students will learn to use compatible numbers to add or subtract.

TRY IT   Use Compatible Numbers to Add or Subtract

Students will practice using compatible numbers to add or subtract. Support will be provided to help students overcome misconceptions.

TRY IT   Practice Using Strategies to Add or Subtract

Students will complete online practice problems. Then they will complete Practice Using Strategies to Add or Subtract from *Summit Math 3 Activity Book*.

TRY IT
Strategies for Exact Sums and Differences (A)

Practice Using Strategies to Add or Subtract

Fill in the boxes and blanks.

1. Use the number line to find 354 + 123.

   a. Model the sum on the number line.

   +100   +10   +10   +3

   354   454   464   474   477

   b. 354 + 123 = 477

2. Use the number line to find 903 − 86.

   a. Model the difference on the number line.

   −3 −3 −10 −10 −10 −10 −10 −10 −10 −10

   817 820 823 833 843 853 863 873 883 893   903

   b. 903 − 86 = 817

STRATEGIES FOR EXACT SUMS AND DIFFERENCES (A)   25

3. Use compatible numbers to find 435 + 357.

   a. A good compatible number for 357 is 360.

   b. Move 3 from 435 to 357 to make the numbers compatible.

   c. The compatible numbers are 432 and 360.

   d. The sum is 792.

4. Use compatible numbers to find 698 − 282.

   a. A good compatible number for 282 is 290.

   b. Add 8 to both numbers to make them compatible.

   c. The compatible numbers are 706 and 290.

   d. The difference is 416.

Note: Students may use a number line instead of compatible numbers to support their work for
Find the sum or difference. Show your work. Problems 5-8.

5. 193 + 236 = 429
   Possible work: +229
                   200
                   229
                   429

6. 968 − 613 = 355
   Possible work: −615
                   970
                   615
                   355

7. 704 − 156 = 548
   Possible work: 708
                 − 160
                   548

8. 615 + 148 = 763
   Possible work: 613
                 + 150
                   763

26   STRATEGIES FOR EXACT SUMS AND DIFFERENCES (A)

WRAP-UP

Using Strategies to Add or Subtract

Students will solve problems to show that they understand how to use strategies to add or subtract.

Strategies for Exact Sums and Differences (B)

Lesson Overview

ACTIVITY	ACTIVITY TITLE	TIME	ONLINE/OFFLINE
GET READY	Introduction to Strategies for Exact Sums and Differences (B)	**2** minutes	🖥️
	Adding and Subtracting 4 and 6 Math Facts Game	**8** minutes	🖥️
LEARN AND **TRY IT**	Using the Identity and Commutative Properties to Add	**7** minutes	🖥️
	Use the Identity and Commutative Properties to Add	**7** minutes	🖥️
	Using the Associative Property to Add	**7** minutes	🖥️
	Use the Associative Property to Add	**7** minutes	🖥️
	Practice Using Properties to Add	**20** minutes	🖥️ and 📄
WRAP-UP	Using Properties to Add	**2** minutes	🖥️

Content Background

Students will learn to use the identity property of addition, the commutative property of addition, and the associative property of addition to add. These properties are often used together to make addition easier to complete mentally. However, before students can use the properties together, they first need to understand them as separate ideas.

Lesson Goals

- Use the identity property of addition to add.
- Use the commutative property of addition to add.
- Use the associative property of addition to add.

GET READY

Introduction to Strategies for Exact Sums and Differences (B)

Students will get a glimpse of what they will learn about in the lesson. They will also read the lesson goals and keywords. Have students select each keyword and preview its definition.

Adding and Subtracting 4 and 6 Math Facts Game

Students will practice adding and subtracting 4 and 6.

LEARN AND TRY IT

LEARN Using the Identity and Commutative Properties to Add

Students will learn to use the identity and commutative properties to add.

TRY IT Use the Identity and Commutative Properties to Add

Students will practice using the identity and commutative properties to add. Support will be provided to help students overcome misconceptions.

LEARN Using the Associative Property to Add

Students will learn to use the associative property to add.

TRY IT Use the Associative Property to Add

Students will practice using the associative property to add. Support will be provided to help students overcome misconceptions.

TRY IT Practice Using Properties to Add

Students will complete online practice problems. Then they will complete Practice Using Properties to Add from *Summit Math 3 Activity Book*.

TRY IT
Strategies for Exact Sums and Differences (B)

Practice Using Properties to Add

Fill in the blanks.

1. You can add 0 to any number using the __identity__ property of addition.

2. You can change the order of addends without changing the sum because of the __commutative__ property of addition.

3. You can group addends differently without changing the sum because of the __associative__ property of addition.

Follow the steps to find the sum.

4. 175 + 0

 a. Remember that the sum of any number and 0 is __that number__.

 b. Apply the property to add. __175__

You can use properties to add and subtract.

STRATEGIES FOR EXACT SUMS AND DIFFERENCES (B)   **27**

---

5. 53 + 89 + 47

 a. Change the order of the numbers.

 __53__ + __47__ + 89

 b. Use mental math to find the sum. __189__

6. 460 + 245 + 140

 a. Change the order of the numbers.

 __460__ + __140__ + __245__

 b. Use mental math to find the sum. __845__

7. 35 + 85 + 72

 a. Place parentheses around the two numbers that should be added first.

 $(35 + 85) + 72$

 b. Use mental math to find the sum. __192__

8. 163 + 172 + 128

 a. Place parentheses around the two numbers that should be added first.

 $163 + (172 + 128)$

 b. Use mental math to find the sum. __463__

28   STRATEGIES FOR EXACT SUMS AND DIFFERENCES (B)

Using Properties to Add

Students will solve a problem to show that they understand how to use properties to add.

Strategies for Exact Sums and Differences (C)

Lesson Overview

ACTIVITY	ACTIVITY TITLE	TIME	ONLINE/OFFLINE
GET READY	Introduction to Strategies for Exact Sums and Differences (C)	**2** minutes	🖥️
	Adding and Subtracting 7 Math Facts	**8** minutes	🖥️
LEARN AND **TRY IT**	Using the Break Apart Strategy to Add	**7** minutes	🖥️
	Use the Break Apart Strategy to Add	**7** minutes	🖥️
	Using the Break Apart Strategy to Subtract	**7** minutes	🖥️
	Use the Break Apart Strategy to Subtract	**7** minutes	🖥️
	Practice Using the Break Apart Strategy	**20** minutes	🖥️ and 📄
WRAP-UP	Using the Break Apart Strategy	**2** minutes	🖥️

Content Background

Students will learn to use the break apart strategy to add and subtract. The main idea of this strategy is to break apart numbers by place value into expanded form. This allows students to add or subtract each place value using mental math. Finally, the sum or difference is converted from expanded form to standard form.

MATERIALS

Supplied
- *Summit Math 3 Activity Book:* Practice Using the Break Apart Strategy

Lesson Goals
- Use the break apart strategy to add and subtract.

GET READY

Introduction to Strategies for Exact Sums and Differences (C)
Students will get a glimpse of what they will learn about in the lesson. They will also read the lesson goals.

Adding and Subtracting 7 Math Facts
Students will practice adding and subtracting 7.

LEARN   Using the Break Apart Strategy to Add
Students will learn to use the break apart strategy to add.

TRY IT   Use the Break Apart Strategy to Add
Students will practice using the break apart strategy to add. Support will be provided to help students overcome misconceptions.

LEARN   Using the Break Apart Strategy to Subtract
Students will learn to use the break apart strategy to subtract.

TRY IT   Use the Break Apart Strategy to Subtract
Students will practice using the break apart strategy to subtract. Support will be provided to help students overcome misconceptions.

TRY IT   Practice Using the Break Apart Strategy
Students will complete online practice problems. Then they will complete Practice Using the Break Apart Strategy from *Summit Math 3 Activity Book*.

TRY IT
Strategies for Exact Sums and Differences (C)

Practice Using the Break Apart Strategy

Follow the steps to find the sum.

1. 174 + 552

   a. Break apart each number into expanded form.

   174 = 100 + 70 + 4

   552 = 500 + 50 + 2

   b. Add each place value. Sum = 600 + 120 + 6

   c. Write the sum in standard form. Sum = 726

2. 286 + 317

   a. Break apart each number into expanded form.

   286 = 200 + 80 + 6

   317 = 300 + 10 + 7

   b. Add each place value. Sum = 500 + 90 + 13

   c. Write the sum in standard form. Sum = 603

STRATEGIES FOR EXACT SUMS AND DIFFERENCES (C)   **29**

Follow the steps to find the difference.

3. 976 − 145

   a. Break apart each number into expanded form.

   976 = 900 + 70 + 6

   145 = 100 + 40 + 5

   b. Subtract each place value.

   Difference = 800 + 30 + 1

   c. Write the difference in standard form.

   Difference = 831

4. 799 − 604

   a. Break apart each number into expanded form.

   799 = 700 + 90 + 9

   604 = 600 + 0 + 4

   b. Subtract each place value.

   Difference = 100 + 90 + 5

   c. Write the difference in standard form.

   Difference = 195

30   STRATEGIES FOR EXACT SUMS AND DIFFERENCES (C)

Using the Break Apart Strategy
Students will solve problems to show that they understand how to use the break apart strategy to add and subtract.

Strategies for Exact Sums and Differences (D)

Lesson Overview

ACTIVITY	ACTIVITY TITLE	TIME	ONLINE/OFFLINE
GET READY	Introduction to Strategies for Exact Sums and Differences (D)	**2** minutes	🖥️
TRY IT	Review Strategies for Exact Sums and Differences	**18** minutes	🖥️
QUIZ	Strategies for Exact Sums and Differences	**25** minutes	🖥️
WRAP-UP	More Math Practice	**15** minutes	🖥️

Lesson Goals

- Review using number lines, friendly numbers, properties, and the break apart strategy to add and subtract.
- Take a quiz.

MATERIALS

There are no materials to gather for this lesson.

GET READY

Introduction to Strategies for Exact Sums and Differences (D)

Students will read the lesson goals.

TRY IT

Review Strategies for Exact Sums and Differences

Students will answer questions to review what they have learned about strategies for exact sums and differences.

QUIZ

Strategies for Exact Sums and Differences

Students will complete the Strategies for Exact Sums and Differences quiz.

More Math Practice

Students will practice skills according to their individual needs.

Using a Standard Addition Algorithm (A)

Lesson Overview

ACTIVITY	ACTIVITY TITLE	TIME	ONLINE/OFFLINE
GET READY	Introduction to Using a Standard Addition Algorithm (A)	**2** minutes	🖥️
	Look Back at Identifying Place Value	**8** minutes	🖥️
LEARN AND **TRY IT**	Adding Vertically to 100 without Regrouping	**7** minutes	🖥️
	Add Vertically to 100 without Regrouping	**7** minutes	🖥️
	Adding Vertically to 100 with Regrouping	**7** minutes	🖥️
	Add Vertically to 100 with Regrouping	**7** minutes	🖥️
	Practice Adding Vertically to 100	**20** minutes	🖥️ and 📄
WRAP-UP	Adding Vertically to 100	**2** minutes	🖥️

Content Background

Students will learn how to add using the standard addition algorithm. Each addend will be a two-digit number, and sums will be 100 or less. Students should be able to use the terms *addend* and *sum* within the context of addition.

Algorithm is a mathematical term for a repeated step-by-step way to solve a problem, such as adding numbers. Regrouping is a critical component of the traditional addition algorithm. The term *regrouping* has replaced the term *carrying*.

Students will begin with sums represented in a place-value chart. This helps to reinforce mental math strategies based on place value. However, they will encounter sums without the chart. This helps students move from concrete to abstract representations.

Lesson Goals

- Add to 100 without regrouping.
- Add to 100 with regrouping.

MATERIALS

Supplied
- *Summit Math 3 Activity Book:* Practice Adding Vertically to 100

KEYWORDS

addend – one of the two or more numbers that are added to find a sum

algorithm – a step-by-step way to solve a problem

place value – the value of a digit depending on its position, or place, in a number

sum – the answer to an addition problem

Introduction to Using a Standard Addition Algorithm (A)

Students will get a glimpse of what they will learn about in the lesson. They will also read the lesson goals and keywords. Have students select each keyword and preview its definition.

Look Back at Identifying Place Value

Students will practice the prerequisite skill of identifying place value.

LEARN AND TRY IT

LEARN   Adding Vertically to 100 without Regrouping

Students will learn to add vertically to 100 without regrouping.

TRY IT   Add Vertically to 100 without Regrouping

Students will practice adding vertically to 100 without regrouping. Support will be provided to help students overcome misconceptions.

LEARN   Adding Vertically to 100 with Regrouping

Students will learn to add vertically to 100 with regrouping.

TRY IT   Add Vertically to 100 with Regrouping

Students will practice adding to 100 with regrouping. Support will be provided to help students overcome misconceptions.

TRY IT   Practice Adding Vertically to 100

Students will complete online practice problems. Then they will complete Practice Adding Vertically to 100 from *Summit Math 3 Activity Book*.

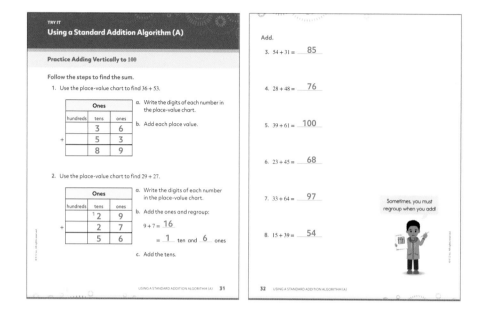

WRAP-UP

Adding Vertically to 100

Students will solve a problem to show that they understand how to add vertically up to 100.

Using a Standard Addition Algorithm (B)

Lesson Overview

ACTIVITY	ACTIVITY TITLE	TIME	ONLINE/OFFLINE
GET READY	Introduction to Using a Standard Addition Algorithm (B)	**2** minutes	🖥️
	Adding and Subtracting 7 with Instant Recall	**8** minutes	🖥️
LEARN AND **TRY IT**	Adding Vertically to 1,000 without Regrouping	**7** minutes	🖥️
	Add Vertically to 1,000 without Regrouping	**7** minutes	🖥️
	Adding Vertically to 1,000 with Regrouping	**7** minutes	🖥️
	Add Vertically to 1,000 with Regrouping	**7** minutes	🖥️
	Practice Adding Vertically to 1,000	**20** minutes	🖥️ and 📄
WRAP-UP	Adding Vertically to 1,000	**2** minutes	🖥️

Content Background

Students will continue to apply the standard addition algorithm. Addends will have one, two, or three digits, and sums will be between 100 and 1,000. At first, problems will not require regrouping, but eventually problems will require one or two regroupings. The steps of the algorithm are still the same. Encourage students to add from right to left, always beginning with the ones place.

SUPPORT   Some students automatically regroup even when it is not needed. Other students forget to regroup even when it is needed. These students may benefit from using base-10 blocks to model addition. Help students pair the base-10 model with the written representation.

> ### Lesson Goals
> - Add to 1,000 without regrouping.
> - Add to 1,000 with regrouping.

MATERIALS

Supplied
- *Summit Math 3 Activity Book:* Practice Adding Vertically to 1,000

Introduction to Using a Standard Addition Algorithm (B)

Students will get a glimpse of what they will learn about in the lesson. They will also read the lesson goals.

Adding and Subtracting 7 with Instant Recall

Students will practice adding and subtracting 7.

LEARN AND TRY IT

LEARN   Adding Vertically to 1,000 without Regrouping

Students will learn to add vertically to 1,000 without regrouping.

TRY IT   Add Vertically to 1,000 without Regrouping

Students will practice adding vertically to 1,000 without regrouping. Support will be provided to help students overcome misconceptions.

LEARN   Adding Vertically to 1,000 with Regrouping

Students will learn to add vertically to 1,000 with regrouping.

TRY IT   Add Vertically to 1,000 with Regrouping

Students will practice adding vertically to 1,000 with regrouping. Support will be provided to help students overcome misconceptions.

TRY IT   Practice Adding Vertically to 1,000

Students will complete online practice problems. Then they will complete Practice Adding Vertically to 1,000 from *Summit Math 3 Activity Book*.

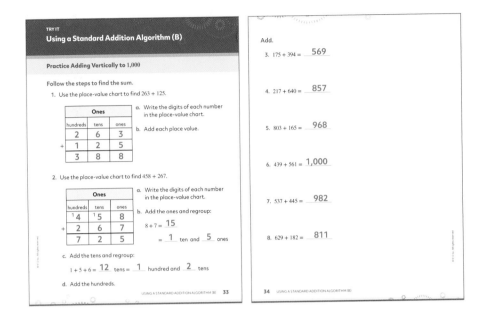

WRAP-UP

Adding Vertically to 1,000

Students will solve problems to show that they understand how to add vertically to 1,000.

Using a Standard Addition Algorithm (C)

Lesson Overview

ACTIVITY	ACTIVITY TITLE	TIME	ONLINE/OFFLINE
GET READY	Introduction to Using a Standard Addition Algorithm (C)	**2** minutes	🖥️
	Adding and Subtracting 7 Math Facts Game	**8** minutes	🖥️
LEARN AND **TRY IT**	Solving Problems with Addition	**15** minutes	🖥️
	Solve Problems with Addition	**10** minutes	🖥️
	OPTIONAL Working with Money	**7** minutes	🖥️
	OPTIONAL Work with Money	**7** minutes	🖥️
	OPTIONAL Practice Working with Money	**10** minutes	🖥️
	Practice Solving Problems with Addition	**20** minutes	🖥️ and 📄
WRAP-UP	Solving Problems with Addition	**5** minutes	🖥️

Content Background

Students will apply what they have learned about addition to solve real-world problems. Real-world addition problems fall mainly into two categories: combine problems and change problems. In combine problems, students combine two or more groups, called parts, to get a sum or total, called the whole. Encourage students to make a part-part-whole chart to organize facts in the problem and discover the relationships among the numbers. In change problems, an amount is added to or increases from a starting amount.

Students may find that using a start-change-result chart will help them understand how to write the number sentence that represents the problem. Using a chart is not necessary. But many students find it helpful to organize information and understand the problem.

MATERIALS

Supplied
- *Summit Math 3 Activity Book:* Practice Solving Problems with Addition

Lesson Goals
- Solve real-world problems by adding.

Introduction to Using a Standard Addition Algorithm (C)

Students will get a glimpse of what they will learn about in the lesson. They will also read the lesson goals.

Adding and Subtracting 7 Math Facts Game

Students will practice adding and subtracting 7.

LEARN AND TRY IT

LEARN   Solving Problems with Addition

Students will learn to solve problems with addition.

TRY IT   Solve Problems with Addition

Students will practice solving problems with addition. Support will be provided to help students overcome misconceptions.

LEARN   OPTIONAL   Working with Money

Students will learn how to represent amounts of money and solve problems by adding amounts of money. Students will be directed to complete or skip this activity by their teacher.

TRY IT   OPTIONAL   Work with Money

Students will practice representing amounts of money and solving problems by adding amounts of money. Support will be provided to help students overcome misconceptions. Students will be directed to complete or skip this activity by their teacher.

TRY IT   OPTIONAL   Practice Working with Money

Students will complete online practice problems. Students will be directed to complete or skip this activity by their teacher.

TRY IT   Practice Solving Problems with Addition

Students will complete online practice problems. Then they will complete Practice Solving Problems with Addition from *Summit Math 3 Activity Book.*

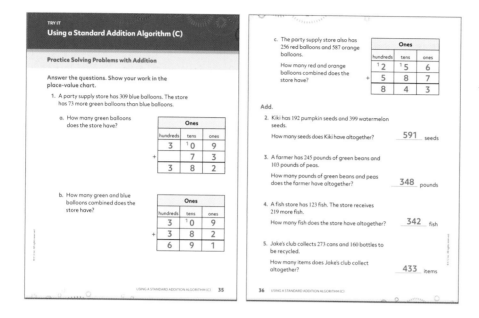

WRAP-UP

Solving Problems with Addition

Students will solve a problem to show that they understand how to solve problems with addition.

Using a Standard Addition Algorithm (D)

Lesson Overview

ACTIVITY	ACTIVITY TITLE	TIME	ONLINE/OFFLINE
GET READY	Introduction to Using a Standard Addition Algorithm (D)	**2** minutes	🖥️
TRY IT	Review Using a Standard Addition Algorithm	**18** minutes	🖥️
QUIZ	Using a Standard Addition Algorithm	**25** minutes	🖥️
WRAP-UP	More Math Practice	**15** minutes	🖥️

Lesson Goals

- Review adding to 1,000 with and without regrouping, and solving real-world problems by adding.

- Take a quiz.

MATERIALS

There are no materials to gather for this lesson.

GET READY

Introduction to Using a Standard Addition Algorithm (D)

Students will read the lesson goals.

TRY IT

Review Using a Standard Addition Algorithm

Students will answer questions to review what they have learned about using a standard addition algorithm.

QUIZ

Using a Standard Addition Algorithm

Students will complete the Using a Standard Addition Algorithm quiz.

More Math Practice

Students will practice skills according to their individual needs.

Using a Standard Subtraction Algorithm (A)

Lesson Overview

ACTIVITY	ACTIVITY TITLE	TIME	ONLINE/OFFLINE
GET READY	Introduction to Using a Standard Subtraction Algorithm (A)	**2** minutes	🖥️
	Look Back at Modeling Subtraction	**8** minutes	🖥️
LEARN AND **TRY IT**	Subtracting Vertically to 1,000 without Regrouping	**15** minutes	🖥️
	Subtract Vertically to 1,000 without Regrouping	**10** minutes	🖥️
	Practice Subtracting Vertically without Regrouping	**20** minutes	🖥️ and 📄
WRAP-UP	Subtracting Vertically without Regrouping	**5** minutes	🖥️

Content Background

Students will learn to subtract using the standard subtraction algorithm. Minuends will have two or three digits, subtrahends will have one, two, or three digits, and differences will be less than 1,000. Students should be able to use the terms *minuend*, *subtrahend*, and *difference* within the context of subtraction.

Algorithm is a mathematical term for a repeated step-by-step way to solve a problem, such as subtracting numbers. Many algorithms exist for performing any given operation. This lesson introduces students to the standard algorithm for subtracting.

Students will begin with differences represented in a place-value chart. This helps to reinforce mental math strategies based on place value. However, they will also encounter differences without the chart. This helps students move from concrete to abstract representations.

Lesson Goals
- Subtract to 1,000 without regrouping.

GET READY

Introduction to Using a Standard Subtraction Algorithm (A)
Students will get a glimpse of what they will learn about in the lesson. They will also read the lesson goals and keywords. Have students select each keyword and preview its definition.

Look Back at Modeling Subtraction

Students will practice the prerequisite skill of representing subtraction problems with models.

LEARN AND TRY IT

LEARN   Subtracting Vertically to 1,000 without Regrouping

Students will learn to subtract vertically to 1,000 without regrouping.

TRY IT   Subtract Vertically to 1,000 without Regrouping

Students will practice subtracting vertically to 1,000 without regrouping. Support will be provided to help students overcome misconceptions.

TRY IT   Practice Subtracting Vertically without Regrouping

Students will complete online practice problems. Then they will complete Practice Subtracting Vertically without Regrouping from *Summit Math 3 Activity Book*.

TRY IT
Using a Standard Subtraction Algorithm (A)

Practice Subtracting Vertically without Regrouping

Follow the steps to find the difference.

1. Use the place-value chart to find 68 – 41.

   a. Write the digits of each number in the place-value chart.

   b. Subtract each place value.

Ones		
hundreds	tens	ones
	6	8
–	4	1
	2	7

2. Use the place-value chart to find 884 – 71.

   a. Write the digits of each number in the place-value chart.

   b. Subtract each place value.

Ones		
hundreds	tens	ones
8	8	4
–	7	1
8	1	3

I always subtract from right to left!

USING A STANDARD SUBTRACTION ALGORITHM (A)   37

3. Use the place-value chart to find 537 – 123.

   a. Write the digits of each number in the place-value chart.

   b. Subtract each place value.

Ones		
hundreds	tens	ones
5	3	7
– 1	2	3
4	1	4

Subtract.

4. 87 – 25 = __62__

5. 708 – 403 = __305__

6. 592 – 71 = __521__

7. 999 – 894 = __105__

38   USING A STANDARD SUBTRACTION ALGORITHM (A)

WRAP-UP

Subtracting Vertically without Regrouping

Students will solve a problem to show that they understand how to subtract vertically without regrouping.

Using a Standard Subtraction Algorithm (B)

Lesson Overview

ACTIVITY	ACTIVITY TITLE	TIME	ONLINE/OFFLINE
GET READY	Introduction to Using a Standard Subtraction Algorithm (B)	**2** minutes	🖥️
	Adding and Subtracting 8 Math Facts	**8** minutes	🖥️
LEARN AND **TRY IT**	Subtracting Vertically to 100 with Regrouping	**15** minutes	🖥️
	Subtract Vertically to 100 with Regrouping	**10** minutes	🖥️
	Practice Subtracting Vertically to 100 with Regrouping	**20** minutes	🖥️ and 📄
WRAP-UP	Subtracting Vertically to 100 with Regrouping	**5** minutes	🖥️

Content Background

Students will continue to apply the standard subtraction algorithm. Minuends and subtrahends will have two digits, and differences will be less than 100. The differences in this lesson require students to regroup a ten into 10 ones. Regrouping is a critical component of the traditional subtraction algorithm. The term *regrouping* has replaced the term *borrowing*. Encourage students to subtract from right to left, always beginning by subtracting the ones place.

SUPPORT   Some students regroup a ten as 10 ones but forget to incorporate the previous ones. For example, students may regroup 4 tens 5 ones as 3 tens 10 ones instead of as 3 tens 15 ones. Sometimes students try to subtract the wrong way. For example, in 23 −16, 6 cannot be subtracted from 3 so they subtract 3 from 6 instead of regrouping. These students may benefit from using base-10 blocks to model regrouping. Help the students pair the base-10 model with the written representation.

MATERIALS

Supplied
- *Summit Math 3 Activity Book:* Practice Subtracting Vertically to 100 with Regrouping

Lesson Goals
- Subtract two-digit numbers with regrouping.

GET READY

Introduction to Using a Standard Subtraction Algorithm (B)
Students will get a glimpse of what they will learn about in the lesson. They will also read the lesson goals.

Adding and Subtracting 8 Math Facts

Students will practice adding and subtracting 8.

LEARN   Subtracting Vertically to 100 with Regrouping

Students will learn to subtract vertically to 100 with regrouping.

TRY IT   Subtract Vertically to 100 with Regrouping

Students will practice subtracting vertically to 100 with regrouping. Support will be provided to help students overcome misconceptions.

TRY IT   Practice Subtracting Vertically to 100 with Regrouping

Students will complete online practice problems. Then they will complete Practice Subtracting Vertically to 100 with Regrouping from *Summit Math 3 Activity Book*.

TRY IT
Using a Standard Subtraction Algorithm (B)

Practice Subtracting Vertically to 100 with Regrouping

Follow the steps to find the difference.

1. Use the place-value chart to find 74 − 25.
   a. Write the digits of each number in the place-value chart.
   b. Regroup one ten.
   c. Subtract each place value.

Ones		
hundreds	tens	ones
	6 7	14 4
−	2	5
	4	9

2. Use the place-value chart to find 86 − 28.
   a. Write the digits of each number in the place-value chart.
   b. Regroup one ten.
   c. Subtract each place value.

Ones		
hundreds	tens	ones
	7 8	16 6
−	2	8
	5	8

3. Use the place-value chart to find 60 − 14.
   a. Write the digits of each number in the place-value chart.
   b. Regroup one ten.
   c. Subtract each place value.

Ones		
hundreds	tens	ones
	5 6	10 0
−	1	4
	4	6

Subtract.

4. 51 − 37 = ___14___

5. 82 − 47 = ___35___

6. 96 − 28 = ___68___

7. 75 − 29 = ___46___

USING A STANDARD SUBTRACTION ALGORITHM (B)   39

40   USING A STANDARD SUBTRACTION ALGORITHM (B)

Subtracting Vertically to 100 with Regrouping

Students will solve a problem to show that they understand how to subtract vertically to 100 with regrouping.

Using a Standard Subtraction Algorithm (C)

Lesson Overview

ACTIVITY	ACTIVITY TITLE	TIME	ONLINE/OFFLINE
GET READY	Introduction to Using a Standard Subtraction Algorithm (C)	**2** minutes	🖥️
	Adding and Subtracting 8 with Instant Recall	**8** minutes	🖥️
LEARN AND **TRY IT**	Subtracting Vertically to 1,000 with Regrouping	**15** minutes	🖥️
	Subtract Vertically to 1,000 with Regrouping	**10** minutes	🖥️
	Practice Subtracting Vertically to 1,000 with Regrouping	**20** minutes	🖥️ and 📄
WRAP-UP	Subtracting Vertically to 1,000 with Regrouping	**5** minutes	🖥️

Content Background

Students will learn how to apply the standard subtraction algorithm to numbers with three digits. The level of difficulty changes depending on whether students must regroup once or twice to subtract. Students may regroup a hundred as 10 tens, a ten as 10 ones, or both.

SUPPORT Some students automatically regroup even when it is not needed. Other students subtract in the wrong direction rather than regroup correctly. These students may benefit from using base-10 blocks to model subtraction. Help the students pair the base-10 model with the written representation.

MATERIALS

Supplied
- *Summit Math 3 Activity Book:* Practice Subtracting Vertically to 1,000 with Regrouping

Lesson Goals
- Subtract three-digit numbers with regrouping.

GET READY

Introduction to Using a Standard Subtraction Algorithm (C)
Students will get a glimpse of what they will learn about in the lesson. They will also read the lesson goals.

Adding and Subtracting 8 with Instant Recall
Students will practice adding and subtracting 8.

LEARN Subtracting Vertically to 1,000 with Regrouping

Students will learn to subtract vertically to 1,000 with regrouping.

TRY IT Subtract Vertically to 1,000 with Regrouping

Students will practice subtracting vertically to 1,000 with regrouping. Support will be provided to help students overcome misconceptions.

TRY IT Practice Subtracting Vertically to 1,000 with Regrouping

Students will complete online practice problems. Then they will complete Practice Subtracting Vertically to 1,000 with Regrouping from *Summit Math 3 Activity Book*.

WRAP-UP

Subtracting Vertically to 1,000 with Regrouping

Students will solve a problem to show that they understand how to subtract vertically to 1,000 with regrouping.

Using a Standard Subtraction Algorithm (D)

Lesson Overview

ACTIVITY	ACTIVITY TITLE	TIME	ONLINE/OFFLINE
GET READY	Introduction to Using a Standard Subtraction Algorithm (D)	**2** minutes	🖥️
	Adding and Subtracting 8 Math Facts Game	**8** minutes	🖥️
LEARN AND **TRY IT**	Solving Problems with Subtraction	**7** minutes	🖥️
	Solve Problems with Subtraction	**7** minutes	🖥️
	Solving Problems with Addition and Subtraction	**7** minutes	🖥️
	Solve Problems with Addition and Subtraction	**7** minutes	🖥️
	OPTIONAL Solving Money Problems	**7** minutes	🖥️
	OPTIONAL Solve Money Problems	**7** minutes	🖥️
	OPTIONAL Practice Solving Money Problems	**10** minutes	🖥️
	Practice Solving Problems with Addition and Subtraction	**20** minutes	🖥️ and 📄
WRAP-UP	Solving Problems with Addition and Subtraction	**2** minutes	🖥️

Content Background

Students will apply what they have learned about subtraction to solve real-world problems. Real-world subtraction problems fall mainly into two categories: combine problems and change problems. In combine problems, students combine two or more groups, called parts, to get a sum or total, called the whole. In addition problems, students are given each part and must find the whole. Subtraction problems are different because students are given the whole and one part is unknown. Students will learn to subtract the part, or parts, from the whole in order to find the missing part. Some students find it helpful to make a part-part-whole chart to get organized.

Change problems involve a starting quantity that changes by having an amount taken away or decreasing by a certain amount. Students can make a start-change-result chart to help them understand how to write the number sentence that represents the problem. Using a chart is not necessary. But many students find it helpful to organize information and understand the problem.

Lesson Goals

- Use subtraction to solve problems.
- Use addition and subtraction to solve problems.

GET READY

Introduction to Using a Standard Subtraction Algorithm (D)

Students will get a glimpse of what they will learn about in the lesson. They will also read the lesson goals.

Adding and Subtracting 8 Math Facts Game

Students will practice adding and subtracting 8.

LEARN AND TRY IT

LEARN   Solving Problems with Subtraction

Students will learn to solve problems with subtraction.

TRY IT   Solve Problems with Subtraction

Students will practice solving problems with subtraction. Support will be provided to help students overcome misconceptions.

LEARN   Solving Problems with Addition and Subtraction

Students will learn to solve problems with addition and subtraction.

TRY IT   Solve Problems with Addition and Subtraction

Students will practice solving problems with addition and subtraction. Support will be provided to help students overcome misconceptions.

LEARN   OPTIONAL   Solving Money Problems

Students will learn how to solve problems by subtracting amounts of money. Students will be directed to complete or skip this activity by their teacher.

TRY IT   OPTIONAL   Solve Money Problems

Students will practice solving problems by subtracting amounts of money. Support will be provided to help students overcome misconceptions. Students will be directed to complete or skip this activity by their teacher.

TRY IT OPTIONAL   Practice Solving Money Problems

Students will complete online practice problems. Students will be directed to complete or skip this activity by their teacher.

TRY IT   Practice Solving Problems with Addition and Subtraction

Students will complete online practice problems. Then they will complete Practice Solving Problems with Addition and Subtraction from *Summit Math 3 Activity Book*.

WRAP-UP

Solving Problems with Addition and Subtraction

Students will solve a problem to show that they understand how to solve problems with addition and subtraction.

Using a Standard Subtraction Algorithm (E)

Lesson Overview

ACTIVITY	ACTIVITY TITLE	TIME	ONLINE/OFFLINE
GET READY	Introduction to Using a Standard Subtraction Algorithm (E)	**2** minutes	🖥
TRY IT	Review Using a Standard Subtraction Algorithm	**18** minutes	🖥
QUIZ	Using a Standard Subtraction Algorithm	**25** minutes	🖥
WRAP-UP	More Math Practice	**15** minutes	🖥

Lesson Goals

- Review subtracting without regrouping, subtracting with regrouping, and subtracting to solve problems.
- Take a quiz.

MATERIALS

There are no materials to gather for this lesson.

GET READY

Introduction to Using a Standard Subtraction Algorithm (E)

Students will read the lesson goals.

TRY IT

Review Using a Standard Subtraction Algorithm

Students will answer questions to review what they have learned about using a standard subtraction algorithm.

QUIZ

Using a Standard Subtraction Algorithm

Students will complete the Using a Standard Subtraction Algorithm quiz.

More Math Practice

Students will practice skills according to their individual needs.

Perimeter (A)

Lesson Overview

ACTIVITY	ACTIVITY TITLE	TIME	ONLINE/OFFLINE
GET READY	Introduction to Perimeter (A)	**2** minutes	🖥
	Look Back at Adding Three or More 2-Digit Numbers	**8** minutes	🖥
LEARN AND **TRY IT**	Finding the Perimeter of a Polygon	**7** minutes	📶
	Find the Perimeter of a Polygon	**7** minutes	📶
	Finding the Perimeter of a Complex Figure	**7** minutes	📶
	Find the Perimeter of a Complex Figure	**7** minutes	🖥
	Practice Finding the Perimeter of Shapes	**20** minutes	🖥 and 📄
WRAP-UP	Finding the Perimeter of Shapes	**2** minutes	📶

Content Background

Students will learn to find the perimeter of a shape. Perimeter is the distance around a figure. To find perimeter, find the sum of the lengths of all the sides. Students will encounter different types of polygons, like triangles, squares, rectangles, and hexagons. They will also encounter more complex figures like this example.

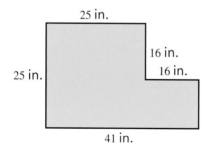

The standard addition algorithm is usually taught for finding the sum of two addends. However, it can be used for any number of addends. Encourage students to use the standard addition algorithm to find perimeter.

Lesson Goals

- Find the perimeter of a figure.

GET READY

Introduction to Perimeter (A)

Students will get a glimpse of what they will learn about in the lesson. They will also read the lesson goals and keywords. Have students select each keyword and preview its definition.

Look Back at Adding Three or More 2-Digit Numbers

Students will practice the prerequisite skill of adding more than two 2-digit numbers.

LEARN AND TRY IT

LEARN   Finding the Perimeter of a Polygon

Students will learn to find the perimeter of a polygon.

TRY IT   Find the Perimeter of a Polygon

Students will practice finding the perimeter of a polygon. Support will be provided to help students overcome misconceptions.

LEARN   Finding the Perimeter of a Complex Figure

Students will learn to find the perimeter of a complex figure.

TRY IT   Find the Perimeter of a Complex Figure

Students will practice finding the perimeter of a complex figure. Support will be provided to help students overcome misconceptions.

TRY IT Practice Finding the Perimeter of Shapes

Students will complete online practice problems. Then they will complete Practice Finding the Perimeter of Shapes from *Summit Math 3 Activity Book*.

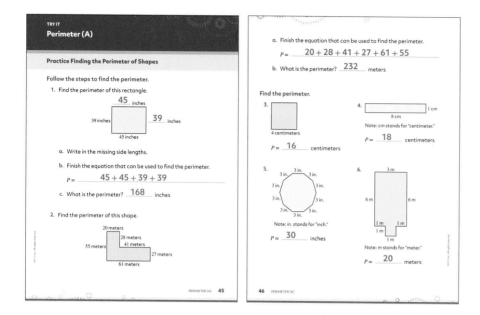

WRAP-UP

Finding the Perimeter of Shapes

Students will solve a problem to show that they understand how to find the perimeter of a shape.

Perimeter (B)

Lesson Overview

ACTIVITY	ACTIVITY TITLE	TIME	ONLINE/OFFLINE
GET READY	Introduction to Perimeter (B)	**2** minutes	🖥️
	Adding and Subtracting 9 Math Facts	**8** minutes	🖥️
LEARN AND **TRY IT**	Finding Missing Side Lengths	**15** minutes	🖥️
	Find Missing Side Lengths	**10** minutes	🖥️
	Practice Finding Missing Side Lengths	**20** minutes	🖥️ and 📄
WRAP-UP	Finding Missing Side Lengths	**5** minutes	🖥️

Content Background

Students will learn to use the idea of perimeter of a figure to find the measure of a missing side length. In each problem, students will be given the perimeter of a figure and all but one side length. To find the missing side length, they will find the sum of the given side lengths and subtract that sum from the given perimeter. Encourage students to use the standard addition algorithm and standard subtraction algorithm in their work.

MATERIALS

Supplied
- *Summit Math 3 Activity Book:* Practice Finding Missing Side Lengths

Lesson Goals
- Find the measure of a missing side length using perimeter.

GET READY

Introduction to Perimeter (B)
Students will get a glimpse of what they will learn about in the lesson. They will also read the lesson goals.

Adding and Subtracting 9 Math Facts
Students will practice adding and subtracting 9.

LEARN   Finding Missing Side Lengths

Students will learn to find missing side lengths.

TRY IT   Find Missing Side Lengths

Students will practice finding missing lengths. Support will be provided to help students overcome misconceptions.

TRY IT   Practice Finding Missing Side Lengths

Students will complete online practice problems. Then they will complete Practice Finding Missing Side Lengths from *Summit Math 3 Activity Book*.

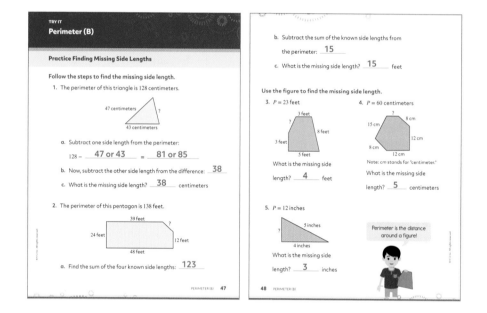

Finding Missing Side Lengths

Students will solve a problem to show that they understand how to find the measure of a missing side of a shape.

Perimeter (C)

Lesson Overview

ACTIVITY	ACTIVITY TITLE	TIME	ONLINE/OFFLINE
GET READY	Introduction to Perimeter (C)	**2** minutes	🖥️
	Adding and Subtracting 9 with Instant Recall	**8** minutes	🖥️
LEARN AND **TRY IT**	Finding Perimeter in Real-World Problems	**15** minutes	🖥️
	Find Perimeter in Real-World Problems	**10** minutes	🖥️
	Practice Finding Perimeter in Real-World Problems	**20** minutes	🖥️ and 📄
WRAP-UP	Finding Perimeter in Real-World Problems	**5** minutes	🖥️

Content Background

Students will apply what they have learned about finding perimeter and finding missing side lengths to solve real-world problems.

TIP Remind students that perimeter is the sum of a shape's side lengths.

Encourage students to continue using the standard addition algorithm and standard subtraction algorithm to show their work.

> ### Lesson Goals
> - Use perimeter to solve problems.

MATERIALS

Supplied
- *Summit Math 3 Activity Book:* Practice Finding Perimeter in Real-World Problems

GET READY

Introduction to Perimeter (C)
Students will get a glimpse of what they will learn about in the lesson. They will also read the lesson goals.

Adding and Subtracting 9 with Instant Recall
Students will practice adding and subtracting 9.

LEARN   Finding Perimeter in Real-World Problems

Students will learn to find perimeter in real-world problems.

TRY IT   Find Perimeter in Real-World Problems

Students will practice finding perimeter in real-world problems. Support will be provided to help students overcome misconceptions.

TRY IT   Practice Finding Perimeter in Real-World Problems

Students will complete online practice problems. Then they will complete Practice Finding Perimeter in Real-World Problems from *Summit Math 3 Activity Book*.

TRY IT
Perimeter (C)

Practice Finding Perimeter in Real-World Problems

Follow the steps to solve the problem.

1. A pillow is in the shape of a triangle. The trim around the edge of the pillow is 87 centimeters long.

   23 centimeters   23 centimeters
   ?

   Find the length of the third side of the pillow.

   a. Subtract one side length from the perimeter:

   $87 - \underline{23} = \underline{64}$

   b. Subtract the other side length from the difference: $\underline{41}$

   c. What is the missing side length? $\underline{41}$ centimeters

2. A designer sews trim around the edges of 2 pillows. Each pillow is in the shape of this rectangle.

   17 centimeters
   51 centimeters

   Find the amount of trim the designer uses.

   PERIMETER (C)   **49**

---

a. Finish the equation that can be used to find the perimeter of one pillow.

$P = \underline{17 + 17 + 51 + 51}$

b. Find the perimeter of one pillow. $\underline{136}$ centimeters

c. Write and solve an equation to find the amount of trim used for two pillows. $\underline{136 + 136 = 272}$

d. How much trim does the designer use? $\underline{272}$ centimeters

Solve.

3. There are 64 squares on this game board. Each small square is 1 inch long.

   What is the perimeter of the game board?

   $\underline{32}$ inches

4. The perimeter of this street sign is 122 inches.

   25 inches   25 inches
   18 inches   18 inches
   ?

   What is the missing side length?

   $\underline{36}$ inches

50   PERIMETER (C)

Finding Perimeter in Real-World Problems

Students will solve a problem to show that they understand how to find perimeter in real-world problems.

Perimeter (D)

Lesson Overview

ACTIVITY	ACTIVITY TITLE	TIME	ONLINE/OFFLINE
GET READY	Introduction to Perimeter (D)	**2** minutes	🖥️
TRY IT	Review Perimeter	**18** minutes	🖥️
QUIZ	Perimeter	**25** minutes	🖥️
WRAP-UP	More Math Practice	**15** minutes	🖥️

Lesson Goals

- Review perimeter.
- Take a quiz.

MATERIALS

There are no materials to gather for this lesson.

GET READY

Introduction to Perimeter (D)

Students will read the lesson goals.

TRY IT

Review Perimeter

Students will answer questions to review what they have learned about perimeter.

QUIZ

Perimeter

Students will complete the Perimeter quiz.

More Math Practice

Students will practice skills according to their individual needs.

Big Ideas: Extended Problems

Lesson Overview

Big Ideas lessons provide students the opportunity to further apply the knowledge and skills acquired throughout previous units. Each Big Ideas lesson consists of two types of activities:

1. **Cumulative Review:** Students keep their skills fresh by reviewing prior content.

2. **Synthesis:** Students complete an assignment that allows them to interweave and apply what they've learned. These synthesis assignments will vary throughout the course.

   In the Synthesis portion of this Big Ideas lesson, students will complete multistep problems that go beyond the short answer and multiple choice problems they encounter in their regular lessons. These problems give students an opportunity to demonstrate problem solving, reasoning, communication, and modeling skills. Students will need to use pencil and paper and/or technology to show their work.

   LEARNING COACH CHECK-IN   This is a graded assessment. Make sure students complete, review, and submit the assignment to their teacher.

All materials needed for this lesson are linked online. The materials are not provided in this Lesson Guide or in the Activity Book.

Exploring Multiplication

Skip Counting Patterns (A)

Lesson Overview

ACTIVITY	ACTIVITY TITLE	TIME	ONLINE/OFFLINE
GET READY	Introduction to Skip Counting Patterns (A)	**2** minutes	🖥️
	Look Back at Adding a Multiple of 10	**8** minutes	🖥️
LEARN AND **TRY IT**	Skip Counting by 10s	**7** minutes	🖥️
	Skip Count by 10s	**7** minutes	🖥️
	Skip Counting by 5s	**7** minutes	🖥️
	Skip Count by 5s	**7** minutes	🖥️
	Practice Skip Counting by 5s and 10s	**20** minutes	🖥️ and 📄
WRAP-UP	Skip Counting by 5s and 10s	**2** minutes	🖥️

Content Background

Students will skip count by 10 and 5. Students will also describe the skip counting pattern in a list of numbers. Patterns of all kinds are part of the study of mathematics. Skip counting patterns build a strong foundation for learning multiplication facts. Skip counting involves counting forwards or backwards by the same number. Another way to think of skip counting is adding or subtracting the same number to each number in a pattern. To skip count by 10, add 10 to each number in the pattern. To skip count by 5, add 5 to each number in the pattern.

Students will start using a number line to show repeated jumps of 10 or 5. Then students will discover that adding 10 or 5 creates different patterns. For example, skip counting by 10 is just adding 1 to the digit in the tens place. Some students have trouble skip counting when starting at a number other than 0, especially when the first number is greater than 100 and does not end in 0 or 5. For example, skip counting by 5 starting at 253 is more challenging than starting at 150, which is more challenging than starting at 0. Encourage students to notice and use patterns.

Lesson Goals

- Skip count by 10.

- Skip count by 5.

- Find patterns in sets of numbers.

Introduction to Skip Counting Patterns (A)

After a quick introductory activity, students will read the lesson goals.

Look Back at Adding a Multiple of 10

Students will practice the prerequisite skill of adding 10 to a number.

LEARN AND TRY IT

LEARN   Skip Counting by 10s

Students will learn to skip count by 10.

TRY IT   Skip Count by 10s

Students will practice skip counting by 10. Support will be provided to help students overcome misconceptions.

LEARN   Skip Counting by 5s

Students will learn to skip count by 5.

TRY IT   Skip Count by 5s

Students will practice skip counting by 5. Support will be provided to help students overcome misconceptions.

Students will complete online practice problems. Then they will complete Practice Skip Counting by 5s and 10s from *Summit Math 3 Activity Book*.

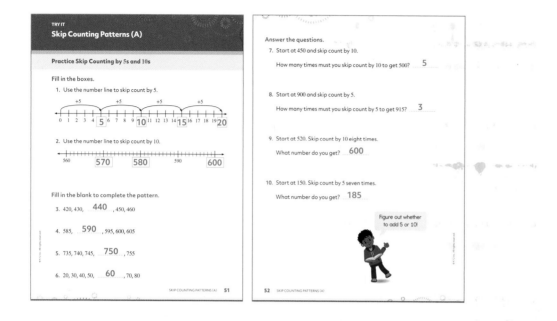

WRAP-UP

Skip Counting by 5s and 10s

Students will solve problems to show that they understand how to skip count by 5 and 10.

Skip Counting Patterns (B)

Lesson Overview

ACTIVITY	ACTIVITY TITLE	TIME	ONLINE/OFFLINE
GET READY	Introduction to Skip Counting Patterns (B)	**2** minutes	🖥️
	Practice Adding and Subtracting 9	**8** minutes	🖥️
LEARN AND **TRY IT**	Skip Counting by 2s	**7** minutes	🖥️
	Skip Count by 2s	**7** minutes	🖥️
	Skip Counting by 3s	**7** minutes	🖥️
	Skip Count by 3s	**7** minutes	🖥️
	Practice Skip Counting by 2s and 3s	**20** minutes	🖥️ and 📄
WRAP-UP	Skip Counting by 2s and 3s	**2** minutes	🖥️

Content Background

Students will learn to skip count by 2 and 3. Skip counting by 2 can be thought of as counting every other number. If you start at an even number, all the numbers you count will be even. If you start at an odd number, all the numbers you count will be odd.

Skip counting by 3 can be more difficult for students since the pattern of the ones digits is not as obvious. Some students may find that they count by 2 and then add 1 until they become proficient at counting by 3.

Lesson Goals

- Skip count by 2.
- Skip count by 3.
- Find patterns in sets of numbers.

GET READY

Introduction to Skip Counting Patterns (B)
Students will get a glimpse of what they will learn about in the lesson. They will also read the lesson goals.

Practice Adding and Subtracting 9

Students will practice adding and subtracting 9.

LEARN   Skip Counting by 2s

Students will learn to skip count by 2.

TRY IT   Skip Count by 2s

Students will practice skip counting by 2. Support will be provided to help students overcome misconceptions.

LEARN   Skip Counting by 3s

Students will learn to skip count by 3.

TRY IT   Skip Count by 3s

Students will practice skip counting by 3. Support will be provided to help students overcome misconceptions.

TRY IT   Practice Skip Counting by 2s and 3s

Students will complete online practice problems. Then they will complete Practice Skip Counting by 2s and 3s from *Summit Math 3 Activity Book*.

TRY IT
Skip Counting Patterns (B)

Practice Skip Counting by 2s and 3s

Fill in the boxes.

1. Use the number line to skip count by 3.

   0 1 2 **3** 4 5 **6** 7 8 **9** 10 11 **12**

2. Use the number line to skip count by 2.

   620 622 **624** 626 **628** 630 632 634 **636**

Fill in the blank to complete the pattern.

3. 447, 450, 453, __456__, 459

4. 963, 966, __969__, 972, 975

5. 36, 38, __40__, 42, 44, 46, 48

6. 192, __194__, 196, 198, 200

SKIP COUNTING PATTERNS (B) 53

Answer the questions.

7. Start at 762 and skip count by 2.

   How many times must you skip count by 2 to get 778? __8__

8. Start at 33 and skip count by 3.

   How many times must you skip count by 3 to get 51? __6__

9. Start at 146. Skip count by 2 four times.

   What number do you get? __154__

10. Start at 270. Skip count by 3 five times.

    What number do you get? __285__

You can use patterns to skip count!

54 SKIP COUNTING PATTERNS (B)

Skip Counting by 2s and 3s

Students will solve problems to show that they understand how to skip count by 2 and 3.

Skip Counting Patterns (C)

Lesson Overview

ACTIVITY	ACTIVITY TITLE	TIME	ONLINE/OFFLINE
GET READY	Introduction to Skip Counting Patterns (C)	**2** minutes	🖥️
	Mixed Addition and Subtraction Math Facts	**8** minutes	🖥️
LEARN AND **TRY IT**	Skip Counting by 4s, 6s, 7s, 8s, or 9s	**7** minutes	🖥️
	Skip Count by 4s, 6s, 7s, 8s, or 9s	**7** minutes	🖥️
	Recognizing and Explaining Skip Counting Patterns	**7** minutes	🖥️
	Recognize and Explain Skip Counting Patterns	**7** minutes	🖥️
	Practice Skip Counting Patterns	**20** minutes	🖥️ and 📄
WRAP-UP	Skip Counting Patterns	**2** minutes	🖥️

Content Background

Students will learn to skip count by 4, 6, 7, 8, and 9. They will also continue to look for patterns within the skip counting sequence. That is, they will look for patterns like all numbers in the sequence are even or the numbers in the sequence alternate between even and odd.

MATERIALS

Supplied
- *Summit Math 3 Activity Book:* Practice Skip Counting Patterns

Lesson Goals

- Skip count by 4, 6, 7, 8, or 9.
- Find patterns in sets of numbers.
- Explain patterns of numbers.

GET READY

Introduction to Skip Counting Patterns (C)
Students will get a glimpse of what they will learn about in the lesson. They will also read the lesson goals.

Mixed Addition and Subtraction Math Facts
Students will practice adding and subtracting.

LEARN   Skip Counting by 4s, 6s, 7s, 8s, or 9s

Students will learn to skip count by 4, 6, 7, 8, and 9.

TRY IT   Skip Count by 4s, 6s, 7s, 8s, or 9s

Students will practice skip counting by 4, 6, 7, 8, and 9. Support will be provided to help students overcome misconceptions.

LEARN   Recognizing and Explaining Skip Counting Patterns

Students will learn to recognize and explain a skip counting pattern.

TRY IT   Recognize and Explain Skip Counting Patterns

Students will practice recognizing and explaining skip counting patterns. Support will be provided to help students overcome misconceptions.

TRY IT   Practice Skip Counting Patterns

Students will complete online practice problems. Then they will complete Practice Skip Counting Patterns from *Summit Math 3 Activity Book*.

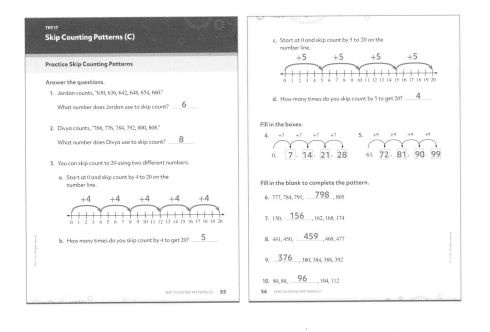

Skip Counting Patterns

Students will solve problems to show that they understand how to skip count and recognize skip counting patterns.

Skip Counting Patterns (D)

Lesson Overview

ACTIVITY	ACTIVITY TITLE	TIME	ONLINE/OFFLINE
GET READY	Introduction to Skip Counting Patterns (D)	**2** minutes	🖥️
TRY IT	Review Skip Counting Patterns	**18** minutes	🖥️
QUIZ	Skip Counting Patterns	**25** minutes	🖥️
WRAP-UP	More Math Practice	**15** minutes	🖥️

Lesson Goals

- Review skip counting by 2 through 10, finding patterns in sets of numbers, and explaining patterns in sets of numbers.

- Take a quiz.

MATERIALS

There are no materials to gather for this lesson.

GET READY

Introduction to Skip Counting Patterns (D)
Students will read the lesson goals.

TRY IT

Review Skip Counting Patterns
Students will answer questions to review what they have learned about skip counting patterns.

QUIZ

Skip Counting Patterns
Students will complete the Skip Counting Patterns quiz.

More Math Practice

Students will practice skills according to their individual needs.

Equal Groups (A)

Lesson Overview

ACTIVITY	ACTIVITY TITLE	TIME	ONLINE/OFFLINE
GET READY	Introduction to Equal Groups (A)	**2** minutes	🖥️
	Look Back at Skip Counting	**8** minutes	🖥️
LEARN AND **TRY IT**	Modeling Multiplication with Equal Groups	**7** minutes	🖥️
	Model Multiplication with Equal Groups	**7** minutes	🖥️
	Representing Equal Groups with Multiplication Expressions	**7** minutes	🖥️
	Represent Equal Groups with Multiplication Expressions	**7** minutes	🖥️
	Practice Modeling and Representing Multiplication	**20** minutes	🖥️ and 📄
WRAP-UP	Modeling and Representing Multiplication	**2** minutes	🖥️

Content Background

Students will learn to model multiplication with equal groups. For example, the expression 5×3 is read as 5 times 3 and it means 5 groups of 3. One way to find the total in 5 groups of 3 is adding the equal groups. Add three 5 times: $3 + 3 + 3 + 3 + 3 = 15$. Therefore, $5 \times 3 = 15$.

Numbers that we multiply are called factors. The answer is called the product. In $5 \times 3 = 15$, 5 and 3 are the factors and 15 is the product.

Students will also learn to represent equal groups with multiplication expressions. This is done by writing an expression in the form: number of groups ✕ number of objects per group.

Lesson Goals

- Model multiplication with equal groups.
- Multiply using equal groups.

MATERIALS

Supplied
- *Summit Math 3 Activity Book:* Practice Modeling and Representing Multiplication

---

KEYWORDS

factor – one of two or more numbers that are multiplied

multiply – to use the shortcut for adding the same number over and over a certain number of times

product – the answer to a multiplication problem

Introduction to Equal Groups (A)

Students will get a glimpse of what they will learn about in the lesson. They will also read the lesson goals and keywords. Have students select each keyword and preview its definition.

Look Back at Skip Counting

Students will practice the prerequisite skill of skip counting.

LEARN AND TRY IT

LEARN   Modeling Multiplication with Equal Groups

Students will learn to model multiplication with equal groups.

TRY IT   Model Multiplication with Equal Groups

Students will practice modeling multiplication with equal groups. Support will be provided to help students overcome misconceptions.

LEARN   Representing Equal Groups with Multiplication Expressions

Students will learn to represent equal groups with multiplication expressions.

TRY IT   Represent Equal Groups with Multiplication Expressions

Students will practice representing equal groups with multiplication expressions. Support will be provided to help students overcome misconceptions.

TRY IT   Practice Modeling and Representing Multiplication

Students will complete online practice problems. Then they will complete Practice Modeling and Representing Multiplication from *Summit Math 3 Activity Book*.

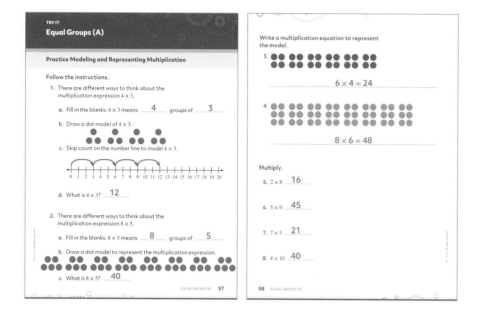

WRAP-UP

Modeling and Representing Multiplication

Students will solve problems to show that they understand how to model and represent multiplication.

Equal Groups (B)

Lesson Overview

ACTIVITY	ACTIVITY TITLE	TIME	ONLINE/OFFLINE
GET READY	Introduction to Equal Groups (B)	**2** minutes	🖥️
	Mixed Addition and Subtraction with Instant Recall	**8** minutes	🖥️
LEARN AND **TRY IT**	Using Arrays to Multiply	**7** minutes	🖥️
	Use Arrays to Multiply	**7** minutes	🖥️
	Working with the Commutative Property	**7** minutes	🖥️
	Work with the Commutative Property	**7** minutes	🖥️
	Practice Using Arrays and Working with Commutative Property	**20** minutes	🖥️ and 📄
WRAP-UP	Using Arrays and Working with Commutative Property	**2** minutes	🖥️

Content Background

Students will learn to use arrays to multiply. An array is an arrangement of objects in rows and columns. Arrays can be used to model multiplication. Students will learn that the first factor is the number of rows and the second factor is the number of objects in each row.

For example, this array has 6 rows with 3 objects in each row, so it models 6×3.

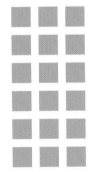

Students will also learn to work with the commutative property. The commutative property says changing the order of the factors does not change the product. The array above also models 3×6. You can use skip counting to determine that there are a total of 18 objects either way.

MATERIALS

Supplied
- *Summit Math 3 Activity Book:* Practice Using Arrays and Working with Commutative Property

KEYWORDS

array – a set of rows with the same number of objects in each row

commutative property of multiplication – a rule that says no matter what order you use to multiply factors, the product will not change

Lesson Goals

- Use arrays to model multiplication.
- Apply the commutative property of multiplication.

Introduction to Equal Groups (B)

Students will get a glimpse of what they will learn about in the lesson. They will also read the lesson goals and keywords. Have students select each keyword and preview its definition.

Mixed Addition and Subtraction with Instant Recall

Students will practice addition and subtraction facts.

LEARN AND TRY IT

LEARN Using Arrays to Multiply

Students will learn to use arrays to multiply.

TRY IT Use Arrays to Multiply

Students will practice using arrays to multiply. Support will be provided to help students overcome misconceptions.

LEARN Working with the Commutative Property

Students will learn to work with the commutative property.

TRY IT Work with the Commutative Property

Students will practice working with the commutative property. Support will be provided to help students overcome misconceptions.

TRY IT Practice Using Arrays and Working with Commutative Property

Students will complete online practice problems. Then they will complete Practice Using Arrays and Working with Commutative Property from *Summit Math 3 Activity Book.*

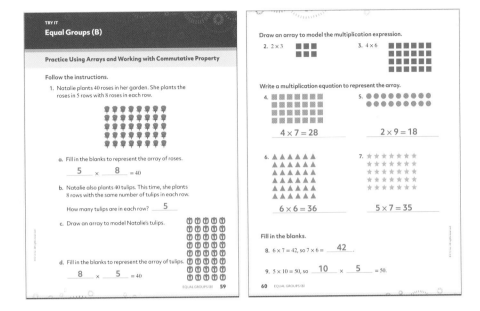

Using Arrays and Working with Commutative Property

Students will solve problems to show that they understand how to use arrays to multiply and work with the commutative property.

Equal Groups (C)

Lesson Overview

ACTIVITY	ACTIVITY TITLE	TIME	ONLINE/OFFLINE
GET READY	Introduction to Equal Groups (C)	**2** minutes	🖥️
	Mixed Addition and Subtraction Math Facts Game	**8** minutes	🖥️
LEARN AND **TRY IT**	Multiplying by 1	**7** minutes	🖥️
	Multiply by 1	**7** minutes	🖥️
	Multiplying by 0	**7** minutes	🖥️
	Multiply by 0	**7** minutes	🖥️
	Practice Multiplying by 0 and 1	**20** minutes	🖥️ and 📄
WRAP-UP	Multiplying by 0 and 1	**2** minutes	🖥️

Content Background

Students will learn to multiply by 1 and 0. The product of a number and 1 is always the original number. This is called the identity property of multiplication. The product of any number and 0 is 0. This is called the zero property of multiplication. Sometimes students confuse these two rules. Encourage students to think about equal groups. For example, 1×8 represents 1 group of 8, which equals 8. But 0×8 represents no groups of 8, which equals 0. Students will also begin to fill out a multiplication table. They will complete additional rows and columns in other lessons until all the multiplication facts have been introduced.

Lesson Goals

- Multiply by 1.
- Multiply by 0.

MATERIALS

Supplied
- *Summit Math 3 Activity Book:* Practice Multiplying by 0 and 1

KEYWORDS

identity property of multiplication – a rule that says that the product of a number and one is always the original number

zero property of multiplication – a rule that says that the product of a number and zero is always zero

Introduction to Equal Groups (C)

Students will get a glimpse of what they will learn about in the lesson. They will also read the lesson goals and keywords. Have students select each keyword and preview its definition.

Mixed Addition and Subtraction Math Facts Game

Students will practice adding and subtracting math facts.

LEARN AND TRY IT

LEARN   Multiplying by 1

Students will learn to multiply by 1.

TRY IT   Multiply by 1

Students will practice multiplying by 1. Support will be provided to help students overcome misconceptions.

LEARN   Multiplying by 0

Students will learn to multiply by 0.

TRY IT   Multiply by 0

Students will practice multiplying by 0. Support will be provided to help students overcome misconceptions.

TRY IT   Practice Multiplying by 0 and 1

Students will complete online practice problems. Then they will complete Practice Multiplying by 0 and 1 from *Summit Math 3 Activity Book*.

WRAP-UP

Multiplying by 0 and 1

Students will solve problems to show that they understand how to multiply by 0 and 1.

Equal Groups (D)

Lesson Overview

ACTIVITY	ACTIVITY TITLE	TIME	ONLINE/OFFLINE
GET READY	Introduction to Equal Groups (D)	**2** minutes	🖥
TRY IT	Review Equal Groups	**18** minutes	🖥
QUIZ	Equal Groups	**25** minutes	🖥
WRAP-UP	More Math Practice	**15** minutes	🖥

Lesson Goals

- Review multiplying using equal groups or arrays and using properties to multiply by 0 and 1.
- Take a quiz.

MATERIALS

There are no materials to gather for this lesson.

GET READY

Introduction to Equal Groups (D)

Students will read the lesson goals.

TRY IT

Review Equal Groups

Students will answer questions to review what they have learned about equal groups.

QUIZ

Equal Groups

Students will complete the Equal Groups quiz.

More Math Practice

Students will practice skills according to their individual needs.

Multiples of 10 and 5 (A)

Lesson Overview

ACTIVITY	ACTIVITY TITLE	TIME	ONLINE/OFFLINE
GET READY	Introduction to Multiples of 10 and 5 (A)	**2** minutes	📶
	Look Back at Skip Counting by 5s and 10s	**8** minutes	📶
LEARN AND TRY IT	Multiplying by 10	**15** minutes	📶
	Multiply by 10	**10** minutes	📶
	Practice Multiplying by 10	**20** minutes	📶 and 📄
WRAP-UP	Multiplying by 10	**5** minutes	📶

Content Background

Students will learn to multiply by 10. To multiply by 10, skip count by 10 the number of times indicated by the other factor. For example, 3×10 means to skip count by 10 three times, so $3 \times 10 = 30$. Students will also identify and explain patterns when multiplying by 10. One pattern is that every product of a number and 10 ends in 0 because 10 ends in 0. Additionally, students will complete the 10 row and column in their multiplication table.

MATERIALS

Supplied
- *Summit Math 3 Activity Book:* Practice Multiplying by 10

Lesson Goals

- Multiply by 10.
- Identify and explain patterns when multiplying by 10.

GET READY

Introduction to Multiples of 10 and 5 (A)

Students will get a glimpse of what they will learn about in the lesson. They will also read the lesson goals.

Look Back at Skip Counting by 5s and 10s

Students will practice the prerequisite skill of skip counting by 5 and 10.

LEARN   Multiplying by 10

Students will learn to multiply by 10.

TRY IT   Multiply by 10

Students will practice multiplying by 10. Support will be provided to help students overcome misconceptions.

TRY IT   Practice Multiplying by 10

Students will complete online practice problems. Then they will complete Practice Multiplying by 10 from *Summit Math 3 Activity Book*.

TRY IT
Multiples of 10 and 5 (A)

Practice Multiplying by 10

Fill in the blanks.

1. The product of 10 and a number always ends in ___0___

2. To multiply by 10, you can skip count by ___10___

3. Jordan has 3 boxes of markers. Each box has 10 markers.
   How many markers does Jordan have?
   $3 \times 10 =$ ___30___   Jordan has ___30___ markers.

4. Eloise has 10 baskets of apples. Each basket has 6 apples.
   How many apples does Eloise have?
   $10 \times 6 =$ ___60___   Eloise has ___60___ apples.

5. A group of children run relay races. There are 5 teams with 10 children on each team.
   How many children run in the relay races?
   $5 \times 10 =$ ___50___   ___50___ children run in the races.

MULTIPLES OF 10 AND 5 (A)   63

Multiply.

6. 7×10 ___70___   7. 4×10 ___40___

8. 10×2 ___20___   9. 10×9 ___90___

10. 3×10 ___30___   11. 10×10 ___100___

12. 1×10 ___10___   13. 10×0 ___0___

14. 2×10 ___20___   15. 10×6 ___60___

16. 10×5 ___50___   17. 9×10 ___90___

18. 10×7 ___70___   19. 8×10 ___80___

64   MULTIPLES OF 10 AND 5 (A)

WRAP-UP

Multiplying by 10

Students will solve a problem to show that they understand how to multiply by 10.

Multiples of 10 and 5 (B)

Lesson Overview

ACTIVITY	ACTIVITY TITLE	TIME	ONLINE/OFFLINE
GET READY	Introduction to Multiples of 10 and 5 (B)	**2** minutes	🖥️
	Multiplying by 0 and 1 Math Facts	**8** minutes	🖥️
LEARN AND **TRY IT**	Multiplying by 5	**15** minutes	🖥️
	Multiply by 5	**10** minutes	🖥️
	Practice Multiplying by 5	**20** minutes	🖥️ and 📄
WRAP-UP	Multiplying by 5	**5** minutes	🖥️

Content Background

Students will learn to multiply by 5. To multiply by 5, skip count by 5 the number of times indicated by the other factor. For example, 6×5 means skip count by 5 six times, so $6 \times 5 = 30$. Students will also identify and explain patterns when multiplying by 5. For example, when you multiply a number by 5, the product ends in 5 or 0. Additionally, students will complete the 5 row and column in their multiplication table.

MATERIALS

Supplied

- *Summit Math 3 Activity Book:* Practice Multiplying by 5

Lesson Goals

- Multiply by 5.
- Identify and explain patterns when multiplying by 5.

GET READY

Introduction to Multiples of 10 and 5 (B)

Students will get a glimpse of what they will learn about in the lesson. They will also read the lesson goals.

Multiplying by 0 and 1 Math Facts

Students will practice multiplying by 0 and 1.

LEARN   Multiplying by 5

Students will learn to multiply by 5.

TRY IT   Multiply by 5

Students will practice multiplying by 5. Support will be provided to help students overcome misconceptions.

TRY IT   Practice Multiplying by 5

Students will complete online practice problems. Then they will complete Practice Multiplying by 5 from *Summit Math 3 Activity Book.*

TRY IT
Multiples of 10 and 5 (B)

Practice Multiplying by 5

Fill in the blanks.

1. The product of 5 and a number always ends in __0__ or __5__.

2. To multiply by 5, you can skip count by __5__.

3. Eloise has 5 bags. Each bag has 6 crackers.
   How many crackers does Eloise have in all?

   $5 \times 6 =$ __30__   Eloise has __30__ crackers.

4. Aisha reads her book for 3 days. She reads 5 pages each day.
   How many pages does Aisha read in all?

   $3 \times 5 =$ __15__   Aisha reads __15__ pages.

5. Cans of paint are placed on 5 shelves. Each shelf has 8 cans of paint.
   How many cans of paint are on the shelves in all?

   $5 \times 8 =$ __40__   The shelves have __40__ cans.

MULTIPLES OF 10 AND 5 (B)   **65**

Multiply.

6. 4×5 __20__   7. 8×5 __40__

8. 5×2 __10__   9. 5×9 __45__

10. 6×5 __30__   11. 5×3 __15__

12. 1×5 __5__   13. 5×0 __0__

14. 7×5 __35__   15. 5×6 __30__

16. 5×5 __25__   17. 9×5 __45__

18. 5×8 __40__   19. 5×4 __20__

66   MULTIPLES OF 10 AND 5 (B)

Multiplying by 5

Students will solve a problem to show that they understand how to multiply by 5.

Multiples of 10 and 5 (C)

Lesson Overview

ACTIVITY	ACTIVITY TITLE	TIME	ONLINE/OFFLINE
GET READY	Introduction to Multiples of 10 and 5 (C)	**2** minutes	
TRY IT	Review Multiples of 10 and 5	**18** minutes	
QUIZ	Multiples of 10 and 5	**25** minutes	
WRAP-UP	More Math Practice	**15** minutes	

Lesson Goals

- Review multiplying by 10 and 5.

- Take a quiz.

MATERIALS

There are no materials to gather for this lesson.

GET READY

Introduction to Multiples of 10 and 5 (C)

Students will read the lesson goals.

TRY IT

Review Multiples of 10 and 5

Students will answer questions to review what they have learned about multiples of 10 and 5.

QUIZ

Multiples of 10 and 5

Students will complete the Multiples of 10 and 5 quiz.

More Math Practice

Students will practice skills according to their individual needs.

Big Ideas: Mini-Project

Lesson Overview

Big Ideas lessons provide students the opportunity to further apply the knowledge and skills acquired throughout previous units. Each Big Ideas lesson consists of two types of activities:

1. **Cumulative Review:** Students keep their skills fresh by reviewing prior content.

2. **Synthesis:** Students complete an assignment that allows them to interweave and apply what they've learned. These synthesis assignments will vary throughout the course.

   In the Synthesis portion of this Big Ideas lesson, students will complete a small, creative project designed to tie together concepts and skills that students have encountered across units. These small projects are designed to emphasize a real-world application that connects mathematics to other subjects, including science, technology, engineering, art, and history. Students will need to use pencil and paper and/or technology to show their work.

   LEARNING COACH CHECK-IN Make sure students complete, review, and submit the assignment to their teacher.

All materials needed for this lesson are linked online. The materials are not provided in this Lesson Guide or in the Activity Book.

MATERIALS

Supplied
- Mini-Project Instructions (printout)

Multiplication Properties and Strategies

Multiplication Patterns (A)

Lesson Overview

ACTIVITY	ACTIVITY TITLE	TIME	ONLINE/OFFLINE
GET READY	Introduction to Multiplication Patterns (A)	**2** minutes	🖥
	Look Back at Understanding Even and Odd Numbers	**8** minutes	🖥
LEARN AND **TRY IT**	Multiplying by 2	**7** minutes	🖥
	Multiply by 2	**7** minutes	🖥
	Multiplying by 4	**7** minutes	🖥
	Multiply by 4	**7** minutes	🖥
	Practice Multiplying by 2 and 4	**20** minutes	🖥 and 📄
WRAP-UP	Multiplying by 2 and 4	**2** minutes	🖥

Content Background

Skip counting provides a firm foundation for multiplication. However, students must memorize and automatically recall their multiplication facts to truly succeed in math. Students have already learned the multiplication facts for 0, 1, 5, and 10, and should continue to practice those. In this lesson, students will learn to multiply fluently by 2 and 4.

You can multiply by 2 and 4 using mental math involving doubles. To double a number, add the number to itself. The product of a number and 2 is double the number. The product of a number and 4 is double the number twice, because 4 is 2×2. For example, to find 4×5, double 5 twice: $5 + 5$ is 10 and $10 + 10$ is 20. The multiplication facts for 4 are double the multiplication facts for 2. Students will complete the columns and rows for 2 and 4 in their multiplication tables.

TIP Knowing how to double a number makes it easier for students to memorize the 2 and 4 multiplication facts. Practice doubling the numbers 1 through 20 using addition: $1 + 1$, $2 + 2$, and so on.

The commutative property of multiplication states that two numbers can be multiplied in any order without changing the product. Even if the property is not yet completely understood by students, they should recognize that once they know the product of 5×2 they also know the product of 2×5. Students can find the product by skip counting by 5 twice or by doubling 5.

MATERIALS

Supplied
- *Summit Math 3 Activity Book:* Practice Multiplying by 2 and 4

Students will also learn to identify patterns in multiplication facts. For example, in the 2 facts, each product is 2 more than the product before it. Another pattern is that each product is even. So, the product of 2 and any number is an even number.

Lesson Goals

- Multiply by 2.

- Multiply by 4.

- Identify and explain the patterns in multiplication facts.

GET READY

Introduction to Multiplication Patterns (A)
After a quick introductory activity, students will read the lesson goals.

Look Back at Understanding Even and Odd Numbers
Students will practice the prerequisite skill of understanding even and odd numbers.

LEARN AND TRY IT

LEARN   Multiplying by 2
Students will learn to multiply by 2.

TRY IT   Multiply by 2
Students will practice multiplying by 2. Support will be provided to help students overcome misconceptions.

LEARN   Multiplying by 4
Students will learn to multiply by 4.

TRY IT   Multiply by 4
Students will practice multiplying by 4. Support will be provided to help students overcome misconceptions.

TRY IT   Practice Multiplying by 2 and 4

Students will complete online practice problems. Then they will complete Practice Multiplying by 2 and 4 from *Summit Math 3 Activity Book.*

Multiplying by 2 and 4

Students will solve problems to show that they understand how to multiply by 2 and 4.

Multiplication Patterns (B)

Lesson Overview

ACTIVITY	ACTIVITY TITLE	TIME	ONLINE/OFFLINE
GET READY	Introduction to Multiplication Patterns (B)	**2** minutes	🖥️
	Multiplying by 0 and 1 with Instant Recall	**8** minutes	🖥️
LEARN AND **TRY IT**	Multiplying by 3	**7** minutes	🖥️
	Multiply by 3	**7** minutes	🖥️
	Multiplying by 6	**7** minutes	🖥️
	Multiply by 6	**7** minutes	🖥️
	Practice Multiplying by 3 and 6	**20** minutes	🖥️ and 📄
WRAP-UP	Multiplying by 3 and 6	**2** minutes	🖥️

Content Background

Students will learn to multiply fluently by 3 and 6. Learning the multiplication facts for 3 relies on skip counting by 3. However, students must work towards memorizing and automatically recalling their multiplication facts. Since 6 is 3×2, multiplying by six combines two strategies. The product of a number and 6 is double the product of the number and 3. For example, 6×5 is double 3×5, or $15 + 15 = 30$. The multiplication facts for 6 are double the multiplication facts for 3.

Students will complete the columns and rows for 3 and 6 in their multiplication tables.

Students should continue to apply the commutative property to recognize that they can multiply two numbers in any order. For example, $6 \times 4 = 4 \times 6$, so students could double 6 twice or double 4×3 to find the product.

Students will also learn to identify and explain patterns in multiplication facts. For example, in the 3 facts, the products alternate between even and odd numbers. And in the 6 facts, all the products are even.

> ### MATERIALS
>
> **Supplied**
> - *Summit Math 3 Activity Book:* Practice Multiplying by 3 and 6

Lesson Goals

- Multiply by 3.

- Multiply by 6.

- Identify and explain patterns in multiplication facts.

Introduction to Multiplication Patterns (B)

Students will get a glimpse of what they will learn about in the lesson. They will also read the lesson goals.

Multiplying by 0 and 1 with Instant Recall

Students will practice multiplying by 0 and 1.

LEARN AND TRY IT

LEARN   Multiplying by 3

Students will learn to multiply by 3.

TRY IT   Multiply by 3

Students will practice multiplying by 3. Support will be provided to help students overcome misconceptions.

LEARN   Multiplying by 6

Students will learn to multiply by 6.

TRY IT   Multiply by 6

Students will practice multiplying by 6. Support will be provided to help students overcome misconceptions.

TRY IT   Practice Multiplying by 3 and 6

Students will complete online practice problems. Then they will complete Practice Multiplying by 3 and 6 from *Summit Math 3 Activity Book.*

WRAP-UP

Multiplying by 3 and 6

Students will solve problems to show that they understand how to multiply by 3 and 6.

Multiplication Patterns (C)

Lesson Overview

ACTIVITY	ACTIVITY TITLE	TIME	ONLINE/OFFLINE
GET READY	Introduction to Multiplication Patterns (C)	**2** minutes	🖥️
	Multiplying by 0 and 1 Math Facts Game	**8** minutes	🖥️
LEARN AND **TRY IT**	Understanding the Distributive Property	**15** minutes	🖥️
	Understand the Distributive Property	**10** minutes	🖥️
	Practice Understanding the Distributive Property	**20** minutes	🖥️ and 📄
WRAP-UP	Understanding the Distributive Property	**5** minutes	🖥️

Content Background

Students will learn about the distributive property of multiplication. This property states that multiplying a number by a sum gives the same answer as multiplying the number by each addend of the sum and then adding the products. For example, $6 \times 9 = 6 \times (5 + 4) = (6 \times 5) + (6 \times 4) = 30 + 24 = 54$.

The distributive property can be used to break apart numbers to make it easier to multiply using mental math. For example, in the product 3×9, you could break apart 9 as $5 + 4$: $3 \times 9 = 3 \times (5 + 4) = (3 \times 5) + (3 \times 4) = 15 + 12 = 27$. Students have already learned the multiplication facts for 0, 1, 2, 3, 4, 5, 6, and 10. When multiplying, it can be helpful to break apart one factor into a sum of these numbers.

Lesson Goals

- Use the distributive property to multiply.

MATERIALS

Supplied
- *Summit Math 3 Activity Book:* Practice Understanding the Distributive Property

KEYWORDS

distributive property – a rule that says that multiplying a number by a sum gives the same answer as multiplying the number by each addend of the sum and then adding the products

GET READY

Introduction to Multiplication Patterns (C)

Students will get a glimpse of what they will learn about in the lesson. They will also read the lesson goals and keywords. Have students select each keyword and preview its definition.

Multiplying by 0 and 1 Math Facts Game

Students will practice multiplying by 0 and 1.

LEARN AND TRY IT

LEARN   Understanding the Distributive Property

Students will learn to use the distributive property to multiply.

TRY IT   Understand the Distributive Property

Students will practice using the distributive property to multiply. Support will be provided to help students overcome misconceptions.

TRY IT   Practice Understanding the Distributive Property

Students will complete online practice problems. Then they will complete Practice Understanding the Distributive Property from *Summit Math 3 Activity Book*.

WRAP-UP

Understanding the Distributive Property

Students will solve problems to show that they understand how to use the distributive property to multiply.

Multiplication Patterns (D)

Lesson Overview

ACTIVITY	ACTIVITY TITLE	TIME	ONLINE/OFFLINE
GET READY	Introduction to Multiplication Patterns (D)	**2** minutes	🖥️
	Multiplying by 10 and 5 Math Facts	**8** minutes	🖥️
LEARN AND **TRY IT**	Multiplying by 7	**15** minutes	🖥️
	Multiply by 7	**10** minutes	🖥️
	Practice Multiplying by 7	**20** minutes	🖥️ and 📄
WRAP-UP	Multiplying by 7	**5** minutes	🖥️

Content Background

Students will learn to fluently multiply by 7. Students have already learned multiplication facts for 0 through 6, and 10, and should continue to practice those. Since students have also learned that the order of the factors does not change the product, students can use multiplication facts they have already memorized to find the product of 7 and a number. For example, to find 5×7, students can skip count by 5 seven times. When multiplying by 7, 8, or 9, students can use the break apart strategy. This strategy uses the distributive property to find the product. Students can break 7 into $5 + 2$.

$$8 \times 7 = 8 \times (5 + 2) = (8 \times 5) + (8 \times 2) = 40 + 16 = 56$$

Students will complete the row and column for 7 in their multiplication tables. They will also learn to identify patterns in multiplication facts.

MATERIALS

Supplied
- *Summit Math 3 Activity Book:* Practice Multiplying by 7

Lesson Goals

- Multiply by 7.
- Identify and explain patterns in multiplication facts.

Introduction to Multiplication Patterns (D)

Students will get a glimpse of what they will learn about in the lesson. They will also read the lesson goals.

Multiplying by 10 and 5 Math Facts

Students will practice multiplying by 10 and 5.

LEARN AND TRY IT

LEARN   Multiplying by 7

Students will learn to multiply by 7.

TRY IT   Multiply by 7

Students will practice multiplying by 7. Support will be provided to help students overcome misconceptions.

TRY IT   Practice Multiplying by 7

Students will complete online practice problems. Then they will complete Practice Multiplying by 7 from *Summit Math 3 Activity Book*.

TRY IT
Multiplication Patterns (D)

Practice Multiplying by 7

Follow the instructions.

1. This array represents 7 × 4.

    a. Draw a line to break the array into two equal groups.

    b. Fill in the boxes to find 7 × 4.

    $7 \times 4 = \left(7 \times \boxed{2}\right) + \left(7 \times \boxed{2}\right)$

    $7 \times 4 = \boxed{14} + \boxed{14}$

    $7 \times 4 = \boxed{28}$

2. Skip count on the number line to find 7 × 3.
    Possible answer:

    0 1 2 3 4 5 6 7 8 9 10 11 12 13 14 15 16 17 18 19 20 21 22 23 24

    $7 \times 3 = \boxed{21}$

MULTIPLICATION PATTERNS (D)   73

3. Describe how to use doubles to find 7 × 6.
Possible answer: Think of 6 as 3 + 3. Multiply 7 by 3 and then double the product. 7 × 3 = 21 and 21 + 21 = 42.

Answer the question.

4. Jane walks her dog 7 miles each week.
    How many miles does she walk her dog in 10 weeks? **70 miles**

Multiply.

5. 7 × 6   **42**   6. 3 × 7   **21**

7. 0 × 7   **0**   8. 7 × 5   **35**

9. 7 × 1   **7**   10. 7 × 7   **49**

11. 8 × 7   **56**   12. 7 × 9   **63**

74   MULTIPLICATION PATTERNS (D)

WRAP-UP

Multiplying by 7

Students will solve a problem to show that they understand how to multiply by 7.

Multiplication Patterns (E)

Lesson Overview

ACTIVITY	ACTIVITY TITLE	TIME	ONLINE/OFFLINE
GET READY	Introduction to Multiplication Patterns (E)	**2** minutes	🖥️
TRY IT	Review Multiplication Patterns	**18** minutes	🖥️
QUIZ	Multiplication Patterns	**25** minutes	🖥️
WRAP-UP	More Math Practice	**15** minutes	🖥️

Lesson Goals

- Review multiplying by 2, 3, 4, 6, and 7, multiplying with the distributive property, and identifying and explaining the patterns in multiplication facts.

- Take a quiz.

MATERIALS

There are no materials to gather for this lesson.

GET READY

Introduction to Multiplication Patterns (E)

Students will read the lesson goals.

TRY IT

Review Multiplication Patterns

Students will answer questions to review what they have learned about multiplication patterns.

QUIZ

Multiplication Patterns

Students will complete the Multiplication Patterns quiz.

More Math Practice

Students will practice skills according to their individual needs.

Strategies for Multiplying (A)

Lesson Overview

ACTIVITY	ACTIVITY TITLE	TIME	ONLINE/OFFLINE
GET READY	Introduction to Strategies for Multiplying (A)	**2** minutes	📶
	Look Back at the Commutative Property of Multiplication	**8** minutes	📶
LEARN AND **TRY IT**	Understanding the Associative Property	**15** minutes	📶
	Understand the Associative Property	**10** minutes	📶
	Practice Understanding the Associative Property	**20** minutes	📶 and 📄
WRAP-UP	Understanding the Associative Property	**5** minutes	📶

Content Background

Students will learn to understand the associative property. The associative property of multiplication allows you to regroup the factors in a multiplication problem. The product is the same no matter which numbers you multiply first. Consider the problem $3 \times 5 \times 2$. To solve the problem, multiply from left to right. You can show the order using parentheses to group the factors: $(3 \times 5) \times 2 = 15 \times 2 = 30$. Some students may struggle to multiply 15 by 2, so it can be helpful to group the factors differently. You can easily multiply by 10 using mental math. Since $5 \times 2 = 10$, it makes sense to multiply 5 and 2 first. Move the parentheses to show the regrouping: $3 \times (5 \times 2) = 3 \times 10 = 30$.

MATERIALS

Supplied
- *Summit Math 3 Activity Book:* Practice Understanding the Associative Property

KEYWORDS

associative property of multiplication – a rule that says no matter how you group factors to multiply, the product will not change

Lesson Goals
- Use the associative property to multiply three factors.

GET READY

Introduction to Strategies for Multiplying (A)

Students will get a glimpse of what they will learn about in the lesson. They will also read the lesson goals and keywords. Have students select each keyword and preview its definition.

Look Back at the Commutative Property of Multiplication

Students will practice the prerequisite skill of understanding the commutative property of multiplication.

LEARN Understanding the Associative Property

Students will learn to understand and use the associative property.

TRY IT Understand the Associative Property

Students will practice using the associative property. Support will be provided to help students overcome misconceptions.

TRY IT Practice Understanding the Associative Property

Students will complete online practice problems. Then they will complete Practice Understanding the Associative Property from *Summit Math 3 Activity Book*.

TRY IT
Strategies for Multiplying (A)

Practice Understanding the Associative Property

Follow the steps to find the product.

1. $9 \times 2 \times 5$

   a. Write parentheses in each expression to group the factors two different ways.

$$9 \times (2 \times 5) \qquad (9 \times 2) \times 5$$

   b. Choose which expression you will use to find the product. Explain your choice.

Possible answer: I would use $9 \times (2 \times 5)$. I think it is easier to multiply 2×5 first. $2 \times 5 = 10$ and it is easy to multiply a number by 10.

   c. Find the product. __90__

Rewrite the expression to regroup the factors. Then find the product.

2. $2 \times (3 \times 7)$ 3. $6 \times (7 \times 2)$ 4. $(6 \times 2) \times 2$ 5. $5 \times (2 \times 4)$

$(2 \times 3) \times 7$ $(6 \times 7) \times 2$ $6 \times (2 \times 2)$ $(5 \times 2) \times 4$

   __42__   __84__   __24__   __40__

STRATEGIES FOR MULTIPLYING (A)   75

Use the associative property to find the product.

6. $7 \times 2 \times 2$ 7. $2 \times 3 \times 9$ 8. $7 \times 9 \times 1$ 9. $4 \times 2 \times 5$

  __28__   __54__   __63__   __40__

10. $2 \times 2 \times 4$ 11. $8 \times 7 \times 1$ 12. $3 \times 0 \times 9$ 13. $6 \times 2 \times 3$

  __16__   __56__   __0__   __36__

Answer the questions.

14. A roller coaster has 4 cars. Each car has 3 rows of seats. Each row has 2 seats.

How many seats does the roller coaster have? __24 seats__

15. Stella feeds her cat twice a day. She gives her cat 4 ounces of food at each feeding.

How many ounces of food does Stella feed her cat in 6 days? __48 ounces__

16. Bela drinks 5 ounces of milk twice each day.

How much milk does he drink in 7 days? __70 ounces__

76   STRATEGIES FOR MULTIPLYING (A)

Understanding the Associative Property

Students will solve a problem to show that they understand the associative property.

Strategies for Multiplying (B)

Lesson Overview

ACTIVITY	ACTIVITY TITLE	TIME	ONLINE/OFFLINE
GET READY	Introduction to Strategies for Multiplying (B)	**2** minutes	🖥️
	Multiplying by 10 and 5 with Instant Recall	**8** minutes	🖥️
LEARN AND **TRY IT**	Multiplying by 8	**7** minutes	🖥️
	Multiply by 8	**7** minutes	🖥️
	Multiplying by 9	**7** minutes	🖥️ and 📄
	Multiply by 9	**7** minutes	🖥️
	Practice Multiplying by 8 and 9	**20** minutes	🖥️ and 📄
WRAP-UP	Multiplying by 8 and 9	**2** minutes	🖥️

Content Background

Students will learn to multiply by 8 and 9. Students have already learned all the other multiplication facts besides 8 and 9 and should continue to practice those. Since students have already learned that the order of the factors does not change the product, they can use facts they have already learned for many of the multiplication facts for 8 and 9.

Students will also learn to use doubles to multiply by 8. Since 8 is $2 \times 2 \times 2$, the product of a number and 8 is double the number 3 times. To find 8×5, double 5 to get 10, double 10 to get 20 and double 20 to get 40.

Students will learn to identify patterns in multiplication facts. There are lots of patterns that can help you multiply by 9. One pattern is in how the tens and ones change from one product to the next. Notice that each product has 1 more ten and 1 less one than the product before.

$1 \times 9 = 9$ 0 tens   9 ones

$2 \times 9 = 18$ 1 ten   8 ones

$3 \times 9 = 27$ 2 tens   7 ones

$4 \times 9 = 36$ 3 tens   6 ones

Add the digits in each product to find another pattern. The sum of the digits in each product is always 9. Also notice that the number of tens is 1 less than the factor that is not 9. You can use these patterns together to multiply by 9. For example, 7×9 must have 6 tens because $7 - 1 = 6$. It must have 3 ones because $6 + 3 = 9$. So $7 \times 9 = 63$.

Students will complete the remaining rows and columns in their multiplication tables.

Lesson Goals

- Multiply by 8.
- Multiply by 9.
- Identify and explain patterns in multiplication facts.

GET READY

Introduction to Strategies for Multiplying (B)
Students will get a glimpse of what they will learn about in the lesson. They will also read the lesson goals.

Multiplying by 10 and 5 with Instant Recall
Students will practice multiplying by 10 and 5.

LEARN AND TRY IT

LEARN   Multiplying by 8
Students will learn to multiply by 8.

TRY IT   Multiply by 8
Students will practice multiplying by 8. Support will be provided to help students overcome misconceptions.

LEARN   Multiplying by 9
Students will learn to multiply by 9.

TRY IT   Multiply by 9
Students will practice multiplying by 9. Support will be provided to help students overcome misconceptions.

TRY IT   Practice Multiplying by 8 and 9

Students will complete online practice problems. Then they will complete Practice Multiplying by 8 and 9 from *Summit Math 3 Activity Book*.

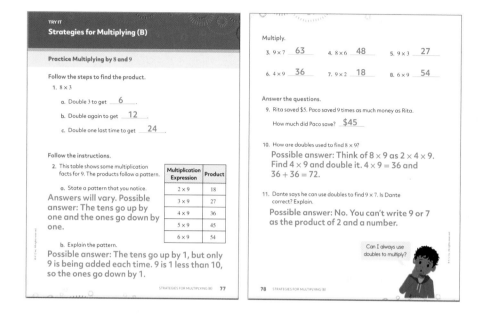

TRY IT
Strategies for Multiplying (B)

Practice Multiplying by 8 and 9

Follow the steps to find the product.

1. 8 × 3

   a. Double 3 to get ___6___

   b. Double again to get ___12___

   c. Double one last time to get ___24___

Follow the instructions.

2. This table shows some multiplication facts for 9. The products follow a pattern.

Multiplication Expression	Product
2 × 9	18
3 × 9	27
4 × 9	36
5 × 9	45
6 × 9	54

   a. State a pattern that you notice.
   Answers will vary. Possible answer: The tens go up by one and the ones go down by one.

   b. Explain the pattern.
   Possible answer: The tens go up by 1, but only 9 is being added each time. 9 is 1 less than 10, so the ones go down by 1.

Multiply.

3. 9 × 7 ___63___   4. 8 × 6 ___48___   5. 9 × 3 ___27___

6. 4 × 9 ___36___   7. 9 × 2 ___18___   8. 6 × 9 ___54___

Answer the questions.

9. Rita saved $5. Paco saved 9 times as much money as Rita.

   How much did Paco save? ___$45___

10. How are doubles used to find 8 × 9?
    Possible answer: Think of 8 × 9 as 2 × 4 × 9. Find 4 × 9 and double it. 4 × 9 = 36 and 36 + 36 = 72.

11. Dante says he can use doubles to find 9 × 7. Is Dante correct? Explain.
    Possible answer: No. You can't write 9 or 7 as the product of 2 and a number.

Can I always use doubles to multiply?

WRAP-UP

Multiplying by 8 and 9

Students will solve problems to show that they understand how to multiply by 8 and 9.

Strategies for Multiplying (C)

Lesson Overview

ACTIVITY	ACTIVITY TITLE	TIME	ONLINE/OFFLINE
GET READY	Introduction to Strategies for Multiplying (C)	**2** minutes	🖥️
	Multiplying by 10 and 5 Math Facts Game	**8** minutes	🖥️
LEARN AND **TRY IT**	Finding an Unknown Factor	**15** minutes	🖥️
	Find an Unknown Factor	**10** minutes	🖥️
	Practice Finding an Unknown Factor	**20** minutes	🖥️ and 📄
WRAP-UP	Finding an Unknown Factor	**5** minutes	🖥️

Content Background

Students will learn to find an unknown factor in a multiplication equation. Previously, students have found a product given two factors. The problems in this lesson are different because students will be given one factor and the product. They must find the unknown, or missing, factor. Working backwards to find an unknown factor requires students to know their multiplication facts. It also lays the foundation for students to learn about division. An unknown factor may be represented as a box or blank to fill in, a question mark, or even a letter such as n. Students will find unknown factors using an array and using their multiplication table.

Lesson Goals

- Identify factors and products.
- Find an unknown factor.

GET READY

Introduction to Strategies for Multiplying (C)

Students will get a glimpse of what they will learn about in the lesson. They will also read the lesson goals and keywords. Have students select each keyword and preview its definition.

Multiplying by 10 and 5 Math Facts Game

Students will practice multiplying by 10 and 5.

LEARN AND TRY IT

LEARN   Finding an Unknown Factor

Students will learn to find an unknown factor in a multiplication equation.

TRY IT   Find an Unknown Factor

Students will practice finding an unknown factor in a multiplication problem. Support will be provided to help students overcome misconceptions.

TRY IT   Practice Finding an Unknown Factor

Students will complete online practice problems. Then they will complete Practice Finding an Unknown Factor from *Summit Math 3 Activity Book*.

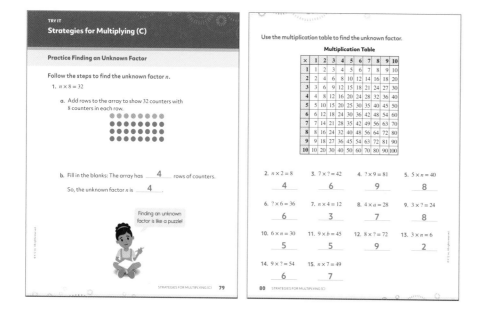

WRAP-UP

Finding an Unknown Factor

Students will solve a problem to show that they understand how to find an unknown factor.

Strategies for Multiplying (D)

Lesson Overview

ACTIVITY	ACTIVITY TITLE	TIME	ONLINE/OFFLINE
GET READY	Introduction to Strategies for Multiplying (D)	**2** minutes	🖥️
	Multiplying by 2 and 4 Math Facts	**8** minutes	🖥️
LEARN AND **TRY IT**	Multiplying by Multiples of 10 Using Place Value	**7** minutes	🖥️
	Multiply by Multiples of 10 Using Place Value	**7** minutes	🖥️
	Multiplying by Multiples of 10 Using Properties	**7** minutes	🖥️
	Multiply by Multiples of 10 Using Properties	**7** minutes	🖥️
	Practice Multiplying by Multiples of 10	**20** minutes	🖥️ and 📄
WRAP-UP	Multiplying by Multiples of 10	**2** minutes	🖥️

Content Background

Students will learn to multiply a number by a multiple of 10. Multiples of 10 end in 0, such as 20, 30, 40, and so on. Students will use base-10 blocks and skip counting to discover that they can multiply by the tens digit of the multiple of 10 and add on a 0 to get the product of a number and a multiple of 10. For example, $5 \times 2 = 10$ so $5 \times 20 = 100$. Another way to think about multiplying by a multiple of 10 is to use the associative property. A multiple of 10 is the product of a number and 10, such as $20 = 2 \times 10$.

$$5 \times 20 = 5 \times (2 \times 10) = (5 \times 2) \times 10 = 10 \times 10 = 100$$

Students may apply this strategy mentally without needing to write out each step. However, students may benefit from writing it out to help them understand the reason for the pattern.

Lesson Goals

• Multiply a number by a multiple of 10.

Introduction to Strategies for Multiplying (D)

Students will get a glimpse of what they will learn about in the lesson. They will also read the lesson goals and keywords. Have students select each keyword and preview its definition.

Multiplying by 2 and 4 Math Facts

Students will practice multiplying by 2 and 4.

LEARN AND TRY IT

LEARN   Multiplying by Multiples of 10 Using Place Value

Students will learn to multiply by multiples of 10 using place value.

TRY IT   Multiply by Multiples of 10 Using Place Value

Students will practice multiplying by multiples of 10 using place value. Support will be provided to help students overcome misconceptions.

LEARN   Multiplying by Multiples of 10 Using Properties

Students will learn to multiply by multiples of 10 using properties.

TRY IT   Multiply by Multiples of 10 Using Properties

Students will practice multiplying by multiples of 10 using properties. Support will be provided to help students overcome misconceptions.

TRY IT   Practice Multiplying by Multiples of 10

Students will complete online practice problems. Then they will complete Practice Multiplying by Multiples of 10 from *Summit Math 3 Activity Book.*

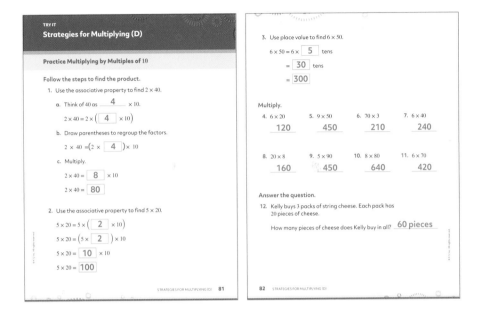

WRAP-UP

Multiplying by Multiples of 10

Students will solve a problem to show that they understand how to multiply by multiples of 10.

Strategies for Multiplying (E)

Lesson Overview

ACTIVITY	ACTIVITY TITLE	TIME	ONLINE/OFFLINE
GET READY	Introduction to Strategies for Multiplying (E)	**2** minutes	📶
TRY IT	Review Strategies for Multiplying	**18** minutes	📶
QUIZ	Strategies for Multiplying	**25** minutes	📶
WRAP-UP	More Math Practice	**15** minutes	📶

Lesson Goals

- Review using the associative property to multiply, multiplying by 8 and 9, identifying and explaining patterns, finding unknown factors, and multiplying by a multiple of 10.

- Take a quiz.

MATERIALS

There are no materials to gather for this lesson.

GET READY

Introduction to Introduction to Strategies for Multiplying (E)
Students will read the lesson goals.

TRY IT

Review Strategies for Multiplying
Students will answer questions to review what they have learned about strategies for multiplying.

QUIZ

Strategies for Multiplying
Students will complete the Strategies for Multiplying quiz.

More Math Practice

Students will practice skills according to their individual needs.

Problem Solving with Multiplication (A)

Lesson Overview

ACTIVITY	ACTIVITY TITLE	TIME	ONLINE/OFFLINE
GET READY	Introduction to Problem Solving with Multiplication (A)	**2** minutes	🖥️
	Look Back at Using an Array to Multiply	**8** minutes	🖥️
LEARN AND **TRY IT**	Finding Unknown Products in Real-World Problems	**15** minutes	🖥️
	Find Unknown Products in Real-World Problems	**10** minutes	🖥️
	Practice Finding Unknown Products in Real-World Problems	**20** minutes	🖥️ and 📄
WRAP-UP	Finding Unknown Products in Real-World Problems	**5** minutes	🖥️

Content Background

Students will learn to solve real-world problems by multiplying to find an unknown product. The real-world situations will include equal groups and arrays. Students will also learn how to represent a real-world problem using a multiplication number sentence or equation. Remind students to read each problem carefully and to organize the information in the problem.

MATERIALS

Supplied
- *Summit Math 3 Activity Book:* Practice Finding Unknown Products in Real-World Problems

Lesson Goals

- Solve a real-world problem to find an unknown product.

GET READY

Introduction to Problem Solving with Multiplication (A)

Students will get a glimpse of what they will learn about in the lesson. They will also read the lesson goals.

Look Back at Using an Array to Multiply

Students will practice the prerequisite skill of using an array to multiply.

LEARN Finding Unknown Products in Real-World Problems

Students will learn to find unknown products in real-world problems.

TRY IT Find Unknown Products in Real-World Problems

Students will practice finding unknown products in real-world problems. Support will be provided to help students overcome misconceptions.

TRY IT Practice Finding Unknown Products in Real-World Problems

Students will complete online practice problems. Then they will complete Practice Finding Unknown Products in Real-World Problems from *Summit Math 3 Activity Book*.

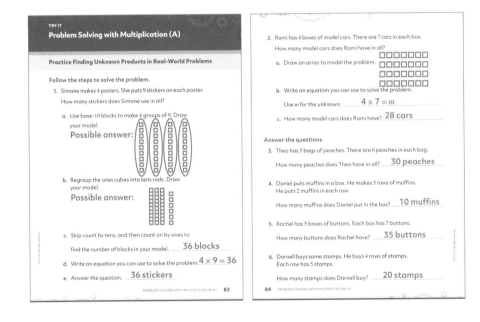

Finding Unknown Products in Real-World Problems

Students will solve a problem to show that they understand how to find unknown products in real-world problems.

Problem Solving with Multiplication (B)

Lesson Overview

ACTIVITY	ACTIVITY TITLE	TIME	ONLINE/OFFLINE
GET READY	Introduction to Problem Solving with Multiplication (B)	**2** minutes	🖥️
	Multiplying by 2 and 4 with Instant Recall	**8** minutes	🖥️
LEARN AND **TRY IT**	Finding Unknown Group Sizes in Real-World Problems	**7** minutes	🖥️
	Find Unknown Group Sizes in Real-World Problems	**7** minutes	🖥️
	Finding Unknown Numbers of Groups in Real-World Problems	**7** minutes	🖥️
	Find Unknown Numbers of Groups in Real-World Problems	**7** minutes	🖥️
	Practice Finding Group Sizes and Numbers of Groups in Problems	**20** minutes	🖥️ and 📄
WRAP-UP	Finding Group Sizes and Numbers of Groups in Problems	**2** minutes	🖥️

Content Background

Students will learn to solve real-world problems by finding a missing factor. That missing factor will either be the size of each equal group or the number of equal groups in the problem. Students will learn how to represent a real-world situation using a multiplication number sentence, or equation. In order to find a missing factor, students will learn how to work backwards using their multiplication facts.

Lesson Goals

- Solve a real-world problem to find an unknown factor.

MATERIALS

Supplied
- *Summit Math 3 Activity Book:* Practice Finding Group Sizes and Numbers of Groups in Problems

GET READY

Introduction to Problem Solving with Multiplication (B)
Students will get a glimpse of what they will learn about in the lesson. They will also read the lesson goals.

Multiplying by 2 and 4 with Instant Recall
Students will practice multiplying by 2 and 4.

LEARN Finding Unknown Group Sizes in Real-World Problems

Students will learn to find unknown group sizes in real-world problems.

TRY IT Find Unknown Group Sizes in Real-World Problems

Students will practice finding unknown group sizes in real-world problems. Support will be provided to help students overcome misconceptions.

LEARN Finding Unknown Numbers of Groups in Real-World Problems

Students will learn to find unknown numbers of groups in real-world problems.

TRY IT Find Unknown Numbers of Groups in Real-World Problems

Students will practice finding unknown numbers of groups in real-world problems. Support will be provided to help students overcome misconceptions.

TRY IT Practice Finding Group Sizes and Numbers of Groups in Problems

Students will complete online practice problems. Then they will complete Practice Finding Group Sizes and Numbers of Groups in Problems from *Summit Math 3 Activity Book*.

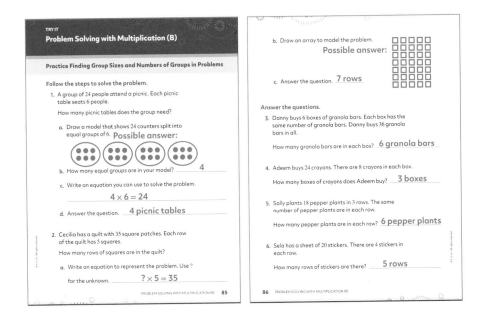

Finding Group Sizes and Numbers of Groups in Problems

Students will solve a problem to show that they understand how to find a group size or number of groups in a real-world problem.

Problem Solving with Multiplication (C)

Lesson Overview

ACTIVITY	ACTIVITY TITLE	TIME	ONLINE/OFFLINE
GET READY	Introduction to Problem Solving with Multiplication (C)	**2** minutes	🖥️
	Multiplying by 2 and 4 Math Facts Game	**8** minutes	🖥️
LEARN AND **TRY IT**	Understanding Order of Operations	**7** minutes	🖥️
	Understand Order of Operations	**7** minutes	🖥️
	Solving Two-Step Real-World Problems with Multiplication	**7** minutes	🖥️
	Solve Two-Step Real-World Problems with Multiplication	**7** minutes	🖥️
	Practice Solving Two-Step Problems with Multiplication	**20** minutes	🖥️ and 📄
WRAP-UP	Solving Two-Step Problems with Multiplication	**2** minutes	🖥️

Content Background

Students will learn to understand the order of operations and solve real-world problems with two steps. The order of operations is necessary to evaluate expressions with more than one step. Consider this problem that has two steps. Sarah buys 3 decks of cards to build a house of cards. Each deck costs $2. She pays with a $10 bill. How much change does she get back?

This problem involves finding the cost of the cards and subtracting that cost from $10. You must multiply then subtract. You get a different answer if you subtract then multiply. The order in which you evaluate the operations is important. When an equation has more than one operation, use the order of operations to know which operation to do first. The order of operations is a set of rules that tells you which operation to do first. First, multiply and divide going from left to right. Then, add and subtract going from left to right.

$$10 - 3 \times 2 = 10 - 6 = 4$$

Lesson Goals

- Evaluate expressions that have more than one operation.

- Solve real-world problems with two steps.

Introduction to Problem Solving with Multiplication (C)

Students will get a glimpse of what they will learn about in the lesson. They will also read the lesson goals and keywords. Have students select each keyword and preview its definition.

Multiplying by 2 and 4 Math Facts Game

Students will practice multiplying by 2 and 4.

LEARN AND TRY IT

LEARN   Understanding Order of Operations

Students will learn to understand the order of operations.

TRY IT   Understand Order of Operations

Students will practice understanding the order of operations. Support will be provided to help students overcome misconceptions.

LEARN   Solving Two-Step Real-World Problems with Multiplication

Students will learn to solve two-step real-world problems with multiplication.

TRY IT   Solve Two-Step Real-World Problems with Multiplication

Students will practice solving two-step real-world problems with multiplication. Support will be provided to help students overcome misconceptions.

TRY IT   Practice Solving Two-Step Problems with Multiplication

Students will complete online practice problems. Then they will complete Practice Solving Two-Step Problems with Multiplication from *Summit Math 3 Activity Book*.

WRAP-UP

Solving Two-Step Problems with Multiplication

Students will solve a problem to show that they understand how to solve two-step problems with multiplication.

Problem Solving with Multiplication (D)

Lesson Overview

ACTIVITY	ACTIVITY TITLE	TIME	ONLINE/OFFLINE
GET READY	Introduction to Problem Solving with Multiplication (D)	**2** minutes	📶
TRY IT	Review Problem Solving with Multiplication	**18** minutes	📶
QUIZ	Problem Solving with Multiplication	**25** minutes	📶
WRAP-UP	More Math Practice	**15** minutes	📶

Lesson Goals

- Review solving real-world multiplication problems with one or two steps, and understanding the order of operations.

- Take a quiz.

MATERIALS

There are no materials to gather for this lesson.

GET READY

Introduction to Problem Solving with Multiplication (D)

Students will read the lesson goals.

TRY IT

Review Problem Solving with Multiplication

Students will answer questions to review what they have learned about problem solving with multiplication.

QUIZ

Problem Solving with Multiplication

Students will complete the Problem Solving with Multiplication quiz.

More Math Practice

Students will practice skills according to their individual needs.

Big Ideas: Extended Problems

Lesson Overview

Big Ideas lessons provide students the opportunity to further apply the knowledge and skills acquired throughout previous units. Each Big Ideas lesson consists of two types of activities:

1. **Cumulative Review:** Students keep their skills fresh by reviewing prior content.

2. **Synthesis:** Students complete an assignment that allows them to interweave and apply what they've learned. These synthesis assignments will vary throughout the course.

   In the Synthesis portion of this Big Ideas lesson, students will complete multistep problems that go beyond the short answer and multiple choice problems they encounter in their regular lessons. These problems give students an opportunity to demonstrate problem solving, reasoning, communication, and modeling skills. Students will need to use pencil and paper and/or technology to show their work.

   LEARNING COACH CHECK-IN This is a graded assessment. Make sure students complete, review, and submit the assignment to their teacher.

All materials needed for this lesson are linked online. The materials are not provided in this Lesson Guide or in the Activity Book.

MATERIALS

Supplied
- Extended Problems Instructions (printout)

Exploring
Division

Division Concepts (A)

Lesson Overview

ACTIVITY	ACTIVITY TITLE	TIME	ONLINE/OFFLINE
GET READY	Introduction to Division Concepts (A)	**2** minutes	🖥
	Look Back at Multiplying Using an Array	**8** minutes	🖥
LEARN AND **TRY IT**	Dividing to Find the Size of Equal Groups	**15** minutes	🖥
	Divide to Find the Size of Equal Groups	**10** minutes	🖥
	Practice Dividing to Find the Size of Equal Groups	**20** minutes	🖥 and 📄
WRAP-UP	Dividing to Find the Size of Equal Groups	**5** minutes	🖥

Content Background

Students will learn to divide to find the size of equal groups. In a division problem, the dividend divided by the divisor is the quotient. For example, in the problem $24 \div 4 = 6$, 24 is the dividend, 4 is the divisor, and 6 is the quotient. Students are expected to learn and use the terms *dividend*, *divisor*, and *quotient*.

One way to understand division is to use equal groups. When you divide a total number of objects by the number of equal groups, you get the size of each group. The dividend is the total number of objects. The divisor is the number of groups. The quotient is the number of objects in each group.

SUPPORT   For students having difficulty finding the size of each equal group, suggest using physical objects to make equal groups. Students can use counters, blocks, coins, or other items. Start with the total number of objects in the problem and place one item into each group until all the items have been placed. Make sure that each group has an equal number of items.

Lesson Goals

- Identify the parts of a division equation.
- Divide to find the size of equal groups.

Introduction to Division Concepts (A)

After a quick introductory activity, students will read the lesson goals and keywords. Have students select each keyword and preview its definition.

Look Back at Multiplying Using an Array

Students will practice the prerequisite skill of multiplying using an array.

LEARN   Dividing to Find the Size of Equal Groups

Students will learn to divide to find the size of equal groups.

TRY IT   Divide to Find the Size of Equal Groups

Students will practice dividing to find the size of equal groups. Support will be provided to help students overcome misconceptions.

TRY IT   Practice Dividing to Find the Size of Equal Groups

Students will complete online practice problems. Then they will complete Practice Dividing to Find the Size of Equal Groups from *Summit Math 3 Activity Book.*

TRY IT
Division Concepts (A)

Practice Dividing to Find the Size of Equal Groups

Follow the instructions.

1. Draw a model of 30 ÷ 5.   **Possible answer:**

2. Write a story problem that models 21 ÷ 7.
   Possible answer: 21 oranges are split into 7 equal groups.

3. Label the dividend, divisor, and quotient in this division problem.

   36   ÷   9   =   4
   dividend   divisor   quotient

Follow the steps to answer the question.

4. 18 bees are split into 2 equal groups.
   How many bees are in each group?

   a. Circle 2 equal groups of bees.
   b. Count the number of bees in each group. **9 bees**

DIVISION CONCEPTS (A)   **89**

5. 24 butterflies are split into 4 equal groups.
   How many butterflies are in each group?

   a. Circle 4 equal groups of butterflies.
   b. Count the number of butterflies in each group. **6 butterflies**

Answer the questions.

6. 35 tennis balls are split into 7 equal groups.
   How many tennis balls are in each group?

   5 tennis balls

7. 32 ladybugs are split into 8 equal groups.
   How many ladybugs are in each group?

   4 ladybugs

90   DIVISION CONCEPTS (A)

Dividing to Find the Size of Equal Groups

Students will solve problems to show that they understand how to find the size of equal groups.

Division Concepts (B)

Lesson Overview

ACTIVITY	ACTIVITY TITLE	TIME	ONLINE/OFFLINE
GET READY	Introduction to Division Concepts (B)	**2** minutes	🖥️
	Multiplying by 3 Math Facts	**8** minutes	🖥️
LEARN AND **TRY IT**	Dividing to Find the Number of Equal Groups	**15** minutes	🖥️
	Divide to Find the Number of Equal Groups	**10** minutes	🖥️
	Practice Dividing to Find the Number of Equal Groups	**20** minutes	🖥️ and 📄
WRAP-UP	Dividing to Find the Number of Equal Groups	**5** minutes	🖥️

Content Background

Students will learn to divide to find the number of equal groups. One way to understand division is to use equal groups. When you divide a total number of objects by the size of each group, you get the number of groups. The dividend is the total number of objects. The divisor is the size of each group. The quotient is the number of groups. Students are expected to learn and use the terms *dividend*, *divisor*, and *quotient*.

SUPPORT   For students having difficulty finding the number of groups, suggest using physical objects to make equal groups. Students can use counters, blocks, coins, or other items. Start with the total number of objects in the problem and put the same number of items into each group until all the items have been placed. Make sure that each group has an equal number of items.

> ### Lesson Goals
> - Divide to find the number of equal groups.

GET READY

Introduction to Division Concepts (B)

Students will get a glimpse of what they will learn about in the lesson. They will also read the lesson goals and keywords. Have students select each keyword and preview its definition.

MATERIALS

Supplied
- *Summit Math 3 Activity Book:* Practice Dividing to Find the Number of Equal Groups

KEYWORDS

dividend – the number to be divided; the dividend divided by the divisor equals the quotient

division – an operation to share equally or group an amount into equal parts

divisor – the number that divides the dividend; the dividend divided by the divisor equals the quotient

quotient – the answer to a division problem; the dividend divided by the divisor equals the quotient

Multiplying by 3 Math Facts

Students will practice multiplying by 3.

LEARN   Dividing to Find the Number of Equal Groups

Students will learn to divide to find the number of equal groups.

TRY IT   Divide to Find the Number of Equal Groups

Students will practice dividing to find the number of equal groups. Support will be provided to help students overcome misconceptions.

TRY IT   Practice Dividing to Find the Number of Equal Groups

Students will complete online practice problems. Then they will complete Practice Dividing to Find the Number of Equal Groups from *Summit Math 3 Activity Book*.

WRAP-UP

Dividing to Find the Number of Equal Groups

Students will solve problems to show that they understand how to divide to find the number of equal groups.

Division Concepts (C)

Lesson Overview

ACTIVITY	ACTIVITY TITLE	TIME	ONLINE/OFFLINE
GET READY	Introduction to Division Concepts (C)	**2** minutes	🖥️
	Multiplying by 3 with Instant Recall	**8** minutes	🖥️
LEARN AND **TRY IT**	Dividing Using Arrays and Repeated Subtraction	**15** minutes	🖥️
	Divide Using Arrays and Repeated Subtraction	**10** minutes	🖥️
	Practice Dividing Using Arrays and Repeated Subtraction	**20** minutes	🖥️ and 📄
WRAP-UP	Dividing Using Arrays and Repeated Subtraction	**5** minutes	🖥️

Content Background

Students will learn to divide using arrays and repeated subtraction. Arrays model multiplication, but they can also model division. The divisor is the total number of objects. The divisor can be the number of rows *or* the number of columns. The quotient is the other dimension.

Division can also be modeled by repeated subtraction. For example, you can model $24 \div 6$ by repeatedly subtracting 6 from 24.

$$24 - 6 = 18$$
$$18 - 6 = 12$$
$$12 - 6 = 6$$
$$6 - 6 = 0$$

Since 6 can be subtracted 4 times from 24, $24 \div 6 = 4$.

Lesson Goals

- Use arrays to divide.
- Use repeated subtraction to divide.

KEYWORDS

array – a set of rows with the same number of objects in each row

dividend – the number to be divided; the dividend divided by the divisor equals the quotient

division – an operation to share equally or group an amount into equal parts

divisor – the number that divides the dividend; the dividend divided by the divisor equals the quotient

quotient – the answer to a division problem; the dividend divided by the divisor equals the quotient

Introduction to Division Concepts (C)

Students will get a glimpse of what they will learn about in the lesson. They will also read the lesson goals and keywords. Have students select each keyword and preview its definition.

Multiplying by 3 with Instant Recall

Students will practice multiplying by 3.

LEARN AND TRY IT

LEARN Dividing Using Arrays and Repeated Subtraction

Students will learn to divide using arrays and repeated subtraction.

TRY IT Divide Using Arrays and Repeated Subtraction

Students will practice dividing using arrays and repeated subtraction. Support will be provided to help students overcome misconceptions.

TRY IT Practice Dividing Using Arrays and Repeated Subtraction

Students will complete online practice problems. Then they will complete Practice Dividing Using Arrays and Repeated Subtraction from *Summit Math 3 Activity Book*.

TRY IT
Division Concepts (C)

Practice Dividing Using Arrays and Repeated Subtraction

Follow the instructions.

1. $6 \div 2$ can be modeled in different ways.

   a. Draw 6 squares in 2 equal groups.

   b. Draw 6 squares with 2 squares in each group.

   c. Draw an array with 6 squares.

   d. Fill in the boxes to subtract 2 from 6 until you get to 0.

   $6 - 2 = 4$
   $4 - 2 = 2$
   $2 - 2 = 0$

   e. What is $6 \div 2$? 3

DIVISION CONCEPTS (C) **93**

2. Draw a model of $36 \div 9$. Use an array.

   or

3. Fill in the boxes to model $28 \div 7$ with repeated subtraction.

   $28 - 7 = 21$
   $21 - 7 = 14$
   $14 - 7 = 7$
   $7 - 7 = 0$

4. Write a story problem that models $21 \div 3$ with an array.

   Answers may vary. Possible answer: 21 coins are arranged in an array with 3 equal rows.

5. What are the parts of $54 \div 9 = 6$? Fill in the blanks.

   The dividend is 54 . The divisor is 9
   The quotient is 6

94 DIVISION CONCEPTS (C)

Dividing Using Arrays and Repeated Subtraction

Students will solve problems to show that they understand how to divide using arrays and repeated subtraction.

Division Concepts (D)

Lesson Overview

ACTIVITY	ACTIVITY TITLE	TIME	ONLINE/OFFLINE
GET READY	Introduction to Division Concepts (D)	**2** minutes	🖥️
	Multiplying by 3 Math Facts Game	**8** minutes	🖥️
LEARN AND **TRY IT**	Dividing with Fact Families	**7** minutes	🖥️
	Divide with Fact Families	**7** minutes	🖥️
	Dividing Using the Multiplication Table	**7** minutes	🖥️
	Divide Using the Multiplication Table	**7** minutes	🖥️
	Practice Solving Division Problems	**20** minutes	🖥️ and 📄
WRAP-UP	Solving Division Problems	**2** minutes	🖥️

Content Background

Students will learn to use the inverse relationship between multiplication and division. Inverse operations are opposite operations that undo each other. You multiply two factors to get a product. But you can also divide a product by one of its factors to get the other factor. Students will first learn to build fact families that consist of two multiplication equations and two division equations that all use the same numbers in different orders. For example, this is the fact family for 4, 8, and 32.

$$4 \times 8 = 32 \qquad 8 \times 4 = 32 \qquad 32 \div 8 = 4 \qquad 32 \div 4 = 8$$

You can use the related equations in a fact family to multiply or divide. For example, to find the missing number in $n \times 8 = 32$, you can use the related equation $32 \div 8 = n$. Or if you must find the missing number $m \div 8 = 4$, you could use the related equation $4 \times 8 = m$.

Students will also apply the inverse relationship between multiplication and division to divide using the multiplication table. In a multiplication table, one factor is listed in the first column and the other factor is listed in the first row. The product is where the column and row meet. However, you can also use the multiplication chart to divide. Find the divisor in the first column. Move across the row until you get to the dividend. Then move up to the top of the column to find the quotient. This multiplication table shows that $6 \times 8 = 48$ and $48 \div 6 = 8$.

×	1	2	3	4	5	6	7	8	9	10
1	1	2	3	4	5	6	7	8	9	10
2	2	4	6	8	10	12	14	16	18	20
3	3	6	9	12	15	18	21	24	27	30
4	4	8	12	16	20	24	28	32	36	40
5	5	10	15	20	25	30	35	40	45	50
6	6	12	18	24	30	36	42	48	54	60
7	7	14	21	28	35	42	49	56	63	70
8	8	16	24	32	40	48	56	64	72	80
9	9	18	27	36	45	54	63	72	81	90
10	10	20	30	40	50	60	70	80	90	100

Lesson Goals

- Write multiplication and division fact families.

- Use multiplication and division to solve problems.

- Divide using a multiplication table.

GET READY

Introduction to Division Concepts (D)

Students will get a glimpse of what they will learn about in the lesson. They will also read the lesson goals and keywords. Have students select each keyword and preview its definition.

Multiplying by 3 Math Facts Game

Students will practice multiplying by 3.

LEARN AND TRY IT

LEARN   Dividing with Fact Families

Students will learn to use fact families to multiply or divide.

TRY IT   Divide with Fact Families

Students will practice using fact families to multiply or divide. Support will be provided to help students overcome misconceptions.

LEARN   Dividing Using the Multiplication Table

Students will learn to divide using the multiplication table.

TRY IT   Divide Using the Multiplication Table

Students will practice dividing using the multiplication table. Support will be provided to help students overcome misconceptions.

TRY IT   Practice Solving Division Problems

Students will complete online practice problems. Then they will complete Practice Solving Division Problems from *Summit Math 3 Activity Book*.

WRAP-UP

Solving Division Problems

Students will solve problems to show that they understand how to solve division problems.

Division Concepts (E)

Lesson Overview

ACTIVITY	ACTIVITY TITLE	TIME	ONLINE/OFFLINE
GET READY	Introduction to Division Concepts (E)	**2** minutes	🖥️
TRY IT	Review Division Concepts	**18** minutes	🖥️
QUIZ	Division Concepts	**25** minutes	🖥️
WRAP-UP	More Math Practice	**15** minutes	🖥️

Lesson Goals

- Review dividing using equal groups, arrays, fact families, and the multiplication table.

- Take a quiz.

MATERIALS

There are no materials to gather for this lesson.

GET READY

Introduction to Division Concepts (E)

Students will read the lesson goals.

TRY IT

Review Division Concepts

Students will answer questions to review what they have learned about division concepts.

QUIZ

Division Concepts

Students will complete the Division Concepts quiz.

More Math Practice

Students will practice skills according to their individual needs.

Division Patterns (A)

Lesson Overview

ACTIVITY	ACTIVITY TITLE	TIME	ONLINE/OFFLINE
GET READY	Introduction to Division Patterns (A)	**2** minutes	🖥️
	Look Back at Multiplying by 1	**8** minutes	🖥️
LEARN AND **TRY IT**	Dividing by 1	**7** minutes	🖥️
	Divide by 1	**7** minutes	🖥️
	Dividing 0 by Any Number	**7** minutes	🖥️
	Divide 0 by Any Number	**7** minutes	🖥️
	Practice Dividing by 1 and Dividing 0 by Any Number	**20** minutes	🖥️ and 📄
WRAP-UP	Dividing by 1 and Dividing 0 by Any Number	**2** minutes	🖥️

Content Background

Students will learn to divide by 1 and divide 0 by any number. Through examples, students will learn two important properties.

Identity Property of Division
A number divided by 1 equals the number.

Zero Property of Division
0 divided by any number, except 0, equals 0.

> **NOTE** Some students are curious about why we don't divide by 0. The reason will be covered in subsequent math courses. If your student asks, you can explain that a divisor of 0 means making 0 groups. You can't split a dividend if there aren't any groups. 0 can be a dividend, but not a divisor.

Encourage students to carefully consider each problem to determine which property to apply.

Lesson Goals
- Divide a number by 1.
- Divide 0 by a number.

Introduction to Division Patterns (A)

Students will get a glimpse of what they will learn about in the lesson. They will also read the lesson goals.

Look Back at Multiplying by 1

Students will practice the prerequisite skill of multiplying by 1.

LEARN AND TRY IT

LEARN   Dividing by 1

Students will learn to divide by 1.

TRY IT   Divide by 1

Students will practice dividing by 1. Support will be provided to help students overcome misconceptions.

LEARN   Dividing 0 by Any Number

Students will learn to divide 0 by any number.

TRY IT   Divide 0 by Any Number

Students will practice dividing 0 by any number. Support will be provided to help students overcome misconceptions.

TRY IT   Practice Dividing by 1 and Dividing 0 by Any Number

Students will complete online practice problems. Then they will complete Practice Dividing by 1 and Dividing 0 by Any Number *Summit Math 3 Activity Book.*

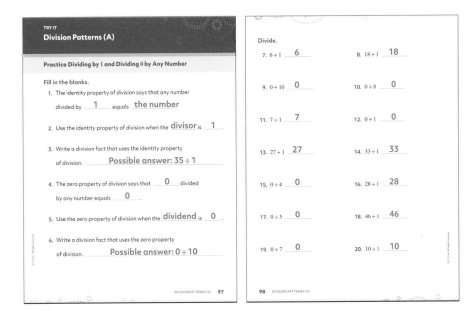

WRAP-UP

Dividing by 1 and Dividing 0 by Any Number

Students will solve problems to show that they understand how to divide by 1 and divide 0 by any number.

Division Patterns (B)

Lesson Overview

ACTIVITY	ACTIVITY TITLE	TIME	ONLINE/OFFLINE
GET READY	Introduction to Division Patterns (B)	**2** minutes	📶
	Multiplying by 6 Math Facts	**8** minutes	📶
LEARN AND **TRY IT**	Dividing by 5	**15** minutes	📶
	Divide by 5	**10** minutes	📶
	Practice Dividing by 5	**20** minutes	📶 and 📄
WRAP-UP	Dividing by 5	**5** minutes	📶

Content Background

Students will learn to divide by 5 fluently using various strategies. Two common strategies for dividing are using repeated subtraction and using a related multiplication fact.

Multiplication is repeated addition. Division is the opposite of multiplication and subtraction is the opposite of addition. Therefore, division is repeated subtraction. A number line can be used to represent repeated subtraction. The quotient is the number of times 5 can be subtracted from the dividend to get to 0.

Since division is the opposite of multiplication, students can also use related multiplication facts to divide. If a student is still working on memorizing their multiplication facts, they may use their multiplication table to find related multiplication facts. This lesson focuses only on dividing by 5, so they will only use the row where 5 is a factor. Encourage students to try both strategies to find the one that makes the most sense.

MATERIALS

Supplied
- *Summit Math 3 Activity Book:* Practice Dividing by 5

Lesson Goals

- Divide by 5 using repeated subtraction.
- Divide by 5 using related multiplication facts.

Introduction to Division Patterns (B)

Students will get a glimpse of what they will learn about in the lesson. They will also read the lesson goals.

Multiplying by 6 Math Facts

Students will practice multiplying by 6.

LEARN AND TRY IT

LEARN   Dividing by 5

Students will learn to divide by 5 using different strategies.

TRY IT   Divide by 5

Students will practice dividing by 5 using different strategies. Support will be provided to help students overcome misconceptions.

TRY IT   Practice Dividing by 5

Students will complete online practice problems. Then they will complete Practice Dividing by 5 from *Summit Math 3 Activity Book*.

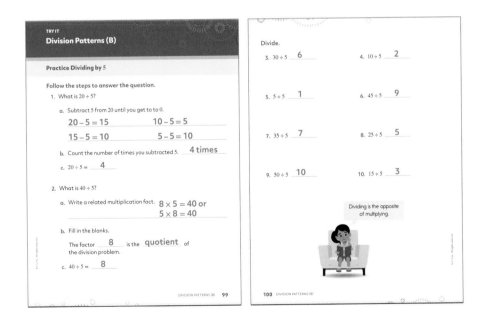

WRAP-UP

Dividing by 5

Students will solve problems to show that they understand how to divide by 5.

Division Patterns (C)

Lesson Overview

ACTIVITY	ACTIVITY TITLE	TIME	ONLINE/OFFLINE
GET READY	Introduction to Division Patterns (C)	**2** minutes	🖥️
	Multiplying by 6 with Instant Recall	**8** minutes	🖥️
LEARN AND **TRY IT**	Dividing by 10	**15** minutes	🖥️
	Divide by 10	**10** minutes	🖥️
	Practice Dividing by 10	**20** minutes	🖥️ and 📄
WRAP-UP	Dividing by 10	**5** minutes	🖥️

Content Background

Students will learn to divide by 10 fluently using various strategies. Students can divide using repeated subtraction, with or without a number line, related multiplication facts, or the pattern for dividing by 10. With repeated subtraction, the quotient is the number of times 10 can be subtracted from the dividend to get to 0. In a related multiplication fact, the quotient is the factor that isn't 10. If students are still working on memorizing their multiplication facts, they may use their multiplication table to find related multiplication facts. This lesson focuses only on dividing by 10, so they will use only the row where 10 is a factor.

There is a pattern when we divide a number that ends in 0 by 10. The quotient is the dividend without the last 0. For example, $40 \div 10 = 4$. The dividend with the zero dropped is 4, which is the quotient. The reason we say that the last zero is dropped is because 100 has two zeros: $100 \div 10 = 10$. Encourage students to try each strategy to find the one that makes the most sense.

> **MATERIALS**
>
> **Supplied**
> - *Summit Math 3 Activity Book:* Practice Dividing by 10

Lesson Goals

- Divide by 10 using repeated subtraction.
- Divide by 10 using related multiplication facts.

Introduction to Division Patterns (C)

Students will get a glimpse of what they will learn about in the lesson. They will also read the lesson goals.

Multiplying by 6 with Instant Recall

Students will practice multiplying by 6.

LEARN AND TRY IT

LEARN Dividing by 10

Students will learn to divide by 10 using different strategies.

TRY IT Divide by 10

Students will practice dividing by 10 using different strategies. Support will be provided to help students overcome misconceptions.

TRY IT Practice Dividing by 10

Students will complete online practice problems. Then they will complete Practice Dividing by 10 from *Summit Math 3 Activity Book*.

TRY IT
Division Patterns (C)

Practice Dividing by 10

Follow the steps to answer the question.

1. What is 80 ÷ 10?

   a. Subtract 10 from 80 until you get to 0.

80 – 10 = 70	40 – 10 = 30
70 – 10 = 60	30 – 10 = 20
60 – 10 = 50	20 – 10 = 10
50 – 10 = 40	10 – 10 = 0

   b. Count the number of times you subtracted 10.   __8 times__

   c. 80 ÷ 10 = __8__

2. What is 40 ÷ 10?

   a. Write a related multiplication fact.   __4 × 10 = 40 or 10 × 4 = 40__

   b. Fill in the blanks.

   The factor __4__ is the __quotient__ of the division problem.

   c. 40 ÷ 10 = __4__

DIVISION PATTERNS (C) **101**

---

3. What is 70 ÷ 10?

   a. Fill in the blanks.

   The pattern for dividing by 10 is to drop the digit __0__ from the end of the __dividend__.

   b. 70 ÷ 10 = __7__

Divide.

4. 20 ÷ 10 __2__   5. 90 ÷ 10 __9__

6. 10 ÷ 10 __1__   7. 100 ÷ 10 __10__

8. 50 ÷ 10 __5__   9. 30 ÷ 10 __3__

10. 60 ÷ 10 __6__

102 DIVISION PATTERNS (C)

WRAP-UP

Dividing by 10

Students will solve problems to show that they understand how to divide by 10.

Division Patterns (D)

Lesson Overview

ACTIVITY	ACTIVITY TITLE	TIME	ONLINE/OFFLINE
GET READY	Introduction to Division Patterns (D)	**2** minutes	🖥️
TRY IT	Review Division Patterns	**18** minutes	🖥️
QUIZ	Division Patterns	**25** minutes	🖥️
WRAP-UP	More Math Practice	**15** minutes	🖥️

Lesson Goals

- Review dividing 0 by a number and dividing by 1, 5, and 10.
- Take a quiz.

MATERIALS

There are no materials to gather for this lesson.

GET READY

Introduction to Division Patterns (D)

Students will read the lesson goals.

TRY IT

Review Division Patterns

Students will answer questions to review what they have learned about division patterns.

QUIZ

Division Patterns

Students will complete the Division Patterns quiz.

More Math Practice

Students will practice skills according to their individual needs.

Big Ideas: Mini-Project

Lesson Overview

Big Ideas lessons provide students the opportunity to further apply the knowledge and skills acquired throughout previous units. Each Big Ideas lesson consists of two types of activities:

1. **Cumulative Review:** Students keep their skills fresh by reviewing prior content.

2. **Synthesis:** Students complete an assignment that allows them to interweave and apply what they've learned. These synthesis assignments will vary throughout the course.

In the Synthesis portion of this Big Ideas lesson, students will complete a small, creative project designed to tie together concepts and skills that students have encountered across units. These small projects are designed to emphasize a real-world application that connects mathematics to other subjects, including science, technology, engineering, art, and history. Students will need to use pencil and paper and/or technology to show their work.

LEARNING COACH CHECK-IN Make sure students complete, review, and submit the assignment to their teacher.

All materials needed for this lesson are linked online. The materials are not provided in this Lesson Guide or in the Activity Book.

> ### MATERIALS
>
> **Supplied**
> - Mini-Project Instructions (printout)

Division Equations
and
Strategies

Division Equations (A)

Lesson Overview

ACTIVITY	ACTIVITY TITLE	TIME	ONLINE/OFFLINE
GET READY	Introduction to Division Equations (A)	**2** minutes	📶
	Look Back at Skip Counting by 2s	**8** minutes	📶
LEARN AND **TRY IT**	Dividing by 2	**7** minutes	📶
	Divide by 2	**7** minutes	📶
	Dividing by 4	**7** minutes	📶
	Divide by 4	**7** minutes	📶
	Practice Dividing by 2 and 4	**20** minutes	📶 and 📄
WRAP-UP	Dividing by 2 and 4	**2** minutes	📶

Content Background

Students have a basic understanding of division. They will apply their understanding to explore division properties and different representations of division specifically when dividing by 2 and 4. Encourage your student to try these strategies when dividing: making equal groups, making an array, using a related multiplication fact, or using the multiplication table. Although one strategy may be emphasized in the lesson, students can use any of these strategies to divide.

Students will learn to represent a division problem using the long-division symbol, as in $2\overline{)6}$. This division problem is read as "6 divided by 2."

> ### Lesson Goals
> - Divide by 2.
> - Divide by 4.

MATERIALS

Supplied
- *Summit Math 3 Activity Book:* Practice Dividing by 2 and 4

KEYWORDS

equation – a number sentence; two expressions that are shown as equal to one another

---

GET READY

Introduction to Division Equations (A)

After a quick introductory activity, students will read the lesson goals and keywords. Have students select each keyword and preview its definition.

Look Back at Skip Counting by 2s

Students will practice the prerequisite skill of skip counting by 2.

LEARN AND TRY IT

LEARN   Dividing by 2

Students will learn to divide by 2.

TRY IT   Divide by 2

Students will practice dividing by 2. Support will be provided to help students overcome misconceptions.

LEARN   Dividing by 4

Students will learn to divide by 4.

TRY IT   Divide by 4

Students will practice dividing by 4. Support will be provided to help students overcome misconceptions.

TRY IT   Practice Dividing by 2 and 4

Students will complete online practice problems. Then they will complete Practice Dividing by 2 and 4 from *Summit Math 3 Activity Book*.

TRY IT
Division Equations (A)

Practice Dividing by 2 and 4

Follow the steps to answer the question.

1. What is $14 \div 2$?

   a. Draw 14 counters split into these two equal groups.

   b. Fill in the blanks: The model has __14__ counters split into __2__ equal groups of __7__ counters.

   c. Write an equation for this model. __$14 \div 2 = 7$__

2. What is $12 \div 4$?

   a. Draw a model of $12 \div 4$.   **Possible answer:**

   b. Fill in the blank.

   $12 \div 4 =$ __3__

DIVISION EQUATIONS (A)   **103**

Fill in the blanks.

3. $12 \div 2 =$ __6__ because __6__ $\times 2 = 12$.

4. $40 \div 4 =$ __10__ because __10__ $\times 4 = 40$.

Divide.

5. $2\overline{)10}$ __5__

6. $4\overline{)32}$ __8__

7. $4\overline{)28}$ __7__

8. $2\overline{)6}$ __3__

9. $36 \div 4$ __9__

10. $20 \div 2$ __10__

11. $8 \div 2$ __4__

12. $24 \div 4$ __6__

13. $4 \div 2$ __2__

14. $8 \div 4$ __2__

104   DIVISION EQUATIONS (A)

Dividing by 2 and 4

Students will solve problems to show that they understand how to divide by 2 and 4.

Division Equations (B)

Lesson Overview

ACTIVITY	ACTIVITY TITLE	TIME	ONLINE/OFFLINE
GET READY	Introduction to Division Equations (B)	**2** minutes	🖥️
	Multiplying by 6 Math Facts Game	**8** minutes	🖥️
LEARN AND **TRY IT**	Dividing by 3	**7** minutes	🖥️
	Divide by 3	**7** minutes	🖥️
	Dividing by 6	**7** minutes	🖥️
	Divide by 6	**7** minutes	🖥️
	Practice Dividing by 3 and 6	**20** minutes	🖥️ and 📄
WRAP-UP	Dividing by 3 and 6	**2** minutes	🖥️

Content Background

Students may benefit from examining the relationship between the quotients that result from dividing the same dividend by 3 and by 6. Students will notice that the quotient after dividing by 6 is half the quotient after dividing by 3.

Dividing by 6 can be difficult for some students, so they might find it easier to first divide a dividend by 3 and then divide that quotient by 2. For example, to find $24 \div 6$, find $24 \div 3 = 8$ and $8 \div 2 = 4$, so $24 \div 6 = 4$.

> ### Lesson Goals
> - Divide by 3.
> - Divide by 6.

MATERIALS

Supplied
- *Summit Math 3 Activity Book:* Practice Dividing by 3 and 6

KEYWORDS

inverse operations – opposite operations that undo each other; subtraction and addition are inverse operations; division and multiplication are inverse operations

GET READY

Introduction to Division Equations (B)

Students will get a glimpse of what they will learn about in the lesson. They will also read the lesson goals and keywords. Have students select each keyword and preview its definition.

Multiplying by 6 Math Facts Game

Students will practice multiplying by 6.

LEARN AND TRY IT

LEARN   Dividing by 3

Students will learn to divide by 3.

TRY IT   Divide by 3

Students will practice dividing by 3. Support will be provided to help students overcome misconceptions.

LEARN   Dividing by 6

Students will learn to divide by 6.

TRY IT   Divide by 6

Students will practice dividing by 6. Support will be provided to help students overcome misconceptions.

TRY IT   Practice Dividing by 3 and 6

Students will complete online practice problems. Then they will complete Practice Dividing by 3 and 6 from *Summit Math 3 Activity Book*.

TRY IT
Division Equations (B)

Practice Dividing by 3 and 6

Follow the steps to answer the question.

1. What is $18 \div 3$?

   a. Draw an array to model $18 \div 3$.

   Possible answer: ●●●●●●
   ●●●●●●
   ●●●●●●

   b. Fill in the blank.

   $18 \div 3 = \underline{6}$

   c. Write another division equation that this array represents. $\underline{18 \div 6 = 3}$

Fill in the blanks.

2. $24 \div 6 = \underline{4}$ because $\underline{4} \times 6 = 24$.

3. $30 \div 3 = \underline{10}$ because $\underline{10} \times 3 = 30$.

DIVISION EQUATIONS (B)   **105**

---

4. $27 \div 3 = \underline{9}$ because $\underline{9} \times 3 = 27$.

5. $12 \div 6 = \underline{2}$ because $\underline{2} \times 6 = 12$.

Divide.

6. $3\overline{)9}$ → 3

7. $3\overline{)15}$ → 5

8. $6\overline{)30}$ → 5

9. $6\overline{)36}$ → 6

10. $54 \div 6$ → 9

11. $60 \div 6$ → 10

12. $3 \div 3$ → 1

13. $27 \div 3$ → 9

14. $21 \div 3$ → 7

15. $42 \div 6$ → 7

106   DIVISION EQUATIONS (B)

Dividing by 3 and 6

Students will solve problems to show that they understand how to divide by 3 and 6.

Division Equations (C)

Lesson Overview

ACTIVITY	ACTIVITY TITLE	TIME	ONLINE/OFFLINE
GET READY	Introduction to Division Equations (C)	**2** minutes	📶
	Multiplying by 9 Math Facts	**8** minutes	📶
LEARN AND **TRY IT**	Dividing by 7, 8, and 9 Using Related Multiplication Facts	**7** minutes	📶
	Divide by 7, 8, and 9 Using Related Multiplication Facts	**7** minutes	📶
	Dividing by 7, 8, and 9 Using Multiplication Tables	**7** minutes	📶
	Divide by 7, 8, and 9 Using Multiplication Tables	**7** minutes	📶
	Practice Dividing by 7, 8, and 9	**20** minutes	📶 and 📄
WRAP-UP	Dividing by 7, 8, and 9	**2** minutes	📶

Content Background

Students have an understanding of the concept that one operation can undo another. They have also learned that multiplication and division undo each other. Students will practice using the inverse relationship between multiplication and division to divide by 7, 8, and 9. Since multiplication and division are inverse operations, a related multiplication fact can help students find the answer to a division problem. For example, $18 \div 9$ must equal 2 because $2 \times 9 = 18$. Students can also use a multiplication table to divide.

MATERIALS

Supplied
- *Summit Math 3 Activity Book:* Practice Dividing by 7, 8, and 9

Lesson Goals

- Divide by 7.
- Divide by 8.
- Divide by 9.

GET READY

Introduction to Division Equations (C)

Students will get a glimpse of what they will learn about in the lesson. They will also read the lesson goals.

Multiplying by 9 Math Facts

Students will practice multiplying by 9.

LEARN   Dividing by 7, 8, and 9 Using Related Multiplication Facts

Students will learn to divide by 7, 8, and 9 using related multiplication facts.

TRY IT   Divide by 7, 8, and 9 Using Related Multiplication Facts

Students will practice dividing by 7, 8, and 9 using related multiplication facts. Support will be provided to help students overcome misconceptions.

LEARN   Dividing by 7, 8, and 9 Using Multiplication Tables

Students will learn to divide by 7, 8, and 9 using multiplication tables.

TRY IT   Divide by 7, 8, and 9 Using Multiplication Tables

Students will practice dividing by 7, 8, and 9 using multiplication tables. Support will be provided to help students overcome misconceptions.

TRY IT   Practice Dividing by 7, 8, and 9

Students will complete online practice problems. Then they will complete Practice Dividing by 7, 8, and 9 from *Summit Math 3 Activity Book*.

TRY IT
Division Equations (C)

Practice Dividing by 7, 8, and 9

Follow the steps to answer the question. Use the multiplication table.

1. What is $49 \div 7$?
   a. The divisor is 7. Point to 7 in the left column.
   b. The dividend is 49. Move right to 49.
   c. Move up to the first row. The number where you end up is the quotient.
   d. Fill in the blank.
      $49 \div 7 =$ __7__

2. What is $81 \div 9$?
   a. The divisor is 9. Point to 9 in the left column.
   b. The dividend is 81. Move right to 81.
   c. Move up to the first row. The number where you end up is the quotient.
   d. Fill in the blank. $81 \div 9 =$ __9__

DIVISION EQUATIONS (C)   **107**

---

3. What is $32 \div 8$?
   a. The divisor is 8. Point to 8 in the left column.
   b. The dividend is 32. Move right to 32.
   c. Move up to the first row. The number where you end up is the quotient.
   d. Fill in the blank.
      $32 \div 8 =$ __4__

Divide.

4. $7 \overline{)21}$ → 3   5. $9 \overline{)36}$ → 4   6. $7 \overline{)70}$ → 10   7. $8 \overline{)48}$ → 6

8. $18 \div 9 =$ 2   9. $42 \div 7 =$ 6

10. $24 \div 8 =$ 3   11. $90 \div 9 =$ 10

12. $42 \div 7 =$ 6   13. $56 \div 8 =$ 7

108   DIVISION EQUATIONS (C)

Dividing by 7, 8, and 9

Students will solve problems to show that they understand how to divide by 7, 8, and 9.

Division Equations (D)

Lesson Overview

ACTIVITY	ACTIVITY TITLE	TIME	ONLINE/OFFLINE
GET READY	Introduction to Division Equations (D)	**2** minutes	🖥️
	Multiplying by 9 with Instant Recall	**8** minutes	🖥️
LEARN AND **TRY IT**	Finding an Unknown Number in a Division Equation	**15** minutes	🖥️
	Find an Unknown Number in a Division Equation	**10** minutes	🖥️
	Practice Finding an Unknown Number in a Division Equation	**20** minutes	🖥️ and 📄
WRAP-UP	Finding an Unknown Number in a Division Equation	**5** minutes	🖥️

Content Background

A division equation is a number sentence that uses division, such as $30 \div 3 = 10$. In division equations with one of the numbers missing, students use what they know about the relationship between multiplication and division to find that missing number. Understanding the relationship between multiplication and division allows students to use multiplication to solve division problems and helps them check their work.

Lesson Goals

- Find a missing number in a division equation.

MATERIALS

Supplied

- *Summit Math 3 Activity Book:* Practice Finding an Unknown Number in a Division Equation

KEYWORDS

dividend – the number to be divided; the dividend divided by the divisor equals the quotient

divisor – the number that divides the dividend; the dividend divided by the divisor equals the quotient

equation – a number sentence; two expressions that are shown as equal to one another

quotient – the answer to a division problem; the dividend divided by the divisor equals the quotient

GET READY

Introduction to Division Equations (D)

Students will get a glimpse of what they will learn about in the lesson. They will also read the lesson goals and keywords. Have students select each keyword and preview its definition.

Multiplying by 9 with Instant Recall

Students will practice multiplying by 9.

LEARN Finding an Unknown Number in a Division Equation

Students will find an unknown number in a division equation.

TRY IT Find an Unknown Number in a Division Equation

Students will practice finding an unknown number in a division equation. Support will be provided to help students overcome misconceptions.

TRY IT Practice Finding an Unknown Number in a Division Equation

Students will complete online practice problems. Then they will complete Practice Finding an Unknown Number in a Division Equation from *Summit Math 3 Activity Book*.

TRY IT
Division Equations (D)

Practice Finding an Unknown Number in a Division Equation

Fill in the blanks.

1. Use the words *dividend, divisor,* and *quotient* in each part.

   a. dividend ÷ divisor = quotient

   b. The product of the quotient and the divisor is the dividend.

Answer the questions to find the missing number.

2. $35 \div ? = 5$

   a. Which number is missing from this equation? Circle your answer.

   dividend (divisor) quotient

   b. How can you find the missing number?
   Possible answer: I can think of which number times 5 equals 35.

   c. What is the missing number? 7

DIVISION EQUATIONS (D) **109**

---

3. $? \div 6 = 9$

   a. Which number is missing? Circle your answer.

   (dividend) divisor quotient

   b. How can you find the missing number?
   Possible answer: I can multiply 6 by 9.

   c. What is the missing number? 54

Fill in the boxes.

4. 24 ÷ 3 = 8 because 8 × 3 = 24 .

5. 28 ÷ 4 = 7 because 7 × 4 = 28.

6. 27 ÷ 9 = 3 because 3 × 9 = 27.

Fill in the box with the missing number.

7. 16 ÷ 2 = 8   8. 45 ÷ 9 = 5   9. 9 ÷ 3 = 3

10. 20 ÷ 4 = 5   11. 42 ÷ 6 = 7   12. 18 ÷ 6 = 3

110 DIVISION EQUATIONS (D)

Finding an Unknown Number in a Division Equation

Students will solve problems to show that they understand how to find an unknown number in a division equation.

Division Equations (E)

Lesson Overview

ACTIVITY	ACTIVITY TITLE	TIME	ONLINE/OFFLINE
GET READY	Introduction to Division Equations (E)	**2** minutes	🖥️
TRY IT	Review Division Equations	**18** minutes	🖥️
QUIZ	Division Equations	**25** minutes	🖥️
WRAP-UP	More Math Practice	**15** minutes	🖥️

Lesson Goals

- Review dividing by 2, 3, 4, 6, 7, 8, and 9, and finding an unknown number in a division equation.

- Take a quiz.

MATERIALS

There are no materials to gather for this lesson.

GET READY

Introduction to Division Equations (E)

Students will read the lesson goals.

TRY IT

Review Division Equations

Students will answer questions to review what they have learned about division equations.

QUIZ

Division Equations

Students will complete the Division Equations quiz.

More Math Practice

Students will practice skills according to their individual needs.

Problem Solving with Division (A)

Lesson Overview

ACTIVITY	ACTIVITY TITLE	TIME	ONLINE/OFFLINE
GET READY	Introduction to Problem Solving with Division (A)	**2** minutes	🖥️
	Look Back at Modeling Division	**8** minutes	🖥️
LEARN AND **TRY IT**	Solving Number of Groups Problems	**7** minutes	🖥️
	Solve Number of Groups Problems	**7** minutes	🖥️
	Solving Number in Group Problems	**7** minutes	🖥️
	Solve Number in Group Problems	**7** minutes	🖥️
	Practice Solving Division Group Problems	**20** minutes	🖥️ and 📄
WRAP-UP	Solving Division Group Problems	**2** minutes	🖥️

Content Background

Students understand that division is an operation that means sharing equally. Students can use division to find the number of equal groups when they know the total number of objects and the number in each group. They can also find the number in each group when they know the total and the number of groups. They have used equal groups to solve simple division problems. Now, students will apply what they have learned to solve real-world problems involving equal groups.

> ### Lesson Goals
> - Solve real-world problems using equal groups.

MATERIALS

Supplied
- *Summit Math 3 Activity Book:* Practice Solving Division Group Problems

GET READY

Introduction to Problem Solving with Division (A)
Students will get a glimpse of what they will learn about in the lesson. They will also read the lesson goals.

Look Back at Modeling Division
Students will practice the prerequisite skill of modeling division.

LEARN Solving Number of Groups Problems

Students will learn to solve problems that involve finding the number of equal groups.

TRY IT Solve Number of Groups Problems

Students will practice solving number of groups problems. Support will be provided to help students overcome misconceptions.

LEARN Solving Number in Group Problems

Students will learn to solve problems that involve finding the number of items in each equal group.

TRY IT Solve Number in Group Problems

Students will practice solving number in group problems. Support will be provided to help students overcome misconceptions.

TRY IT Practice Solving Division Group Problems

Students will complete online practice problems. Then they will complete Practice Solving Division Group Problems from *Summit Math 3 Activity Book.*

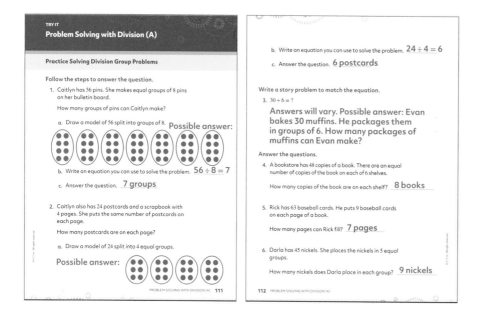

Solving Division Group Problems

Students will solve a problem to show that they understand how to solve division problems involving equal groups.

Problem Solving with Division (B)

Lesson Overview

ACTIVITY	ACTIVITY TITLE	TIME	ONLINE/OFFLINE
GET READY	Introduction to Problem Solving with Division (B)	**2** minutes	🖥️
	Multiplying by 9 Math Facts Game	**8** minutes	🖥️
LEARN AND TRY IT	Solving Real-World Division Problems	**15** minutes	🖥️
	Solve Real-World Division Problems	**10** minutes	🖥️
	Practice Solving Real-World Division Problems	**20** minutes	🖥️ and 📄
WRAP-UP	Solving Real-World Division Problems	**5** minutes	🖥️

Content Background

Students have an understanding of the inverse relationship between multiplication and division. They will learn to use this inverse relationship to solve real-world division problems, using both arrays and related multiplication facts. If students are not given an array, they should be encouraged to make their own. Students who have memorized their multiplication facts may find it easier to solve division problems by recalling multiplication facts.

An array can be used to model multiplication or division because multiplication and division are inverse operations. For example, an array of objects with 5 rows and 6 objects has 30 objects in all. This array could be used to find 5×6, 6×5, $30 \div 6$, and $30 \div 5$. Understanding the relationship between multiplication and division allows students to use multiplication to solve division problems.

> ### Lesson Goals
> - Solve real-world division problems using arrays.
> - Solve real-world division problems using related multiplication facts.

MATERIALS

Supplied
- *Summit Math 3 Activity Book:* Practice Solving Real-World Division Problems

GET READY

Introduction to Problem Solving with Division (B)

Students will get a glimpse of what they will learn about in the lesson. They will also read the lesson goals.

Multiplying by 9 Math Facts Game

Students will practice multiplying by 9.

LEARN AND TRY IT

LEARN   Solving Real-World Division Problems

Students will learn to solve real-world division problems using arrays and related multiplication facts.

TRY IT   Solve Real-World Division Problems

Students will practice solving real-world division problems. Support will be provided to help students overcome misconceptions.

TRY IT   Practice Solving Real-World Division Problems

Students will complete online practice problems. Then they will complete Practice Solving Real-World Division Problems from *Summit Math 3 Activity Book*.

TRY IT
Problem Solving with Division (B)

Practice Solving Real-World Division Problems

Follow the steps to answer the question.

1. Dean makes a quilt from 54 squares of fabric. The quilt has 9 rows of squares.

   How many squares are in each row of the quilt?

   a. Draw an array with 54 squares. Make 9 equal rows of squares.

   Possible answer:

   b. Write an equation you can use to solve the problem. $54 \div 9 = 6$

   c. Answer the question.   6 squares

Write a story problem to match the equation.

2. $20 \div 4 = ?$
   Answers will vary. Possible answer: Molly has 20 stickers. She puts them into 4 equal rows. How many stickers are in each row?

PROBLEM SOLVING WITH DIVISION (B)   **113**

Follow the steps to answer the question.

3. A pet store has 21 fish. There are an equal number of fish in each of 3 fish tanks.

   How many fish are in each tank?

   a. Write a division equation you can use to solve the problem.

      Use a question mark for the unknown number. $21 \div 3 = ?$

   b. Write a related multiplication equation you can use

      to solve the problem. $7 \times 3 = 21$

   c. Answer the question.   7 fish

Answer the questions.

4. Amelia buys 42 cucumber plants for her garden. She puts the same number of plants in each of 6 rows.

   How many plants does Amelia put in each row?   7 plants

5. A party store has 64 balloons. The store makes bunches of 8 balloons.

   How many bunches does the store have?   8 bunches

6. A bakery makes 24 bagels. Four bagels are put into each bag.

   How many bags of bagels does the bakery make?   6 bags

114   PROBLEM SOLVING WITH DIVISION (B)

WRAP-UP

Solving Real-World Division Problems

Students will solve a problem to show that they understand how to solve real-world division problems.

Problem Solving with Division (C)

Lesson Overview

ACTIVITY	ACTIVITY TITLE	TIME	ONLINE/OFFLINE
GET READY	Introduction to Problem Solving with Division (C)	**2** minutes	🖥️
	Multiplying by 7 Math Facts	**8** minutes	🖥️
LEARN AND **TRY IT**	Solving Two-Step Division Problems Not Including Multiplication	**7** minutes	🖥️
	Solve Two-Step Division Problems Not Including Multiplication	**7** minutes	🖥️
	Solving Two-Step Division Problems Including Multiplication	**7** minutes	🖥️
	Solve Two-Step Division Problems Including Multiplication	**7** minutes	🖥️
	Practice Solving Two-Step Division Problems	**20** minutes	🖥️ and 📄
WRAP-UP	Solving Two-Step Division Problems	**2** minutes	🖥️

Content Background

Students should be comfortable dividing. They will learn to identify and solve real-world division problems with two steps. One step will require division and the other will require addition, subtraction, or multiplication. Encourage students to read each problem carefully because the order in which operations are performed is important.

TIP Students might quickly read through a problem and immediately begin calculating, often choosing the wrong operations because they did not take time to read through and understand the context of the problem. Students need to learn "slow-down" mechanisms that can help them concentrate on thoroughly understanding a problem before solving.

As students work through the variety of two-step division problems, they may notice that certain types of problems recur. Some types are sharing an amount, making equal groups from an amount, figuring out equal measures, and finding the cost of one item when the cost of many items is known. Although students are not expected to identify or explain these types of problems, encourage them to recognize the variety of story problems that can be solved with division or with division in combination with other operations.

MATERIALS

Supplied
- *Summit Math 3 Activity Book:* Practice Solving Two-Step Division Problems

Lesson Goals

- Solve real-world problems with two steps.

Introduction to Problem Solving with Division (C)

Students will get a glimpse of what they will learn about in the lesson. They will also read the lesson goals.

Multiplying by 7 Math Facts

Students will practice multiplying by 7.

LEARN AND TRY IT

LEARN Solving Two-Step Division Problems Not Including Multiplication

Students will learn to solve two-step division problems that include addition or subtraction.

TRY IT Solve Two-Step Division Problems Not Including Multiplication

Students will practice solving two-step division problems that include addition or subtraction. Support will be provided to help students overcome misconceptions.

LEARN Solving Two-Step Division Problems Including Multiplication

Students will learn to solve two-step division problems that also include multiplication.

TRY IT Solve Two-Step Division Problems Including Multiplication

Students will practice solving two-step division problems that also include multiplication. Support will be provided to help students overcome misconceptions.

TRY IT   Practice Solving Two-Step Division Problems

Students will complete online practice problems. Then they will complete Practice Solving Two-Step Division Problems from *Summit Math 3 Activity Book.*

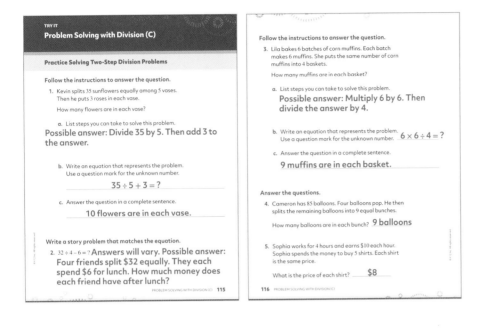

WRAP-UP

Solving Two-Step Division Problems

Students will solve a problem to show that they understand how to solve two-step division problems.

Problem Solving with Division (D)

Lesson Overview

ACTIVITY	ACTIVITY TITLE	TIME	ONLINE/OFFLINE
GET READY	Introduction to Problem Solving with Division (D)	**2** minutes	🖥️
TRY IT	Review Problem Solving with Division	**18** minutes	🖥️
QUIZ	Problem Solving with Division	**25** minutes	🖥️
WRAP-UP	More Math Practice	**15** minutes	🖥️

Lesson Goals

- Review solving real-world division problems with one or two steps.
- Take a quiz.

MATERIALS

There are no materials to gather for this lesson.

GET READY

Introduction to Problem Solving with Division (D)

Students will read the lesson goals.

TRY IT

Review Problem Solving with Division

Students will answer questions to review what they have learned about problem solving with division.

QUIZ

Problem Solving with Division

Students will complete the Problem Solving with Division quiz.

More Math Practice

Students will practice skills according to their individual needs.

Big Ideas: Extended Problems

Lesson Overview

Big Ideas lessons provide students the opportunity to further apply the knowledge and skills acquired throughout previous units. Each Big Ideas lesson consists of two types of activities:

1. **Cumulative Review:** Students keep their skills fresh by reviewing prior content.

2. **Synthesis:** Students complete an assignment that allows them to interweave and apply what they've learned. These synthesis assignments will vary throughout the course.

   In the Synthesis portion of this Big Ideas lesson, students will complete multistep problems that go beyond the short answer and multiple choice problems they encounter in their regular lessons. These problems give students an opportunity to demonstrate problem solving, reasoning, communication, and modeling skills. Students will need to use pencil and paper and/or technology to show their work.

   LEARNING COACH CHECK-IN This is a graded assessment. Make sure students complete, review, and submit the assignment to their teacher.

All materials needed for this lesson are linked online. The materials are not provided in this Lesson Guide or in the Activity Book.

MATERIALS

Supplied
- Extended Problems Instructions (printout)

Shapes

Exploring Shapes and Shared Attributes (A)

Lesson Overview

ACTIVITY	ACTIVITY TITLE	TIME	ONLINE/OFFLINE
GET READY	Introduction to Exploring Shapes and Shared Attributes (A)	**2** minutes	📶
	Look Back at Parts of Shapes	**8** minutes	📶
LEARN AND TRY IT	Describing Two-Dimensional Shapes	**15** minutes	📶
	Describe Two-Dimensional Shapes	**10** minutes	📶
	Practice Describing Two-Dimensional Shapes	**20** minutes	📶 and 📄
WRAP-UP	Describing Two-Dimensional Shapes	**5** minutes	📶

Content Background

Students will learn to describe individual two-dimensional shapes. Students will focus on a shape's sides, vertices, and whether the shape is open or closed. The number of sides refers to the number of straight sides. A curved figure, such as a circle or oval, is said to have no sides.

A vertex is a corner. *Vertices* is the plural form of the word *vertex*. A vertex is formed when two sides come together. A vertex, or corner, can be either square or not square. Students should be encouraged to compare vertices of shapes to a square corner on an index card or a piece of construction paper.

NOTE In future math courses, students will learn that two sides form an *angle* and a square corner is called a *right angle*. Students are not expected to learn or use these terms in this course.

Lesson Goals

- Describe shapes.

GET READY

Introduction to Exploring Shapes and Shared Attributes (A)

After a quick introductory activity, students will read the lesson goals and keywords. Have students select each keyword and preview its definition.

MATERIALS

Supplied
- *Summit Math 3 Activity Book:* Practice Describing Two-Dimensional Shapes

KEYWORDS

closed shape – a shape that starts and ends at the same point

open shape – a shape that starts at one point and ends at a different point

side – one of the line segments that makes a shape

square corner – a corner in a flat shape that is formed by two line segments and is the same shape as the corner of an index card

vertex – the point where two sides of a shape meet; the plural of *vertex* is *vertices*

Look Back at Parts of Shapes

Students will practice the prerequisite skill of identifying defining attributes of shapes.

LEARN AND TRY IT

LEARN Describing Two-Dimensional Shapes

Students will learn how to describe two-dimensional shapes.

TRY IT Describe Two-Dimensional Shapes

Students will practice describing two-dimensional shapes. Support will be provided to help students overcome misconceptions.

TRY IT Practice Describing Two-Dimensional Shapes

Students will complete online practice problems. Then they will complete Practice Describing Two-Dimensional Shapes from *Summit Math 3 Activity Book*.

WRAP-UP

Describing Two-Dimensional Shapes

Students will solve problems to show that they understand how to describe shapes.

Exploring Shapes and Shared Attributes (B)

Lesson Overview

ACTIVITY	ACTIVITY TITLE	TIME	ONLINE/OFFLINE
GET READY	Introduction to Exploring Shapes and Shared Attributes (B)	**2** minutes	🖥️
	Multiplying by 7 with Instant Recall	**8** minutes	🖥️
LEARN AND **TRY IT**	Identifying a Shape with Given Features	**15** minutes	🖥️
	Identify a Shape with Given Features	**10** minutes	🖥️
	Practice Identifying a Shape with Given Features	**20** minutes	🖥️ and 📄
WRAP-UP	Identifying a Shape with Given Features	**5** minutes	🖥️

Content Background

Students will learn to identify or draw a shape given a description of the features of the shape. Features include the number of sides and vertices or whether the shape has square corners or opposite sides that are the same length. In math, there is often one correct answer. Drawing a shape to match a description is different because there are often many correct ways to draw a shape for a given description. For example, each of these triangles has one square corner.

> **MATERIALS**
>
> **Supplied**
> - *Summit Math 3 Activity Book:* Practice Identifying a Shape with Given Features

OPTIONAL You can extend a challenge to your students when drawing a shape to match a description. After they draw one shape, ask them to draw another one that is bigger, smaller, or is positioned differently. You can even make it a game where you take turns drawing lines of the shape to still match the description.

Lesson Goals

- Identify or draw a shape with given features.

Introduction to Exploring Shapes and Shared Attributes (B)

Students will get a glimpse of what they will learn about in the lesson. They will also read the lesson goals.

Multiplying by 7 with Instant Recall

Students will practice multiplying by 7.

LEARN AND TRY IT

LEARN   Identifying a Shape with Given Features

Students will learn how to identify and draw shapes with given features.

TRY IT   Identify a Shape with Given Features

Students will practice identifying and drawing shapes with given features. Support will be provided to help students overcome misconceptions.

TRY IT   Practice Identifying a Shape with Given Features

Students will complete online practice problems. Then they will complete Practice Identifying a Shape with Given Features from *Summit Math 3 Activity Book*.

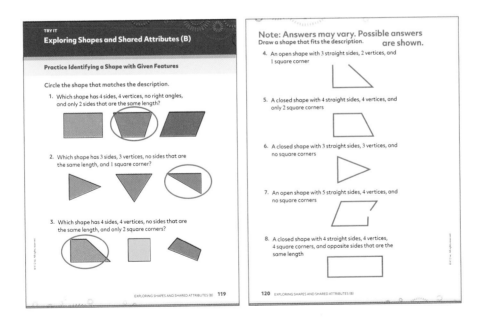

Identifying a Shape with Given Features

Students will solve problems to show that they understand how to identify or draw a shape with given features.

Exploring Shapes and Shared Attributes (C)

Lesson Overview

ACTIVITY	ACTIVITY TITLE	TIME	ONLINE/OFFLINE
GET READY	Introduction to Exploring Shapes and Shared Attributes (C)	**2** minutes	🖥
	Multiplying by 7 Math Facts Game	**8** minutes	🖥
LEARN AND **TRY IT**	Identifying Shared Features of Shapes	**15** minutes	🖥
	Identify Shared Features of Shapes	**10** minutes	🖥
	Practice Identifying Shared Features of Shapes	**20** minutes	🖥 and 📄
WRAP-UP	Identifying Shared Features of Shapes	**5** minutes	🖥

Content Background

Students will learn to compare shapes to identify features they have in common. For example, if students are given a square and a rectangle they should notice that both shapes have 4 sides, 4 square corners, and opposite sides that are the same length. You can direct students to count the number of sides, vertices, and square corners and to compare those numbers.

Lesson Goals

- Identify the features that two or more shapes share.

GET READY

Introduction to Exploring Shapes and Shared Attributes (C)

Students will get a glimpse of what they will learn about in the lesson. They will also read the lesson goals.

Multiplying by 7 Math Facts Game

Students will practice multiplying by 7.

LEARN   Identifying Shared Features of Shapes

Students will learn how to identify shared features of two or more shapes.

TRY IT   Identify Shared Features of Shapes

Students will practice identifying shared features of two or more shapes. Support will be provided to help students overcome misconceptions.

TRY IT   Practice Identifying Shared Features of Shapes

Students will complete online practice problems. Then they will complete Practice Identifying Shared Features of Shapes from *Summit Math 3 Activity Book.*

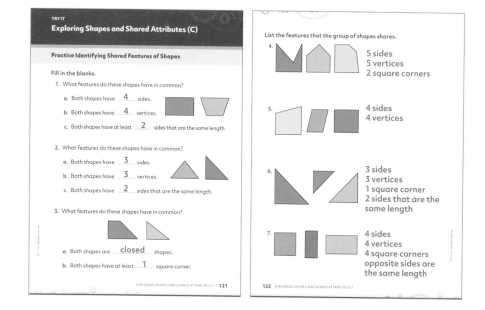

Identifying Shared Features of Shapes

Students will solve a problem to show that they understand how to identify shared features of shapes.

Exploring Shapes and Shared Attributes (D)

Lesson Overview

ACTIVITY	ACTIVITY TITLE	TIME	ONLINE/OFFLINE
GET READY	Introduction to Exploring Shapes and Shared Attributes (D)	**2** minutes	🖥
	Multiplying by 8 Math Facts	**8** minutes	🖥
LEARN AND **TRY IT**	Classifying Shapes	**15** minutes	🖥
	Classify Shapes	**10** minutes	🖥
	Practice Classifying Shapes	**20** minutes	🖥 and 📄
WRAP-UP	Classifying Shapes	**5** minutes	🖥

Content Background

Students will learn to group and sort shapes based on common features. For example, students can sort shapes into groups by their number of sides or whether they have square corners or not. Students should individually examine each shape in a group and then compare the shapes' features. Some common features are the number of sides or vertices, open or closed shapes, square corners, sides that are all the same length, and opposite sides that are the same length.

MATERIALS

Supplied
- *Summit Math 3 Activity Book:* Practice Classifying Shapes

Lesson Goals
- Classify shapes based on their features.

GET READY

Introduction to Exploring Shapes and Shared Attributes (D)
Students will get a glimpse of what they will learn about in the lesson. They will also read the lesson goals.

Multiplying by 8 Math Facts
Students will practice multiplying by 8.

LEARN   Classifying Shapes

Students will learn how to classify shapes.

TRY IT   Classify Shapes

Students will practice classifying shapes. Support will be provided to help students overcome misconceptions.

TRY IT   Practice Classifying Shapes

Students will complete online practice problems. Then they will complete Practice Classifying Shapes from *Summit Math 3 Activity Book*.

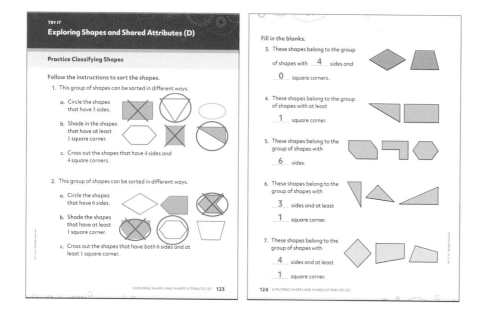

Classifying Shapes

Students will solve a problem to show that they understand how to classify shapes.

Exploring Shapes and Shared Attributes (E)

Lesson Overview

ACTIVITY	ACTIVITY TITLE	TIME	ONLINE/OFFLINE
GET READY	Introduction to Exploring Shapes and Shared Attributes (E)	**2** minutes	🖥️
TRY IT	Review Exploring Shapes and Shared Attributes	**18** minutes	🖥️
QUIZ	Exploring Shapes and Shared Attributes	**25** minutes	🖥️
WRAP-UP	More Math Practice	**15** minutes	🖥️

Lesson Goals

- Review features of shapes.
- Take a quiz.

MATERIALS

There are no materials to gather for this lesson.

GET READY

Introduction to Exploring Shapes and Shared Attributes (E)

Students will read the lesson goals.

TRY IT

Exploring Shapes and Shared Attributes

Students will answer questions to review what they have learned about exploring shapes and shared attributes.

QUIZ

Exploring Shapes and Shared Attributes

Students will complete the Exploring Shapes and Shared Attributes quiz.

More Math Practice

Students will practice skills according to their individual needs.

Polygons (A)

Lesson Overview

ACTIVITY	ACTIVITY TITLE	TIME	ONLINE/OFFLINE
GET READY	Introduction to Polygons (A)	**2** minutes	🖥️
	Look Back at Shared Attributes of Shapes	**8** minutes	🖥️
LEARN AND **TRY IT**	Identifying Polygons	**10** minutes	🖥️
	Identify Polygons	**15** minutes	🖥️
	Practice Identifying Polygons	**20** minutes	🖥️ and 📄
WRAP-UP	Identifying Polygons	**5** minutes	🖥️

Content Background

Students will learn that the term *polygon* refers to a closed shape with 3 or more straight sides. Then students will determine whether a shape is a polygon. There are many shapes that fit into the broad category of polygons. Eventually students will learn to further categorize shapes. Recognizing polygons is an important foundation for categorizing shapes.

Lesson Goals
- Define and identify polygons.

MATERIALS

Supplied
- *Summit Math 3 Activity Book:* Practice Identifying Polygons

KEYWORDS

polygon – a closed shape that has three or more sides

GET READY

Introduction to Polygons (A)

Students will get a glimpse of what they will learn about in the lesson. They will also read the lesson goals and keywords. Have students select each keyword and preview its definition.

Look Back at Shared Attributes of Shapes

Students will practice the prerequisite skill of comparing the shared attributes of shapes.

LEARN   Identifying Polygons

Students will learn how to identify polygons.

TRY IT   Identify Polygons

Students will practice identifying polygons. Support will be provided to help students overcome misconceptions.

TRY IT   Practice Identifying Polygons

Students will complete online practice problems. Then they will complete Practice Identifying Polygons from *Summit Math 3 Activity Book.*

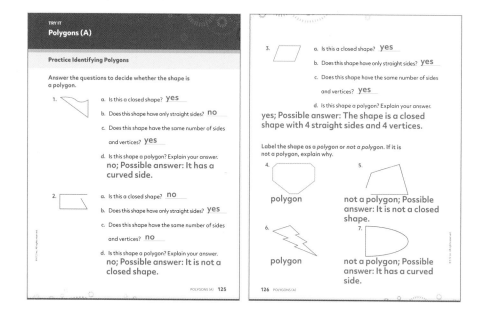

WRAP-UP

Identifying Polygons

Students will solve a problem to show that they understand how to identify polygons.

Polygons (B)

Lesson Overview

ACTIVITY	ACTIVITY TITLE	TIME	ONLINE/OFFLINE
GET READY	Introduction to Polygons (B)	**2** minutes	🖥️
	Multiplying by 8 with Instant Recall	**8** minutes	🖥️
LEARN AND TRY IT	Classifying Polygons	**15** minutes	🖥️
	Classify Polygons	**10** minutes	🖥️
	Practice Classifying Polygons	**20** minutes	🖥️ and 📄
WRAP-UP	Classifying Polygons	**5** minutes	🖥️

Content Background

Students will learn to identify four subcategories of polygons based on the number of sides: triangles, quadrilaterals, pentagons, and hexagons. There are many ways to draw each type of polygon. Students should be encouraged to count the number of straight sides in each shape they must classify.

Lesson Goals

- Identify and describe types of polygons.
- Classify polygons.

GET READY

Introduction to Polygons (B)

Students will get a glimpse of what they will learn about in the lesson. They will also read the lesson goals and keywords. Have students select each keyword and preview its definition.

Multiplying by 8 with Instant Recall

Students will practice multiplying by 8.

MATERIALS

Supplied
- *Summit Math 3 Activity Book:* Practice Classifying Polygons

---

KEYWORDS

hexagon – a 6-sided polygon

pentagon – a 5-sided polygon

quadrilateral – a polygon with four sides

triangle – a polygon with three sides

LEARN   Classifying Polygons

Students will learn how to classify polygons.

TRY IT   Classify Polygons

Students will practice classifying polygons. Support will be provided to help students overcome misconceptions.

TRY IT   Practice Classifying Polygons

Students will complete online practice problems. Then they will complete Practice Classifying Polygons from *Summit Math 3 Activity Book*.

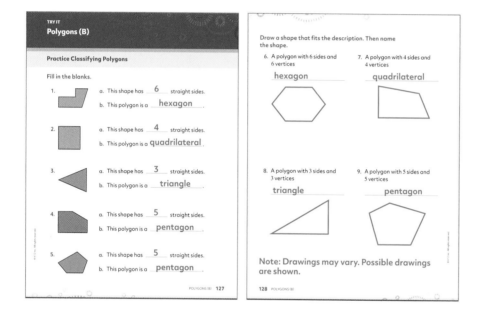

Classifying Polygons

Students will solve a problem to show that they understand how to classify polygons.

Polygons (C)

Lesson Overview

ACTIVITY	ACTIVITY TITLE	TIME	ONLINE/OFFLINE
GET READY	Introduction to Polygons (C)	**2** minutes	🖥️
TRY IT	Review Polygons	**18** minutes	🖥️
QUIZ	Polygons	**25** minutes	🖥️
WRAP-UP	More Math Practice	**15** minutes	🖥️

Lesson Goals

- Review polygons.

- Take a quiz.

MATERIALS

There are no materials to gather for this lesson.

GET READY

Introduction to Polygons (C)

Students will read the lesson goals.

TRY IT

Review Polygons

Students will answer questions to review what they have learned about polygons.

QUIZ

Polygons

Students will complete the Polygons quiz.

More Math Practice

Students will practice skills according to their individual needs.

Quadrilaterals (A)

Lesson Overview

ACTIVITY	ACTIVITY TITLE	TIME	ONLINE/OFFLINE
GET READY	Introduction to Quadrilaterals (A)	**2** minutes	🖥️
	Look Back at Identifying Polygons	**8** minutes	🖥️
LEARN AND **TRY IT**	Identifying Types of Quadrilaterals	**15** minutes	🖥️
	Identify Types of Quadrilaterals	**10** minutes	🖥️
	OPTIONAL Identifying Other Quadrilaterals	**7** minutes	🖥️
	OPTIONAL Identify Other Quadrilaterals	**7** minutes	🖥️
	OPTIONAL Practice Identifying Other Quadrilaterals	**10** minutes	🖥️
	Practice Identifying Types of Quadrilaterals	**20** minutes	🖥️ and 📄
WRAP-UP	Identifying Types of Quadrilaterals	**5** minutes	🖥️

Content Background

Students will learn to identify rectangles, rhombuses, and squares. Each of these shapes is a special type of quadrilateral because each has 4 sides. Students will name shapes given as images and as descriptions. In the next lesson, students will learn that squares are both a special type of rhombus and a special type of rectangle. For this lesson only, squares will be treated as their own category.

Lesson Goals

- Identify types of quadrilaterals.

MATERIALS

Supplied
- *Summit Math 3 Activity Book:* Practice Identifying Types of Quadrilaterals

KEYWORDS

rectangle – a quadrilateral with four square corners and opposite sides that have equal length

rhombus – a quadrilateral in which all sides are the same length

square – a quadrilateral that has four square corners and four sides that are the same length

Introduction to Quadrilaterals (A)

Students will get a glimpse of what they will learn about in the lesson. They will also read the lesson goals and keywords. Have students select each keyword and preview its definition.

Look Back at Identifying Polygons

Students will practice the prerequisite skill of identifying polygons.

LEARN AND TRY IT

LEARN   Identifying Types of Quadrilaterals

Students will learn how to identify types of quadrilaterals.

TRY IT   Identify Types of Quadrilaterals

Students will practice identifying types of quadrilaterals. Support will be provided to help students overcome misconceptions.

LEARN   OPTIONAL   Identifying Other Quadrilaterals

Students will learn how to identify trapezoids and parallelograms. Students will be directed to complete or skip this activity by their teacher.

TRY IT   OPTIONAL   Identify Other Quadrilaterals

Students will practice identifying trapezoids and parallelograms. Support will be provided to help students overcome misconceptions. Students will be directed to complete or skip this activity by their teacher.

TRY IT   OPTIONAL   Practice Identifying Other Quadrilaterals

Students will complete online practice problems. Students will be directed to complete or skip this activity by their teacher.

TRY IT   Practice Identifying Types of Quadrilaterals

Students will complete online practice problems. Then they will complete Practice Identifying Types of Quadrilaterals from *Summit Math 3 Activity Book*.

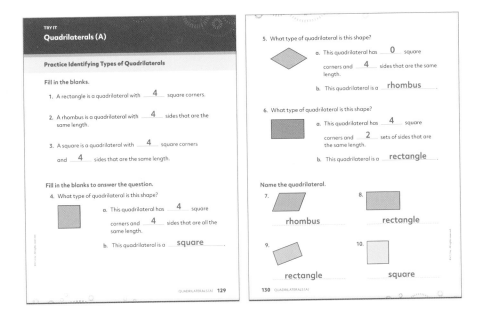

WRAP-UP

Identifying Types of Quadrilaterals

Students will solve a problem to show that they understand how to identify types of quadrilaterals.

Quadrilaterals (B)

Lesson Overview

ACTIVITY	ACTIVITY TITLE	TIME	ONLINE/OFFLINE
GET READY	Introduction to Quadrilaterals (B)	**2** minutes	🖥️
	Multiplying by 8 Math Facts Game	**8** minutes	🖥️
LEARN AND **TRY IT**	Classifying Quadrilaterals	**15** minutes	🖥️
	Classify Quadrilaterals	**10** minutes	🖥️
	Practice Classifying Quadrilaterals	**20** minutes	🖥️ and 📄
WRAP-UP	Classifying Quadrilaterals	**5** minutes	🖥️

Content Background

Students will learn that shapes belong to more than one category. For example, a square is also a polygon, a quadrilateral, a rectangle, and a rhombus.

Some students inappropriately use *converse reasoning* when classifying shapes. For example, they might say, "All squares have 4 sides. This shape has 4 sides, so it must be a square." It may help to make a checklist of features for each of these shapes: polygon, quadrilateral, rectangle, rhombus, square. A shape can be classified into a category when it matches all the features on that checklist.

MATERIALS

Supplied
- *Summit Math 3 Activity Book:* Practice Classifying Quadrilaterals

Lesson Goals

- Classify quadrilaterals.

GET READY

Introduction to Quadrilaterals (B)

Students will get a glimpse of what they will learn about in the lesson. They will also read the lesson goals.

Multiplying by 8 Math Facts Game

Students will practice multiplying by 8.

LEARN AND TRY IT

LEARN   Classifying Quadrilaterals

Students will learn how to classify quadrilaterals.

TRY IT   Classify Quadrilaterals

Students will practice classifying quadrilaterals. Support will be provided to help students overcome misconceptions.

TRY IT   Practice Classifying Quadrilaterals

Students will complete online practice problems. Then they will complete Practice Classifying Quadrilaterals from *Summit Math 3 Activity Book*.

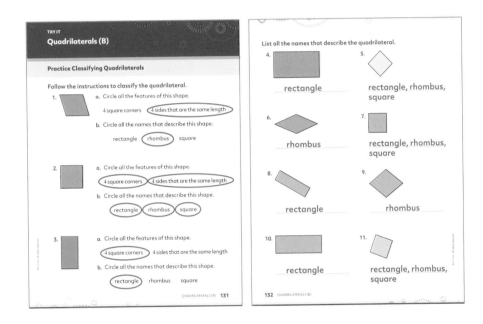

WRAP-UP

Classifying Quadrilaterals

Students will solve a problem to show that they understand how to classify quadrilaterals.

Quadrilaterals (C)

Lesson Overview

ACTIVITY	ACTIVITY TITLE	TIME	ONLINE/OFFLINE
GET READY	Introduction to Quadrilaterals (C)	**2** minutes	🖥
	Multiplying Math Facts	**8** minutes	🖥
LEARN AND **TRY IT**	Describing and Drawing Quadrilaterals	**15** minutes	🖥
	Describe and Draw Quadrilaterals	**10** minutes	🖥
	Practice Describing and Drawing Quadrilaterals	**20** minutes	🖥 and 📄
WRAP-UP	Describing and Drawing Quadrilaterals	**5** minutes	🖥

Content Background

Students will learn to describe quadrilaterals and draw quadrilaterals based on a list of features. It may help to make a checklist of key features for each of these shapes: polygon, quadrilateral, rectangle, rhombus, square. Once students draw a shape, they can compare it to its list of key features.

Lesson Goals

- Describe and draw quadrilaterals.

MATERIALS

Supplied
- *Summit Math 3 Activity Book:* Practice Describing and Drawing Quadrilaterals

GET READY

Introduction to Quadrilaterals (C)

Students will get a glimpse of what they will learn about in the lesson. They will also read the lesson goals.

Multiplying Math Facts

Students will practice multiplying using any factors from 0 to 10.

LEARN   Describing and Drawing Quadrilaterals

Students will learn how to describe and draw quadrilaterals.

TRY IT   Describe and Draw Quadrilaterals

Students will practice describing and drawing quadrilaterals. Support will be provided to help students overcome misconceptions.

TRY IT   Practice Describing and Drawing Quadrilaterals

Students will complete online practice problems. Then they will complete Practice Describing and Drawing Quadrilaterals from *Summit Math 3 Activity Book*.

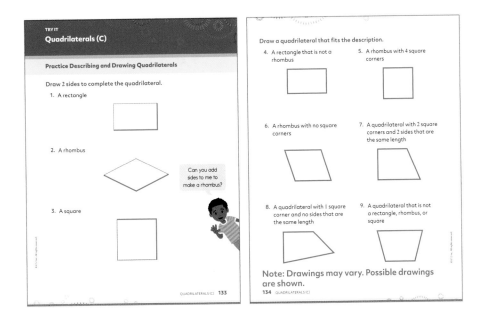

Describing and Drawing Quadrilaterals

Students will solve a problem to show that they understand how to describe and draw quadrilaterals.

Quadrilaterals (D)

Lesson Overview

ACTIVITY	ACTIVITY TITLE	TIME	ONLINE/OFFLINE
GET READY	Introduction to Quadrilaterals (D)	**2** minutes	🖥️
TRY IT	Review Quadrilaterals	**18** minutes	🖥️
QUIZ	Quadrilaterals	**25** minutes	🖥️
WRAP-UP	More Math Practice	**15** minutes	🖥️

Lesson Goals

- Review quadrilaterals.
- Take a quiz.

MATERIALS

There are no materials to gather for this lesson.

GET READY

Introduction to Quadrilaterals (D)

Students will read the lesson goals.

TRY IT

Review Quadrilaterals

Students will answer questions to review what they have learned about quadrilaterals.

QUIZ

Quadrilaterals

Students will complete the Quadrilaterals quiz.

More Math Practice

Students will practice skills according to their individual needs.

Big Ideas: **Challenge Problems**

Lesson Overview

Big Ideas lessons provide students the opportunity to apply the knowledge and skills acquired throughout previous units. Each Big Ideas lesson consists of two types of activities:

1. **Cumulative Review:** Students keep their skills fresh by reviewing prior content.

2. **Synthesis:** Students complete an assignment that allows them to interweave and apply what they've learned. These synthesis assignments will vary throughout the course.

In the Synthesis portion of this Big Ideas lesson, students will complete one or more challenge problems that will guide them to discover new concepts. Through hard work and perseverance, students will learn that they can use the math they already know combined with logical thinking to solve problems about new concepts.

Geometric Measurement: Area

Area Concepts (A)

Lesson Overview

ACTIVITY	ACTIVITY TITLE	TIME	ONLINE/OFFLINE
GET READY	Introduction to Area Concepts (A)	**2** minutes	🖥️
	Look Back at Solving Perimeter Problems	**8** minutes	🖥️
LEARN AND TRY IT	Understanding Area	**15** minutes	🖥️
	Understand Area	**10** minutes	🖥️
	Practice Understanding Area	**20** minutes	🖥️ and 📄
WRAP-UP	Understanding Area	**5** minutes	🖥️

Content Background

Students will learn that area is the measure of the space inside two-dimensional figures. They'll learn that area is measured in square units. The area of a plane figure is the number of unit squares that cover the shape with no gaps or overlaps. The shapes in this lesson include rectangles and rectangular shapes that can be covered in unit squares. Students will find the area of a shape by counting unit squares.

MATERIALS

Supplied
- *Summit Math 3 Activity Book:* Practice Understanding Area

Lesson Goals

- Understand the meaning of area.
- Express the area of a figure in square units.

KEYWORDS

area – the amount of space on a flat surface, most often measured in square units

plane figure – a flat shape with only two dimensions: length and width

square unit – a unit used to measure area; equal to the area of a square that is one unit on each side

unit square – a square that has a length of one unit on each side

GET READY

Introduction to Area Concepts (A)

After a quick introductory activity, students will read the lesson goals and keywords. Have students select each keyword and preview its definition.

Look Back at Solving Perimeter Problems

Students will practice the prerequisite skill of solving perimeter problems.

LEARN   Understanding Area

Students will learn about the area of a shape.

TRY IT   Understand Area

Students will practice explaining what the area of a shape is. Support will be provided to help students overcome misconceptions.

TRY IT   Practice Understanding Area

Students will complete online practice problems. Then they will complete Practice Understanding Area from *Summit Math 3 Activity Book*.

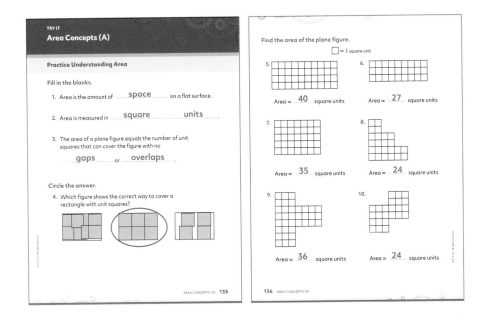

Understanding Area

Students will solve a problem to show that they understand the meaning of the area of a shape.

Area Concepts (B)

Lesson Overview

ACTIVITY	ACTIVITY TITLE	TIME	ONLINE/OFFLINE
GET READY	Introduction to Area Concepts (B)	**2** minutes	🖥️
	Multiplying with Instant Recall	**8** minutes	🖥️
LEARN AND **TRY IT**	Understanding Area Units	**15** minutes	🖥️
	Understand Area Units	**10** minutes	🖥️
	Practice Understanding Area Units	**20** minutes	🖥️ and 📄
WRAP-UP	Understanding Area Units	**5** minutes	🖥️

Content Background

Students will learn to distinguish between units of length and units of area using both metric and U.S. customary measurements. They will also see that the units used to determine the length of a side of a rectangle can be used to create square units. For example, a rectangle with sides measured in meters has an area measured in square meters. Students need to understand that saying "the rectangle has an area of 20" has no meaning unless the units are identified, such as 20 square centimeters, 20 square inches, or 20 of some other square units.

NOTE Students might think of all measurements as length. For example, they might perceive area as a distance—something that they can measure with a ruler. Consequently, they often measure the perimeter instead of the area. Continue to remind students that area is the space inside a plane figure.

Lesson Goals

- Understand the difference between units of length and square units.

GET READY

Introduction to Area Concepts (B)

Students will get a glimpse of what they will learn about in the lesson. They will also read the lesson goals and keywords. Have students select each keyword and preview its definition.

Multiplying with Instant Recall

Students will practice multiplying by any factor from 0 to 10.

LEARN AND TRY IT

LEARN   Understanding Area Units

Students will learn to understand area units.

TRY IT   Understand Area Units

Students will practice understanding area units. Support will be provided to help students overcome misconceptions.

TRY IT   Practice Understanding Area Units

Students will complete online practice problems. Then they will complete Practice Understanding Area Units from *Summit Math 3 Activity Book*.

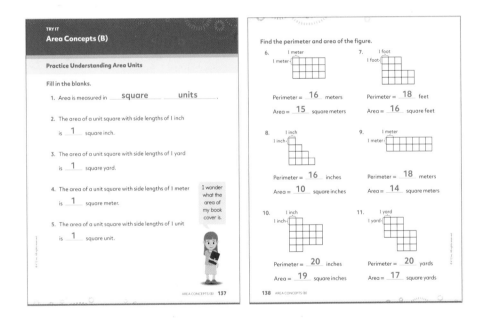

WRAP-UP

Understanding Area Units

Students will solve a problem to show that they understand area units.

Area Concepts (C)

Lesson Overview

ACTIVITY	ACTIVITY TITLE	TIME	ONLINE/OFFLINE
GET READY	Introduction to Area Concepts (C)	**2** minutes	🖥️
TRY IT	Review Area Concepts	**18** minutes	🖥️
QUIZ	Area Concepts	**25** minutes	🖥️
WRAP-UP	More Math Practice	**15** minutes	🖥️

Lesson Goals

- Review understanding the concept of area.
- Take a quiz.

MATERIALS

There are no materials to gather for this lesson.

GET READY

Introduction to Area Concepts (C)

Students will read the lesson goals.

TRY IT

Review Area Concepts

Students will answer questions to review what they have learned about area concepts.

QUIZ

Area Concepts

Students will complete the Area Concepts quiz.

More Math Practice

Students will practice skills according to their individual needs.

Measuring and Calculating Area (A)

Lesson Overview

ACTIVITY	ACTIVITY TITLE	TIME	ONLINE/OFFLINE
GET READY	Introduction to Measuring and Calculating Area (A)	**2** minutes	🖥
	Look Back at Using an Array to Multiply	**8** minutes	🖥
LEARN AND **TRY IT**	Finding Areas by Tiling	**15** minutes	🖥
	Find Areas by Tiling	**10** minutes	🖥
	Practice Finding Areas by Tiling	**20** minutes	🖥 and 📄
WRAP-UP	Finding Areas by Tiling	**5** minutes	🖥

Content Background

Students will learn to find the area of a rectangle by covering it in unit squares. This process is also known as tiling. The area of a rectangle equals the number of unit squares that cover it without gaps or overlaps. In previous lessons, students were given rectangles that were already tiled correctly. The purpose of this lesson is for students to learn to tile a rectangle themselves. This experience helps students recognize that the tiles are arranged in rows with the same number of tiles in each row. In other words, a rectangle tiled with unit squares is very similar to an array used to model multiplication. In a future lesson, students will discover the formula for the area of a rectangle. If students discover the connection between tiling and an array on their own, they may use it to multiply to find the area of a rectangle.

Lesson Goals

- Find the area of a rectangle by covering it with unit squares.

MATERIALS

Supplied

- *Summit Math 3 Activity Book:* Practice Finding Areas by Tiling

KEYWORDS

area – the amount of space on a flat surface, most often measured in square units

unit square – a square that has a length of one unit on each side

GET READY

Introduction to Measuring and Calculating Area (A)

Students will get a glimpse of what they will learn about in the lesson. They will also read the lesson goals and keywords. Have students select each keyword and preview its definition.

Look Back at Using an Array to Multiply

Students will practice the prerequisite skill of using an array to multiply.

LEARN   Finding Areas by Tiling

Students will learn how to find area by tiling.

TRY IT   Find Areas by Tiling

Students will practice finding area by tilling. Support will be provided to help students overcome misconceptions.

TRY IT   Practice Finding Areas by Tiling

Students will complete online practice problems. Then they will complete Practice Finding Areas by Tiling from *Summit Math 3 Activity Book*.

WRAP-UP

Finding Areas by Tiling

Students will solve a problem to show that they understand how to find area by tiling.

Measuring and Calculating Area (B)

Lesson Overview

ACTIVITY	ACTIVITY TITLE	TIME	ONLINE/OFFLINE
GET READY	Introduction to Measuring and Calculating Area (B)	**2** minutes	🖥️
	Multiplying Math Facts Game	**8** minutes	🖥️
LEARN AND **TRY IT**	Finding Areas of Rectangles with Measurement Units	**7** minutes	🖥️
	Find Areas of Rectangles with Measurement Units	**7** minutes	🖥️
	Finding Areas of Figures with Measurement Units	**7** minutes	🖥️
	Find Areas of Figures with Measurement Units	**7** minutes	🖥️
	Practice Finding Areas with Units	**20** minutes	🖥️ and 📄
WRAP-UP	Finding Areas with Units	**2** minutes	🖥️

Content Background

Students will learn how to find the areas of rectangles and rectangular shapes by counting unit squares in metric and U.S. customary units. Units include square meters, square centimeters, square inches, and square feet. Students will use information given in a problem to discover which units of area are appropriate. Students will also learn that unit squares are not all the same size. For example, 1 square centimeter is smaller than 1 square meter because 1 centimeter is smaller than 1 meter.

Lesson Goals

- Find the area of a figure by counting unit squares.
- Understand that a square centimeter is smaller than a square meter.
- Understand that a square inch is smaller than a square foot.

MATERIALS

Supplied
- *Summit Math 3 Activity Book:* Practice Finding Areas with Units

KEYWORDS

area – the amount of space on a flat surface, most often measured in square units

unit square – a square that has a length of one unit on each side

GET READY

Introduction to Measuring and Calculating Area (B)

Students will get a glimpse of what they will learn about in the lesson. They will also read the lesson goals and keywords. Have students select each keyword and preview its definition.

Multiplying Math Facts Game

Students will practice multiplication facts using any factors from 0 to 10.

LEARN AND TRY IT

LEARN   Finding Areas of Rectangles with Measurement Units

Students will learn how to find the area of a rectangle with measurement units.

TRY IT   Find Areas of Rectangles with Measurement Units

Students will practice finding areas of rectangles with measurement units. Support will be provided to help students overcome misconceptions.

LEARN   Finding Areas of Figures with Measurement Units

Students will learn how to find the area of a rectangular figure with measurement units.

TRY IT   Find Areas of Figures with Measurement Units

Students will practice finding areas of rectangular figures with measurement units. Support will be provided to help students overcome misconceptions.

TRY IT   Practice Finding Areas with Units

Students will complete online practice problems. Then they will complete Practice Finding Areas with Units from *Summit Math 3 Activity Book*.

Finding Areas with Units

Students will solve a problem to show that they understand how to find the area of a rectangle with units.

Measuring and Calculating Area (C)

Lesson Overview

ACTIVITY	ACTIVITY TITLE	TIME	ONLINE/OFFLINE
GET READY	Introduction to Measuring and Calculating Area (C)	**2** minutes	🖥️
	Dividing by 1 Math Facts	**8** minutes	📶
LEARN AND **TRY IT**	Finding the Area Formula	**7** minutes	🖥️
	Find the Area Formula	**7** minutes	📶
	Multiplying to Find Area	**7** minutes	📶
	Multiply to Find Area	**7** minutes	🖥️
	Practice Multiplying to Find Area	**20** minutes	📶 and 📄
WRAP-UP	Multiplying to Find Area	**2** minutes	📶

Content Background

Students will discover the formula for the area of a rectangle. Through counting unit squares, some students may have recognized that it's easier to count the number of rows and the number of squares in each row and multiply those values. In other words, the area of a rectangle is the product of its dimensions. Students will formalize this reasoning in the formula $A = l \times w$ or Area = length × width. Continue to remind students that the area of a shape is measured in square units. Students will also learn to find the area of a shape using improvised units. For example, students might use the area of a rectangular tile to find the area of a wall.

Lesson Goals

- Multiply side lengths to find the area of a rectangle.
- Use a formula to find the area of a rectangle.

GET READY

Introduction to Measuring and Calculating Area (C)
Students will get a glimpse of what they will learn about in the lesson. They will also read the lesson goals.

Dividing by 1 Math Facts

Students will practice dividing by 1.

LEARN   Finding the Area Formula

Students will discover the area formula for the area of a rectangle.

TRY IT   Find the Area Formula

Students will practice finding the area formula. Support will be provided to help students overcome misconceptions.

LEARN   Multiplying to Find Area

Students will learn how to multiply to find the area of a rectangle.

TRY IT   Multiply to Find Area

Students will practice multiplying to find area. Support will be provided to help students overcome misconceptions.

TRY IT   Practice Multiplying to Find Area

Students will complete online practice problems. Then they will complete Practice Multiplying to Find Area from *Summit Math 3 Activity Book*.

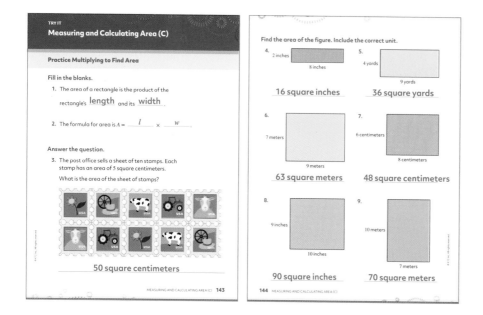

Multiplying to Find Area

Students will solve a problem to show that they understand how to multiply to find the area of a rectangle.

Measuring and Calculating Area (D)

Lesson Overview

ACTIVITY	ACTIVITY TITLE	TIME	ONLINE/OFFLINE
GET READY	Introduction to Measuring and Calculating Area (D)	**2** minutes	📶
TRY IT	Review Measuring and Calculating Area	**18** minutes	📶
QUIZ	Measuring and Calculating Area	**25** minutes	📶
WRAP-UP	More Math Practice	**15** minutes	📶

Lesson Goals

- Review key concepts about measuring and calculating area.
- Take a quiz.

MATERIALS

There are no materials to gather for this lesson.

GET READY

Introduction to Measuring and Calculating Area (D)

Students will read the lesson goals.

TRY IT

Review Measuring and Calculating Area

Students will answer questions to review what they have learned about measuring and calculating area.

QUIZ

Measuring and Calculating Area

Students will complete the Measuring and Calculating Area quiz.

More Math Practice

Students will practice skills according to their individual needs.

Applying Formulas and Properties (A)

Lesson Overview

ACTIVITY	ACTIVITY TITLE	TIME	ONLINE/OFFLINE
GET READY	Introduction to Applying Formulas and Properties (A)	**2** minutes	🖥️
	Look Back at Area of Rectangles	**8** minutes	🖥️
LEARN AND **TRY IT**	Finding Areas of Different Shapes	**15** minutes	🖥️
	Find Areas of Different Shapes	**10** minutes	🖥️
	Practice Finding Areas of Different Shapes	**20** minutes	🖥️ and 📄
WRAP-UP	Finding Areas of Different Shapes	**5** minutes	🖥️

Content Background

Students will use the additive property of area to find the area of a complex figure that can be divided into two or more rectangles or squares. As students work through this lesson, they will learn how to break apart, or decompose, a complex figure into two or more simpler rectangles or squares. By finding the area of each simpler figure and then finding the sum of those areas, they can determine the area of the original figure. A complex figure can often be broken apart in more than one way, providing different paths for determining the area. Encourage students to look for alternative ways to break apart complex figures. Point out that calculating the area of a complex figure in more than one way is a good way to check their answers.

> ### MATERIALS
>
> **Supplied**
> - *Summit Math 3 Activity Book:* Practice Finding Areas of Different Shapes

Lesson Goals
- Find the area of a figure by dividing it into rectangles.

GET READY

Introduction to Applying Formulas and Properties (A)
Students will get a glimpse of what they will learn about in the lesson. They will also read the lesson goals.

Look Back at Area of Rectangles
Students will practice the prerequisite skill of finding the area of a rectangle.

LEARN   Finding Areas of Different Shapes

Students will learn how to find the areas of different shapes.

TRY IT   Find Areas of Different Shapes

Students will practice finding the areas of different shapes. Support will be provided to help students overcome misconceptions.

TRY IT   Practice Finding Areas of Different Shapes

Students will complete online practice problems. Then they will complete Practice Finding Areas of Different Shapes from *Summit Math 3 Activity Book*.

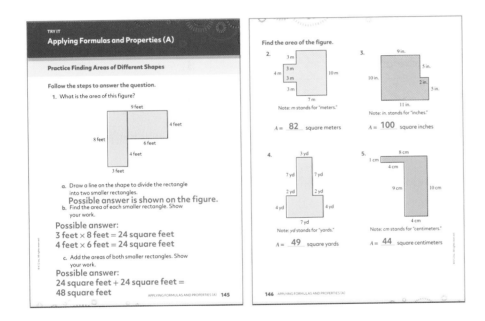

Finding Areas of Different Shapes

Students will solve a problem to show that they understand how to find the area of a rectangular shape.

Applying Formulas and Properties (B)

Lesson Overview

ACTIVITY	ACTIVITY TITLE	TIME	ONLINE/OFFLINE
GET READY	Introduction to Applying Formulas and Properties (B)	**2** minutes	🖥
	Dividing by 1 with Instant Recall	**8** minutes	🖥
LEARN AND **TRY IT**	Solving Area Problems Using Multiplication	**15** minutes	🖥
	Solve Area Problems Using Multiplication	**10** minutes	🖥
	Practice Solving Area Problems Using Multiplication	**20** minutes	🖥 and 📄
WRAP-UP	Solving Area Problems Using Multiplication	**5** minutes	🖥

Content Background

Students have learned that the area of a rectangle is the product of its length and width. Students will apply this knowledge to find the area of rectangles in the real world. Continue to emphasize that square units are the units for area and linear units are the units for the length and width of the rectangle.

MATERIALS

Supplied
- *Summit Math 3 Activity Book:* Practice Solving Area Problems Using Multiplication

Lesson Goals
- Solve real-world area problems using multiplication.

GET READY

Introduction to Applying Formulas and Properties (B)

Students will get a glimpse of what they will learn about in the lesson. They will also read the lesson goals.

Dividing by 1 with Instant Recall

Students will practice dividing by 1.

LEARN Solving Area Problems Using Multiplication

Students will learn to solve real-world area problems using multiplication.

TRY IT Solve Area Problems Using Multiplication

Students will practice solving real-world area problems using multiplication. Support will be provided to help students overcome misconceptions.

TRY IT Practice Solving Area Problems Using Multiplication

Students will complete online practice problems. Then they will complete Practice Solving Area Problems Using Multiplication from *Summit Math 3 Activity Book*.

TRY IT
Applying Formulas and Properties (B)

Practice Solving Area Problems Using Multiplication

Follow the steps to answer the question.

1. A poster is in the shape of a rectangle. The poster has a length of 7 feet and a width of 4 feet.

   What is the area of the poster?

   a. Draw a rectangle to represent the poster.

   Possible answer: 4 feet 7 feet

   b. Write a multiplication equation that you can use to solve the problem. $A = 7 \times 4$

   c. Multiply to find the area of the poster. Include the correct unit in your answer. 28 square feet

2. A rectangular wall is 10 feet long and 9 feet tall.

   What is the area of the wall?

   a. Draw a rectangle to represent the wall.

   Possible answer: 9 feet 10 feet

   APPLYING FORMULAS AND PROPERTIES (B) 147

   b. Write a multiplication equation that you can use to solve the problem. $A = 10 \times 9$

   c. Multiply to find the area of the poster. Include the correct unit in your answer. 90 square feet

   Answer the question. Include the correct unit in your answer.

3. Christian plants a garden in the shape of a rectangle. His garden is 9 meters long and 6 meters wide.

   What is the area of Christian's garden? 54 square meters

4. Lara tiles a floor in the shape of a rectangle. The floor is 7 yards long and 5 yards wide.

   What is the area of the floor? 35 square yards

5. A small notecard is 10 centimeters long and 8 centimeters wide.

   What is the area of the notecard? 80 square centimeters

6. An artist has a canvas. It is a rectangle that is 9 meters long and 5 meters wide.

   What is the area of the canvas? 45 square meters

   148 APPLYING FORMULAS AND PROPERTIES (B)

WRAP-UP

Solving Area Problems Using Multiplication

Students will solve a problem to show that they understand how to solve a real-world area problem using multiplication.

Applying Formulas and Properties (C)

Lesson Overview

ACTIVITY	ACTIVITY TITLE	TIME	ONLINE/OFFLINE
GET READY	Introduction to Applying Formulas and Properties (C)	**2** minutes	🖥
	Dividing by 1 Math Facts Game	**8** minutes	🖥
LEARN AND **TRY IT**	Solving Area Problems Using Division	**15** minutes	🖥
	Solve Area Problems Using Division	**10** minutes	🖥
	Practice Solving Area Problems Using Division	**20** minutes	🖥 and 📄
WRAP-UP	Solving Area Problems Using Division	**5** minutes	🖥

Content Background

Students have learned that the area of a rectangle is the product of its length and width. This means you can divide the area of a rectangle by one dimension in order to find the other dimension. Students learn to divide to find the length or width of a real-world rectangle given the rectangle's area. To emphasize the relationship between length, width, and area, students will practice writing equations using a letter to represent the unknown length or width of a rectangle. Continue to emphasize that square units are the units for area and linear units are the units for the length and width of the rectangle.

Lesson Goals

- Solve real-world area problems using division.
- Use an equation to solve a real-world problem.
- Use a letter to represent an unknown number.

> **MATERIALS**
>
> **Supplied**
> - *Summit Math 3 Activity Book:* Practice Solving Area Problems Using Division

GET READY

Introduction to Applying Formulas and Properties (C)

Students will get a glimpse of what they will learn about in the lesson. They will also read the lesson goals.

Dividing by 1 Math Facts Game

Students will practice dividing by 1.

LEARN Solving Area Problems Using Division

Students will learn how to solve real-world area problems using division.

TRY IT Solve Area Problems Using Division

Students will practice solving real-world area problems using division. Support will be provided to help students overcome misconceptions.

TRY IT Practice Solving Area Problems Using Division

Students will complete online practice problems. Then they will complete Practice Solving Area Problems Using Division from *Summit Math 3 Activity Book*.

TRY IT
Applying Formulas and Properties (C)

Practice Solving Area Problems Using Division

Follow the steps to answer the question.

1. A picture is 10 inches long. It has an area of 80 square inches. How wide is the picture?

   a. Draw a rectangle to represent the picture.

   Possible answer: ? inches / 10 inches

   b. Write a division equation that you can use to solve the problem. $80 \div 10 = w$

   c. Divide to find the width of the picture. Include the correct unit in your answer. 8 inches

2. A desk in the shape of a rectangle is 2 feet wide. It has an area of 16 square feet. How long is the desk?

   a. Draw a rectangle to represent the desk.

   Possible answer: 2 feet / ? feet

   APPLYING FORMULAS AND PROPERTIES (C) **149**

   b. Write a division equation that you can use to solve the problem. $16 \div 2 = l$

   c. Divide to find the length of the desk. Include the correct unit in your answer. 8 feet

   Answer the question. Include the correct unit in your answer.

3. A banner in the shape of a rectangle has an area of 81 square feet. The banner is 9 feet long. How wide is the banner? 9 feet

4. A sidewalk has an area of 50 square meters. The sidewalk is 5 meters wide. How long is the sidewalk? 10 meters

5. A window has 56 square feet of glass. The window is 8 feet long. How wide is the window? 7 feet

6. A placemat in the shape of a rectangle has an area of 63 square inches. The placemat is 7 inches wide. How long is the placemat? 9 inches

   150 APPLYING FORMULAS AND PROPERTIES (C)

Solving Area Problems Using Division

Students will solve a problem to show that they understand how to solve real-world area problems using division.

Applying Formulas and Properties (D)

Lesson Overview

ACTIVITY	ACTIVITY TITLE	TIME	ONLINE/OFFLINE
GET READY	Introduction to Applying Formulas and Properties (D)	**2** minutes	🖥️
	Dividing by 10 and 5 Math Facts	**8** minutes	🖥️
LEARN AND **TRY IT**	Using Area to Model the Distributive Property	**15** minutes	🖥️
	Use Area to Model the Distributive Property	**10** minutes	🖥️
	Practice Using Area to Model the Distributive Property	**20** minutes	🖥️ and 📄
WRAP-UP	Using Area to Model the Distributive Property	**5** minutes	🖥️

Content Background

Students have developed an understanding of the distributive property as a strategy to break apart numbers in order to make it easier to multiply using mental math. Students have also learned that area is additive. In this lesson, students will model the distributive property by adding the areas of two parts of the same rectangle. For example, this rectangle composed of 42 unit squares models $(6 \times 5) + (6 \times 2)$. The area is split into two parts, but the sum of those areas equals the area of the whole rectangle.

MATERIALS

Supplied
- *Summit Math 3 Activity Book:* Practice Using Area to Model the Distributive Property

KEYWORDS

distributive property – a rule that says that multiplying a number by a sum gives the same answer as multiplying the number by each addend of the sum and then adding the products

Lesson Goals

- Use area to represent the distributive property.

Introduction to Applying Formulas and Properties (D)

Students will get a glimpse of what they will learn about in the lesson. They will also read the lesson goals and keywords. Have students select each keyword and preview its definition.

Dividing by 10 and 5 Math Facts

Students will practice dividing by 10 and 5.

LEARN AND TRY IT

LEARN   Using Area to Model the Distributive Property

Students will learn to use areas to model the distributive property.

TRY IT   Use Area to Model the Distributive Property

Students will practice using area to model the distributive property. Support will be provided to help students overcome misconceptions.

TRY IT   Practice Using Area to Model the Distributive Property

Students will complete online practice problems. Then they will complete Practice Using Area to Model the Distributive Property from *Summit Math 3 Activity Book*.

Using Area to Model the Distributive Property

Students will solve a problem to show that they understand how to use area to model the distributive property.

Applying Formulas and Properties (E)

Lesson Overview

ACTIVITY	ACTIVITY TITLE	TIME	ONLINE/OFFLINE
GET READY	Introduction to Applying Formulas and Properties (E)	**2** minutes	📶
	Dividing by 10 and 5 with Instant Recall	**8** minutes	📶
LEARN AND **TRY IT**	Representing Products as Area	**7** minutes	🖥️
	Represent Products as Area	**7** minutes	🖥️
	Solving Problems with Perimeter and Area	**7** minutes	🖥️
	Solve Problems with Perimeter and Area	**7** minutes	📶
	Practice Solving Problems with Perimeter and Area	**20** minutes	📶 and 📄
WRAP-UP	Solving Problems with Perimeter and Area	**2** minutes	📶

Content Background

Students will learn to represent a multiplication equation by creating a rectangle. The rectangle's length and width represent the factors and the area represents the product.

Students will also learn that rectangles that have the same area can have different perimeters and that rectangles that have the same perimeter can have different areas. For example, the four rectangles listed in this table all have the same area, 48 square inches, but they have different perimeters.

RECTANGLES: SAME AREA, DIFFERENT PERIMETERS			
Length	**Width**	**Perimeter**	**Area**
48 inches	1 inch	98 inches	48 square inches
24 inches	2 inches	52 inches	48 square inches
12 inches	4 inches	32 inches	48 square inches
8 inches	6 inches	28 inches	48 square inches

MATERIALS

Supplied
- *Summit Math 3 Activity Book:* Practice Solving Problems with Perimeter and Area

KEYWORDS

area – the amount of space on a flat surface, most often measured in square units

perimeter – the distance around the edge of a shape

The six rectangles listed in this table all have the same perimeter, 26 inches, but they have different areas.

RECTANGLES: SAME PERIMETER, DIFFERENT AREAS			
Length	Width	Perimeter	Area
12 inches	1 inch	12 inches	26 square inches
11 inches	2 inches	22 inches	26 square inches
10 inches	3 inches	30 inches	26 square inches
9 inches	4 inches	36 inches	26 square inches
8 inches	5 inches	40 inches	26 square inches
7 inches	6 inches	42 inches	26 square inches

Continue to emphasize that square units are the units for area and linear units are the units for perimeter.

Lesson Goals

- Show that rectangles can have the same area and different perimeters.
- Show that rectangles can have the same perimeter and different areas.
- Use a multiplication equation to represent the area of the rectangle.

GET READY

Introduction to Applying Formulas and Properties (E)
Students will get a glimpse of what they will learn about in the lesson. They will also read the lesson goals and keywords. Have students select each keyword and preview its definition.

Dividing by 10 and 5 with Instant Recall
Students will practice dividing by 10 and 5.

LEARN AND TRY IT

LEARN   Representing Products as Areas
Students will learn to represent products as the area of a rectangle.

TRY IT Represent Products as Areas

Students will practice representing products as the area of a rectangle. Support will be provided to help students overcome misconceptions.

LEARN Solving Problems with Perimeter and Area

Students will learn to solve problems with perimeter and area.

TRY IT Solve Problems with Perimeter and Area

Students will practice solving problems with perimeter and area. Support will be provided to help students overcome misconceptions.

TRY IT Practice Solving Problems with Perimeter and Area

Students will complete online practice problems. Then they will complete Practice Solving Problems with Perimeter and Area from *Summit Math 3 Activity Book*.

TRY IT
Applying Formulas and Properties (E)

Practice Solving Problems with Perimeter and Area

Follow the instructions.

1. There are 3 different rectangles that have an area of 18 square units.
   Note: Answers may be arranged differently.
   a. Draw each rectangle on this grid.

   b. Complete the table for the 3 rectangles you drew in part **a**. Include the correct units.

Length	Width	Perimeter	Area
18 units	1 unit	38 units	18 square units
9 units	2 units	22 units	18 square units
6 units	3 units	18 units	18 square units

   c. The area of these 3 rectangles is the same. Is the perimeter of each rectangle the same? Explain.
   No. Possible answer: Rectangles can have the same area and different perimeters.

   APPLYING FORMULAS AND PROPERTIES (E) 153

2. Some of these rectangles have the same perimeter.

   a. Circle the 3 rectangles that have a perimeter of 16 meters.
   b. Complete the table for the 3 rectangles you circled in part **a**. Include the correct units for each measurement.

Length	Width	Perimeter	Area
4 meters	4 meters	16 meters	16 square meters
6 meters	2 meters	16 meters	12 square meters
7 meters	1 meter	16 meters	7 square meters

   c. The perimeter of these 3 rectangles is the same. Is the area of each rectangle the same? Explain.
   No. Possible answer: Rectangles can have the same perimeter and different areas.

   Draw and label a rectangle that models the equation.

   3. $3 \times 7 = 21$ 3 units / 7 units
   4. $5 \times 2 = 10$ 2 units / 5 units

   154 APPLYING FORMULAS AND PROPERTIES (E)

WRAP-UP

Solving Problems with Perimeter and Area

Students will solve problems to show that they understand how to solve problems with perimeter and area.

Applying Formulas and Properties (F)

Lesson Overview

ACTIVITY	ACTIVITY TITLE	TIME	ONLINE/OFFLINE
GET READY	Introduction to Applying Formulas and Properties (F)	**2** minutes	🖥️
TRY IT	Review Applying Formulas and Properties	**18** minutes	🖥️
QUIZ	Applying Formulas and Properties	**25** minutes	🖥️
WRAP-UP	More Math Practice	**15** minutes	🖥️

Lesson Goals

- Review key concepts about applying formulas and properties of area.
- Take a quiz.

MATERIALS

There are no materials to gather for this lesson.

GET READY

Introduction to Applying Formulas and Properties (F)

Students will read the lesson goals.

TRY IT

Review Applying Formulas and Properties

Students will answer questions to review what they have learned about applying formulas and properties.

QUIZ

Applying Formulas and Properties

Students will complete the Applying Formulas and Properties quiz.

More Math Practice

Students will practice skills according to their individual needs.

Big Ideas: Extended Problems

Lesson Overview

Big Ideas lessons provide students the opportunity to further apply the knowledge and skills acquired throughout previous units. Each Big Ideas lesson consists of two types of activities:

1. **Cumulative Review:** Students keep their skills fresh by reviewing prior content.

2. **Synthesis:** Students complete an assignment that allows them to interweave and apply what they've learned. These synthesis assignments will vary throughout the course.

   In the Synthesis portion of this Big Ideas lesson, students will complete multistep problems that go beyond the short answer and multiple choice problems they encounter in their regular lessons. These problems give students an opportunity to demonstrate problem solving, reasoning, communication, and modeling skills. Students will need to use pencil and paper and/or technology to show their work.

   LEARNING COACH CHECK-IN   This is a graded assessment. Make sure students complete, review, and submit the assignment to their teacher.

All materials needed for this lesson are linked online. The materials are not provided in this Lesson Guide or in the Activity Book.

MATERIALS

Supplied
- Extended Problems Instructions (printout)

Fractions

Unit Fractions (A)

Lesson Overview

ACTIVITY	ACTIVITY TITLE	TIME	ONLINE/OFFLINE
GET READY	Introduction to Unit Fractions (A)	**2** minutes	🖥
	Look Back at Using Unit Squares to Find Area	**8** minutes	🖥
LEARN AND **TRY IT**	Working with Unit Fractions and Shapes	**15** minutes	🖥
	Work with Unit Fractions and Shapes	**10** minutes	🖥
	Practice Working with Unit Fractions and Shapes	**20** minutes	🖥 and 📄
WRAP-UP	Working with Unit Fractions and Shapes	**5** minutes	🖥

Content Background

Students will learn that a fraction can represent the relationship of a part to a whole using shape models. A fraction is a single number that has two parts, a numerator and a denominator. In a shape model, the denominator of the fraction is the number of equal parts in the shape and the numerator is the number of shaded parts.

When modeling fractions with shapes, the whole can be any shape. However, the parts of the whole must be equal in size, or have the same area. Students may believe that in the diagram on the left the green triangle represents $\frac{1}{3}$, since the whole is divided into 3 parts. This is incorrect, because all 3 parts must be the same size, as is shown in the diagram on the right. In that diagram, each rhombus does represent $\frac{1}{3}$.

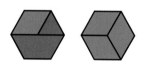

Some students might mistakenly think that a fraction compares one part to another part. Throughout this unit, continue to emphasize that a fraction should be thought of as a single number that shows a comparison between parts of the whole and the entire whole.

This concept focuses only on fractions that have a numerator of 1 and are called *unit fractions*. Students will be introduced to fractions with other numerators in future lessons.

Lesson Goals

- Name a unit fraction of a shape.
- Represent a unit fraction using a shape.

Introduction to Unit Fractions (A)

After a quick introductory activity, students will read the lesson goals and keywords. Have students select each keyword and preview its definition.

Look Back at Using Unit Squares to Find Area

Students will practice the prerequisite skill of using unit squares to find area.

LEARN AND TRY IT

LEARN   Working with Unit Fractions and Shapes

Students will learn to name and represent a unit fraction using a shape.

TRY IT   Work with Unit Fractions and Shapes

Students will practice naming and representing a unit fraction using a shape. Support will be provided to help students overcome misconceptions.

TRY IT   Practice Working with Unit Fractions and Shapes

Students will complete online practice problems. Then they will complete Practice Working with Unit Fractions and Shapes from *Summit Math 3 Activity Book*.

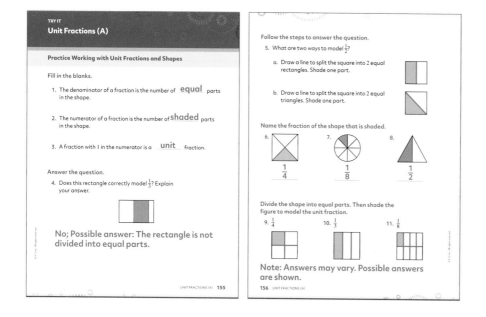

WRAP-UP

Working with Unit Fractions and Shapes

Students will solve a problem to show that they understand how to name a unit fraction using a shape.

Unit Fractions (B)

Lesson Overview

ACTIVITY	ACTIVITY TITLE	TIME	ONLINE/OFFLINE
GET READY	Introduction to Unit Fractions (B)	**2** minutes	🖥️
	Dividing by 10 and 5 Math Facts Game	**8** minutes	🖥️
LEARN AND **TRY IT**	Working with Unit Fractions and Number Lines	**15** minutes	🖥️
	Work with Unit Fractions and Number Lines	**10** minutes	🖥️
	Practice Working with Unit Fractions and Number Lines	**20** minutes	🖥️ and 📄
WRAP-UP	Working with Unit Fractions and Number Lines	**5** minutes	🖥️

Content Background

Students will learn that a fraction can represent the relationship of a part to a whole using number lines. Every fraction has a unique location on a number line. For example, $\frac{1}{4}$ is located at the point exactly $\frac{1}{4}$ of the distance between 0 and 1 on the number line.

A fraction is a single number that has two parts, a numerator and denominator. On a number line, the denominator is the number of equal parts between 0 and 1. The numerator is the number of hops starting from 0. Since this concept focuses on unit fractions, students will make only one hop from 0 to plot a fraction with a numerator of 1. Students will be introduced to fractions with other numerators in future lessons.

Lesson Goals

- Name a unit fraction on a number line.
- Represent a unit fraction on a number line.

GET READY

Introduction to Unit Fractions (B)

Students will get a glimpse of what they will learn about in the lesson. They will also read the lesson goals.

Dividing by 10 and 5 Math Facts Game

Students will practice dividing by 10 and 5.

LEARN   Working with Unit Fractions and Number Lines

Students will learn to name and plot unit fractions on a number line.

TRY IT   Work with Unit Fractions and Number Lines

Students will practice naming and plotting unit fractions on a number line. Support will be provided to help students overcome misconceptions.

TRY IT   Practice Working with Unit Fractions and Number Lines

Students will complete online practice problems. Then they will complete Practice Working with Unit Fractions and Number Lines from *Summit Math 3 Activity Book*.

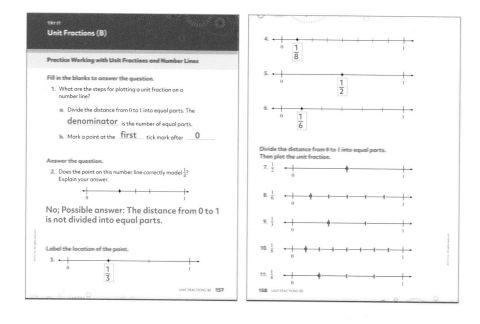

Working with Unit Fractions and Number Lines

Students will solve a problem to show that they understand how to name a unit fraction on a number line.

Unit Fractions (C)

Lesson Overview

ACTIVITY	ACTIVITY TITLE	TIME	ONLINE/OFFLINE
GET READY	Introduction to Unit Fractions (C)	**2** minutes	🖥️
	Dividing by 2 and 4 Math Facts	**8** minutes	🖥️
LEARN AND **TRY IT**	Working with Unit Fractions and Sets	**15** minutes	🖥️
	Work with Unit Fractions and Sets	**10** minutes	🖥️
	Practice Working with Unit Fractions and Sets	**20** minutes	🖥️ and 📄
WRAP-UP	Working with Unit Fractions and Sets	**5** minutes	🖥️

Content Background

Students will learn that a fraction can show the relationship of equal parts to a set, as well as equal parts to a whole. For example, if they have 3 objects and 1 of them is red, they can say that $\frac{1}{3}$ of the objects are red (or that $\frac{1}{3}$ of the set is red). Students will continue to represent and name unit fractions. Students will be introduced to fractions with other numerators in future lessons.

When working with sets, some students might mistakenly think that a fraction compares one part to another part. Continue to emphasize that a fraction should be thought of as a single number that shows a comparison between parts of the whole and the entire whole.

MATERIALS

Supplied
- *Summit Math 3 Activity Book:* Practice Working with Unit Fractions and Sets

Lesson Goals

- Name a unit fraction of a set of objects.
- Represent a unit fraction of a set of objects.

GET READY

Introduction to Unit Fractions (C)

Students will get a glimpse of what they will learn about in the lesson. They will also read the lesson goals.

Dividing by 2 and 4 Math Facts

Students will practice dividing by 2 and 4.

LEARN   Working with Unit Fractions and Sets

Students will learn to name and represent a unit fraction of a set of objects.

TRY IT   Work with Unit Fractions and Sets

Students will practice naming and representing a unit fraction of a set of objects. Support will be provided to help students overcome misconceptions.

TRY IT   Practice Working with Unit Fractions and Sets

Students will complete online practice problems. Then they will complete Practice Working with Unit Fractions and Sets from *Summit Math 3 Activity Book*.

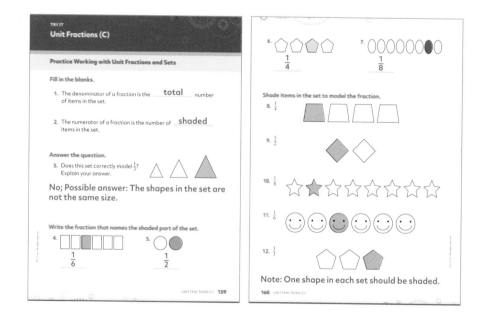

WRAP-UP

Working with Unit Fractions and Sets

Students will solve problems to show that they understand how to name and represent a fraction of a set of objects.

Unit Fractions (D)

Lesson Overview

ACTIVITY	ACTIVITY TITLE	TIME	ONLINE/OFFLINE
GET READY	Introduction to Unit Fractions (D)	**2** minutes	🖥️
TRY IT	Review Unit Fractions	**18** minutes	🖥️
QUIZ	Unit Fractions	**25** minutes	🖥️
WRAP-UP	More Math Practice	**15** minutes	🖥️

Lesson Goals

- Review naming and representing unit fractions using shapes, number lines, and groups of objects.
- Take a quiz.

MATERIALS

There are no materials to gather for this lesson.

GET READY

Introduction to Unit Fractions (D)

Students will read the lesson goals.

TRY IT

Review Unit Fractions

Students will answer questions to review what they have learned about unit fractions.

QUIZ

Unit Fractions

Students will complete the Unit Fractions quiz.

More Math Practice

Students will practice skills according to their individual needs.

Non-Unit Fractions (A)

Lesson Overview

ACTIVITY	ACTIVITY TITLE	TIME	ONLINE/OFFLINE
GET READY	Introduction to Non-Unit Fractions (A)	**2** minutes	📶
	Look Back at Unit Fractions on a Number Line	**8** minutes	📶
LEARN AND TRY IT	Naming Fractions Modeled with Shapes	**15** minutes	📶
	Name Fractions Modeled with Shapes	**10** minutes	📶
	Practice Naming Fractions Modeled with Shapes	**20** minutes	📶 and 📄
WRAP-UP	Naming Fractions Modeled with Shapes	**5** minutes	📶

Content Background

Students have an understanding that a fraction is a single number that has two parts, a numerator and denominator. They have learned that the denominator represents the number of equal parts in a shape model and the numerator is the number of shaded parts. The previous concept focused only on fractions with a numerator of 1, called *unit fractions*. In this concept, students will work with fractions with other numbers in the numerator. These fractions are called *non-unit fractions*. Students will learn how to name a fraction that is represented by a shape model. Students will count the number of equal parts to find the denominator. Then they will count the number of shaded parts to find the numerator.

TIP Remind students that a shape model can be any shape. However, the parts of the shape must be equal. Continue to emphasize that each fraction compares a part to a whole.

Lesson Goals

- Name a fraction of a shape.

MATERIALS

Supplied

- *Summit Math 3 Activity Book:* Practice Naming Fractions Modeled with Shapes

KEYWORDS

non-unit fraction – a fraction with a numerator that is any number except 1, such as $\frac{2}{3}$ or $\frac{5}{8}$

Introduction to Non-Unit Fractions (A)

Students will get a glimpse of what they will learn about in the lesson. They will also read the lesson goals and keywords. Have students select each keyword and preview its definition.

Look Back at Unit Fractions on a Number Line

Students will practice the prerequisite skill of identifying a unit fraction on a number line.

LEARN AND TRY IT

LEARN   Naming Fractions Modeled with Shapes

Students will learn how to name a fraction modeled with a shape.

TRY IT   Name Fractions Modeled with Shapes

Students will practice naming fractions modeled by shapes. Support will be provided to help students overcome misconceptions.

TRY IT   Practice Naming Fractions Modeled with Shapes

Students will complete online practice problems. Then they will complete Practice Naming Fractions Modeled with Shapes from *Summit Math 3 Activity Book*.

Naming Fractions Modeled with Shapes

Students will solve a problem to show that they understand how to name a fraction from a shape model.

Non-Unit Fractions (B)

Lesson Overview

ACTIVITY	ACTIVITY TITLE	TIME	ONLINE/OFFLINE
GET READY	Introduction to Non-Unit Fractions (B)	**2** minutes	🖥️
	Dividing by 2 and 4 with Instant Recall	**8** minutes	🖥️
LEARN AND **TRY IT**	Representing Fractions with Shape Models	**15** minutes	🖥️
	Represent Fractions with Shape Models	**10** minutes	🖥️
	Practice Representing Fractions with Shape Models	**20** minutes	🖥️ and 📄
WRAP-UP	Representing Fractions with Shape Models	**5** minutes	🖥️

Content Background

Students will learn to create shape models to represent fractions with a numerator greater than 1. When modeling fractions with shapes, the whole can be any shape. However, each part of a whole must be equal in size, or have the same area. Students will be given some models that are already divided into equal parts and some models that they must divide into equal parts. Continue to emphasize that the denominator represents the number of equal parts and the numerator represents the number of shaded parts.

MATERIALS

Supplied
- *Summit Math 3 Activity Book:* Practice Representing Fractions with Shape Models

Lesson Goals
- Model a fraction using a shape.

GET READY

Introduction to Non-Unit Fractions (B)

Students will get a glimpse of what they will learn about in the lesson. They will also read the lesson goals.

Dividing by 2 and 4 with Instant Recall

Students will practice dividing by 2 and 4.

LEARN   Representing Fractions with Shape Models

Students will learn to represent a fraction using a shape model.

TRY IT   Represent Fractions with Shape Models

Students will practice representing fractions using shape models. Support will be provided to help students overcome misconceptions.

TRY IT   Practice Representing Fractions with Shape Models

Students will complete online practice problems. Then they will complete Practice Representing Fractions with Shape Models from *Summit Math 3 Activity Book*.

Representing Fractions with Shape Models

Students will solve a problem to show that they understand how to represent a fraction with a shape model.

Non-Unit Fractions (C)

Lesson Overview

ACTIVITY	ACTIVITY TITLE	TIME	ONLINE/OFFLINE
GET READY	Introduction to Non-Unit Fractions (C)	**2** minutes	🖥️
	Dividing by 2 and 4 Math Facts Game	**8** minutes	🖥️
LEARN AND **TRY IT**	Naming Fractions on a Number Line	**15** minutes	🖥️
	Name Fractions on a Number Line	**10** minutes	🖥️
	Practice Naming Fractions on a Number Line	**20** minutes	🖥️ and 📄
WRAP-UP	Naming Fractions on a Number Line	**5** minutes	🖥️

Content Background

Students will learn to label the location of a point on a number line. Each fraction in this lesson is a fraction between 0 and 1 with a numerator that is greater than 1. Every fraction has a unique location on the number line. For example, $\frac{3}{4}$ is located at the point exactly $\frac{3}{4}$ of the distance between 0 and 1 on the number line. A fraction is a single number that has two parts, a numerator and denominator. On a number line, the denominator is the number of equal parts between 0 and 1. The numerator is the number of hops starting from 0. Students will focus on counting the number of equal parts and hops to write the fraction that represents the location of a point.

Lesson Goals

- Name a fraction on a number line.

MATERIALS

Supplied

- *Summit Math 3 Activity Book:* Practice Naming Fractions on a Number Line

GET READY

Introduction to Non-Unit Fractions (C)
Students will get a glimpse of what they will learn about in the lesson. They will also read the lesson goals.

Dividing by 2 and 4 Math Facts Game
Students will practice dividing by 2 and 4.

LEARN Naming Fractions on a Number Line

Students will learn how to name fractions on a number line.

TRY IT Name Fractions on a Number Line

Students will practice naming fractions on a number line. Support will be provided to help students overcome misconceptions.

TRY IT Practice Naming Fractions on a Number Line

Students will complete online practice problems. Then they will complete Practice Naming Fractions on a Number Line from *Summit Math 3 Activity Book.*

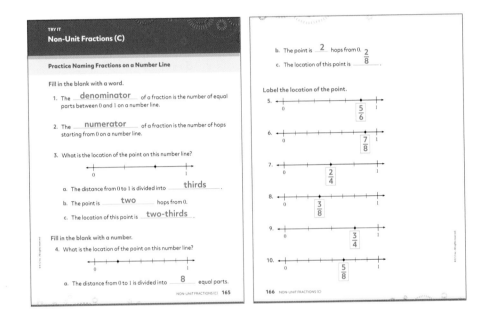

Naming Fractions on a Number Line

Students will solve a problem to show that they understand how to name a fraction on a number line.

Non-Unit Fractions (D)

Lesson Overview

ACTIVITY	ACTIVITY TITLE	TIME	ONLINE/OFFLINE
GET READY	Introduction to Non-Unit Fractions (D)	**2** minutes	🖥️
	Dividing by 3 Math Facts	**8** minutes	🖥️
LEARN AND **TRY IT**	Representing Fractions on a Number Line	**15** minutes	🖥️
	Represent Fractions on a Number Line	**10** minutes	🖥️
	Practice Representing Fractions on a Number Line	**20** minutes	🖥️ and 📄
WRAP-UP	Representing Fractions on a Number Line	**5** minutes	🖥️

Content Background

Students will learn to plot points on a number line to represent fractions with numerators greater than 1. A fraction is a single number that has two parts, a numerator and denominator. Students will be given some number lines that are already divided into equal parts and some number lines that they must divide into equal parts. Continue to emphasize that the denominator represents the number of equal parts and the numerator represents the number of hops starting from 0.

MATERIALS

Supplied
- *Summit Math 3 Activity Book:* Practice Representing Fractions on a Number Line

Lesson Goals

- Represent a fraction on a number line.

GET READY

Introduction to Non-Unit Fractions (D)

Students will get a glimpse of what they will learn about in the lesson. They will also read the lesson goals.

Dividing by 3 Math Facts

Students will practice dividing by 3.

LEARN AND TRY IT

LEARN   Representing Fractions on a Number Line

Students will learn to represent a fraction on a number line.

TRY IT   Represent Fractions on a Number Line

Students will practice representing fractions on a number line. Support will be provided to help students overcome misconceptions.

TRY IT   Practice Representing Fractions on a Number Line

Students will complete online practice problems. Then they will complete Practice Representing Fractions on a Number Line from *Summit Math 3 Activity Book*.

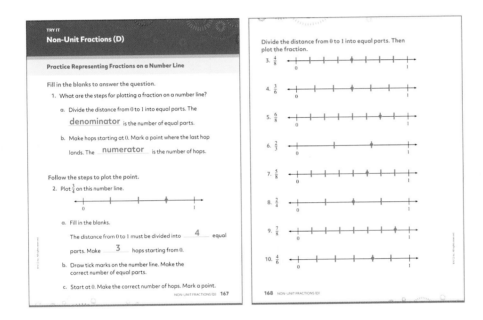

WRAP-UP

Representing Fractions on a Number Line

Students will solve a problem to show that they understand how to represent a fraction on a number line.

Non-Unit Fractions (E)

Lesson Overview

ACTIVITY	ACTIVITY TITLE	TIME	ONLINE/OFFLINE
GET READY	Introduction to Non-Unit Fractions (E)	**2** minutes	🖥️
TRY IT	Review Non-Unit Fractions	**18** minutes	🖥️
QUIZ	Non-Unit Fractions	**25** minutes	🖥️
WRAP-UP	More Math Practice	**15** minutes	🖥️

Lesson Goals

- Review naming and modeling fractions using shapes and number lines.
- Take a quiz.

MATERIALS

There are no materials to gather for this lesson.

GET READY

Introduction to Non-Unit Fractions (E)

Students will read the lesson goals.

TRY IT

Review Non-Unit Fractions

Students will answer questions to review what they have learned about non-unit fractions.

QUIZ

Non-Unit Fractions

Students will complete the Non-Unit Fractions quiz.

More Math Practice

Students will practice skills according to their individual needs.

Reasoning with Fractions (A)

Lesson Overview

ACTIVITY	ACTIVITY TITLE	TIME	ONLINE/OFFLINE
GET READY	Introduction to Reasoning with Fractions (A)	**2** minutes	📶
	Look Back at Finding a Unit Fraction of a Group	**8** minutes	📶
LEARN AND **TRY IT**	Naming Fractions Modeled with Sets	**15** minutes	📶
	Name Fractions Modeled with Sets	**10** minutes	📶
	Practice Naming Fractions Modeled with Sets	**20** minutes	📶 and 📄
WRAP-UP	Naming Fractions Modeled with Sets	**5** minutes	📶

Content Background

Students have learned that fractions can be shown as parts of a whole or as a location on a number line. They have also named and modeled unit fractions using a set of objects. Students will learn how to name non-unit fractions using a set of objects. Students will count the number of objects in the set to find the denominator. Then students will count the number of objects that are circled or shaded to find the numerator.

When working with sets, some students might mistakenly think that a fraction compares one part to another part. Continue to emphasize that a fraction should be thought of as a single number that shows a comparison between parts of the whole and the entire whole.

> ### Lesson Goals
> • Name a fraction of a set of objects.

MATERIALS

Supplied
• *Summit Math 3 Activity Book:* Practice Naming Fractions Modeled with Sets

GET READY

Introduction to Reasoning with Fractions (A)

Students will get a glimpse of what they will learn about in the lesson. They will also read the lesson goals.

Look Back at Finding a Unit Fraction of a Group

Students will get a glimpse of what they will learn about in the lesson. They will also read the lesson goals.

LEARN Naming Fractions Modeled with Sets

Students will learn how to name a fraction of a set of objects.

TRY IT Name Fractions Modeled with Sets

Students will practice naming a fraction of a set of objects. Support will be provided to help students overcome misconceptions.

TRY IT Practice Naming Fractions Modeled with Sets

Students will complete online practice problems. Then they will complete Practice Naming Fractions Modeled with Sets from *Summit Math 3 Activity Book*.

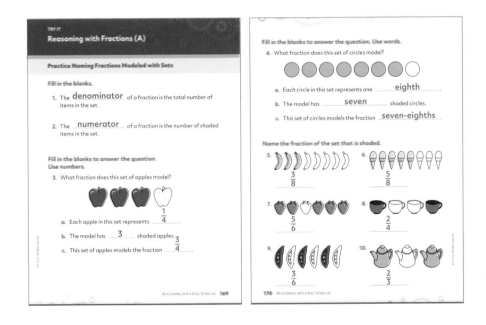

Naming Fractions Modeled with Sets

Students will solve a problem to show that they understand how to name a fraction of a set of objects.

Reasoning with Fractions (B)

Lesson Overview

ACTIVITY	ACTIVITY TITLE	TIME	ONLINE/OFFLINE
GET READY	Introduction to Reasoning with Fractions (B)	**2** minutes	🖥️
	Dividing by 3 with Instant Recall	**8** minutes	🖥️
LEARN AND TRY IT	Representing Fractions with Sets	**15** minutes	🖥️
	Represent Fractions with Sets	**10** minutes	🖥️
	Practice Representing Fractions with Sets	**20** minutes	🖥️ and 📄
WRAP-UP	Representing Fractions with Sets	**5** minutes	🖥️

Content Background

Students will learn to create models using sets of objects to represent fractions with numerators greater than 1. When modeling fractions with sets, any objects can be used. However, it helps if the objects are similar in shape, size, or type. The denominator of the fraction is the number of objects in the set. The numerator of the fraction is the number of objects that students must circle, shade, or select.

TIP   Many students benefit from working with real-life objects. Your student can practice modeling a fraction with a set of everyday objects like toys, foods, eating utensils, coins, or art supplies. Gather a group of 2, 3, 4, 6, or 8 similar objects and ask your student to identify a fraction of the group. Encourage your student to practice writing and saying the fractions created.

> ### MATERIALS
>
> **Supplied**
> - *Summit Math 3 Activity Book:* Practice Representing Fractions with Sets

Lesson Goals
- Model a fraction using a set of objects.

GET READY

Introduction to Reasoning with Fractions (B)
Students will get a glimpse of what they will learn about in the lesson. They will also read the lesson goals.

Dividing by 3 with Instant Recall

Students will practice dividing by 3.

LEARN AND TRY IT

LEARN   Representing Fractions with Sets

Students will learn to model a fraction with a set of objects.

TRY IT   Represent Fractions with Sets

Students will practice modeling fractions with sets of objects. Support will be provided to help students overcome misconceptions.

TRY IT   Practice Representing Fractions with Sets

Students will complete online practice problems. Then they will complete Practice Representing Fractions with Sets from *Summit Math 3 Activity Book*.

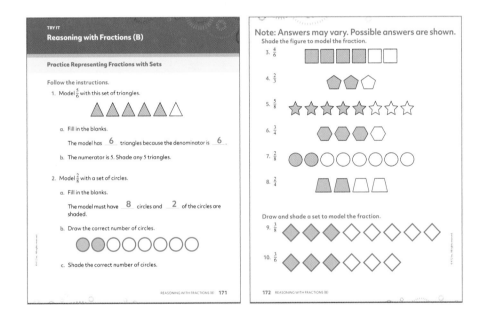

WRAP-UP

Representing Fractions with Sets

Students will solve a problem to show that they understand how to model a fraction with a set of objects.

Reasoning with Fractions (C)

Lesson Overview

ACTIVITY	ACTIVITY TITLE	TIME	ONLINE/OFFLINE
GET READY	Introduction to Reasoning with Fractions (C)	**2** minutes	🖥️
	Dividing by 3 Math Facts Game	**8** minutes	📶
LEARN AND **TRY IT**	Naming Fractions Modeled with Equal Groups	**7** minutes	📶
	Name Fractions Modeled with Equal Groups	**7** minutes	📶
	Representing Fractions Modeled with Equal Groups	**7** minutes	📶
	Represent Fractions Modeled with Equal Groups	**7** minutes	📶
	Practice Working with Fractions Modeled with Equal Groups	**20** minutes	📶 and 📄
WRAP-UP	Working with Fractions Modeled with Equal Groups	**2** minutes	🖥️

Content Background

Students have learned that fractions can be shown as parts of a set. So far, the denominator of the fraction has been the number of objects in the set. For example, if students have 3 objects and 2 of them are red, they can say that two-thirds of the objects are red. In this lesson, students will work with sets of objects that must first be divided into equal groups. For example, 24 oranges are split into 8 equal groups and 5 of the groups are circled.

These oranges model the fraction $\frac{5}{8}$.

In the models in this lesson, the denominator is the number of equal groups and the numerator is the number of groups that are circled or shaded. Students will name fractions and create models using sets split into equal groups.

Lesson Goals

- Name a fraction made from equal groups in a set.
- Model a fraction using equal groups in a set.

GET READY

Introduction to Reasoning with Fractions (C)

Students will get a glimpse of what they will learn about in the lesson. They will also read the lesson goals.

Dividing by 3 Math Facts Game

Students will practice dividing by 3.

LEARN AND TRY IT

LEARN Naming Fractions Modeled with Equal Groups

Students will learn to name a fraction that is modeled with equal groups in a set of objects.

TRY IT Name Fractions Modeled with Equal Groups

Students will practice naming fractions modeled with equal groups in a set of objects. Support will be provided to help students overcome misconceptions.

LEARN Representing Fractions Modeled with Equal Groups

Students will learn to model fractions using equal groups in a set of objects.

TRY IT Represent Fractions Modeled with Equal Groups

Students will practice modeling fractions with equal groups in sets of objects. Support will be provided to help students overcome misconceptions.

TRY IT Practice Working with Fractions Modeled with Equal Groups

Students will complete online practice problems. Then they will complete Practice Working with Fractions Modeled with Equal Groups from *Summit Math 3 Activity Book*.

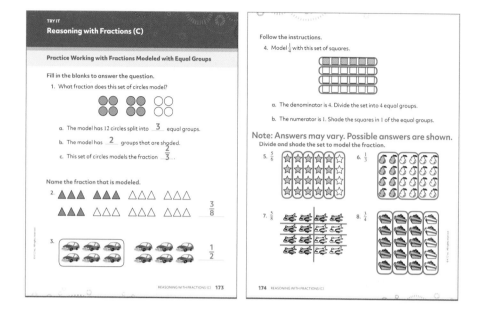

Working with Fractions Modeled with Equal Groups

Students will solve a problem to show that they understand how to name and represent a fraction modeled with equal groups of a set of objects.

Reasoning with Fractions (D)

Lesson Overview

ACTIVITY	ACTIVITY TITLE	TIME	ONLINE/OFFLINE
GET READY	Introduction to Reasoning with Fractions (D)	**2** minutes	🖥️
TRY IT	Review Reasoning with Fractions	**18** minutes	🖥️
QUIZ	Reasoning with Fractions	**25** minutes	🖥️
WRAP-UP	More Math Practice	**15** minutes	🖥️

Lesson Goals

- Review naming and modeling fractions with sets of objects.
- Take a quiz.

MATERIALS

There are no materials to gather for this lesson.

GET READY

Introduction to Reasoning with Fractions (D)

Students will read the lesson goals.

TRY IT

Review Reasoning with Fractions

Students will answer questions to review what they have learned about reasoning with fractions.

QUIZ

Reasoning with Fractions

Students will complete the Reasoning with Fractions quiz.

More Math Practice

Students will practice skills according to their individual needs.

Big Ideas: Challenge Problems

Lesson Overview

Big Ideas lessons provide students the opportunity to apply the knowledge and skills acquired throughout previous units. Each Big Ideas lesson consists of two types of activities:

1. **Cumulative Review:** Students keep their skills fresh by reviewing prior content.

2. **Synthesis:** Students complete an assignment that allows them to interweave and apply what they've learned. These synthesis assignments will vary throughout the course.

   In the Synthesis portion of this Big Ideas lesson, students will complete one or more challenge problems that will guide them to discover new concepts. Through hard work and perseverance, students will learn that they can use the math they already know combined with logical thinking to solve problems about new concepts.

Equivalent Fractions
and
Comparisons

Fraction Equivalence (A)

Lesson Overview

ACTIVITY	ACTIVITY TITLE	TIME	ONLINE/OFFLINE
GET READY	Introduction to Fraction Equivalence (A)	**2** minutes	🖥️
	Look Back at Naming a Fraction of a Circle	**8** minutes	🖥️
LEARN AND **TRY IT**	Using Shapes to Identify Equivalent Fractions	**7** minutes	🖥️
	Use Shapes to Identify Equivalent Fractions	**7** minutes	🖥️
	Using Fraction Strips to Identify Equivalent Fractions	**7** minutes	🖥️
	Use Fraction Strips to Identify Equivalent Fractions	**7** minutes	🖥️
	Practice Identifying Equivalent Fractions	**20** minutes	🖥️ and 📄
WRAP-UP	Identifying Equivalent Fractions	**2** minutes	🖥️

Content Background

Students will learn about equivalent fractions and explain why two fractions are equivalent. Students may already have a basic understanding of the different interpretations of fractions as part of a whole.

Fractions are equivalent when they represent the same amount or same part of a whole. For example, $\frac{1}{2} = \frac{2}{4} = \frac{3}{6}$. Some students might have difficulty understanding that numbers can look different, but still represent the same amount. Students will learn to recognize the same part of a whole by using fraction models and fraction strips.

Lesson Goals
- Identify equivalent fractions using models.

> **MATERIALS**
>
> **Supplied**
> - *Summit Math 3 Activity Book:* Practice Identifying Equivalent Fractions
> - Fraction Strips (printout)

> **KEYWORDS**
>
> **equivalent fractions** – fractions that name the same amount, such as $\frac{1}{2}$ and $\frac{3}{6}$

GET READY

Introduction to Fraction Equivalence (A)

After a quick introductory activity, students will read the lesson goals and keywords. Have students select each keyword and preview its definition.

Look Back at Naming a Fraction of a Circle

Students will practice the prerequisite skill of writing a fraction from a model.

LEARN   Using Shapes to Identify Equivalent Fractions

Students will learn to use shapes to identify equivalent fractions.

TRY IT   Use Shapes to Identify Equivalent Fractions

Students will practice using shapes to identify equivalent fractions. Support will be provided to help students overcome misconceptions.

LEARN   Using Fraction Strips to Identify Equivalent Fractions

Students will learn to use fraction strips to identify equivalent fractions.

OPTIONAL   Students can print Fraction Strips, which is attached in the online activity. Students can use the printed fraction strips as an alternative to the online Fraction Strip Tool.

TRY IT   Use Fraction Strips to Identify Equivalent Fractions

Students will practice using fraction strips to identify equivalent fractions. Support will be provided to help students overcome misconceptions.

TRY IT   Practice Identifying Equivalent Fractions

Students will complete online practice problems. Then they will complete Practice Identifying Equivalent Fractions from *Summit Math 3 Activity Book*.

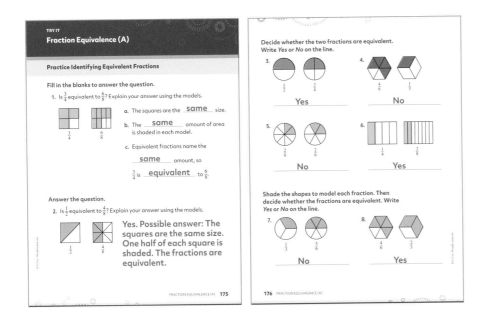

Identifying Equivalent Fractions

Students will solve problems to show that they understand how to identify equivalent fractions and explain why two fractions are equivalent.

Fraction Equivalence (B)

Lesson Overview

ACTIVITY	ACTIVITY TITLE	TIME	ONLINE/OFFLINE
GET READY	Introduction to Fraction Equivalence (B)	**2** minutes	🖥️
	Dividing by 6 Math Facts	**8** minutes	🖥️
LEARN AND **TRY IT**	Finding Equivalent Fractions	**15** minutes	🖥️
	Find Equivalent Fractions	**10** minutes	🖥️
	Practice Finding Equivalent Fractions	**20** minutes	🖥️ and 📄
WRAP-UP	Finding Equivalent Fractions	**5** minutes	🖥️

Content Background

Students will find an equivalent fraction using models. Equivalent fractions are often represented as the same part of a whole. They can also be represented as the same part of a group. For example, this set of 8 stars is divided into 4 equal groups.

Two out of 8 stars are in 1 out of 4 groups, so $\frac{2}{8} = \frac{1}{4}$. Students will use fraction models, fraction strips, and groups of objects to find equivalent fractions.

> ### Lesson Goals
> - Write equivalent fractions using models.

MATERIALS

Supplied
- *Summit Math 3 Activity Book:* Practice Finding Equivalent Fractions
- Fraction Strips (printout)

KEYWORDS

equivalent fractions – fractions that name the same amount, such as $\frac{1}{2}$ and $\frac{3}{6}$

GET READY

Introduction to Fraction Equivalence (B)

Students will get a glimpse of what they will learn about in the lesson. They will also read the lesson goals and keywords. Have students select each keyword and preview its definition.

Dividing by 6 Math Facts

Students will practice dividing by 6.

LEARN Finding Equivalent Fractions

Students will learn how to find an equivalent fraction using models.

OPTIONAL   Students can print Fraction Strips, which is attached in the online activity. Students can use the printed fraction strips as an alternative to the online Fraction Strip Tool.

TRY IT Find Equivalent Fractions

Students will practice finding equivalent fractions using models. Support will be provided to help students overcome misconceptions.

TRY IT Practice Finding Equivalent Fractions

Students will complete online practice problems. Then they will complete Practice Finding Equivalent Fractions from *Summit Math 3 Activity Book*.

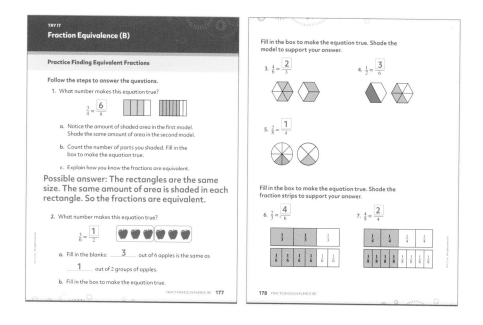

WRAP-UP

Finding Equivalent Fractions

Students will solve a problem to show that they understand how to find an equivalent fraction using a model.

Fraction Equivalence (C)

Lesson Overview

ACTIVITY	ACTIVITY TITLE	TIME	ONLINE/OFFLINE
GET READY	Introduction to Fraction Equivalence (C)	**2** minutes	🖥️
	Dividing by 6 with Instant Recall	**8** minutes	🖥️
LEARN AND **TRY IT**	Using Number Lines to Identify Equivalent Fractions	**15** minutes	🖥️
	Use Number Lines to Identify Equivalent Fractions	**10** minutes	🖥️
	Practice Using Number Lines to Identify Equivalent Fractions	**20** minutes	🖥️ and 📄
WRAP-UP	Using Number Lines to Identify Equivalent Fractions	**5** minutes	🖥️

Content Background

Students will identify equivalent fractions using number lines. Equivalent fractions name the same amount. On a number line, two points that are the same distance from 0 represent the same amount. When the distance between 0 and 1 is the same and the number lines are aligned at 0, equivalent fractions will have points that also align vertically. For example, these number lines show that $\frac{4}{6} = \frac{2}{3}$.

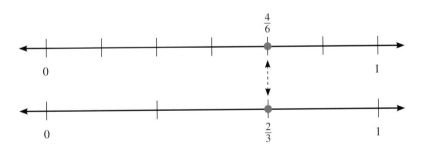

MATERIALS

Supplied
- *Summit Math 3 Activity Book:* Practice Using Number Lines to Identify Equivalent Fractions

KEYWORDS

equivalent fractions – fractions that name the same amount, such as $\frac{1}{2}$ and $\frac{3}{6}$

Lesson Goals
- Identify equivalent fractions using number lines.

Introduction to Fraction Equivalence (C)

Students will get a glimpse of what they will learn about in the lesson. They will also read the lesson goals and keywords. Have students select each keyword and preview its definition.

Dividing by 6 with Instant Recall

Students will practice dividing by 6.

LEARN AND TRY IT

LEARN   Using Number Lines to Identify Equivalent Fractions

Students will learn to use number lines to identify equivalent fractions.

TRY IT   Use Number Lines to Identify Equivalent Fractions

Students will practice using number lines to identify equivalent fractions. Support will be provided to help students overcome misconceptions.

TRY IT   Practice Using Number Lines to Identify Equivalent Fractions

Students will complete online practice problems. Then they will complete Practice Using Number Lines to Identify Equivalent Fractions from *Summit Math 3 Activity Book*.

Using Number Lines to Identify Equivalent Fractions

Students will solve a problem to show that they understand how to identify equivalent fractions using number lines.

Fraction Equivalence (D)

Lesson Overview

ACTIVITY	ACTIVITY TITLE	TIME	ONLINE/OFFLINE
GET READY	Introduction to Fraction Equivalence (D)	**2** minutes	🛜
	Dividing by 6 Math Facts Game	**8** minutes	🛜
LEARN AND **TRY IT**	Using Number Lines to Find Equivalent Fractions	**15** minutes	🛜
	Use Number Lines to Find Equivalent Fractions	**10** minutes	🛜
	Practice Using Number Lines to Find Equivalent Fractions	**20** minutes	🛜 and 📄
WRAP-UP	Using Number Lines to Find Equivalent Fractions	**5** minutes	🛜

Content Background

Students will find an equivalent fraction using number lines. Two points that are the same distance from 0 on a number line represent the same amount. When students use number lines that are aligned correctly, the equivalent fraction will align vertically with the given fraction.

> ### Lesson Goals
> - Find equivalent fractions using number lines.

MATERIALS

Supplied
- *Summit Math 3 Activity Book:* Practice Using Number Lines to Find Equivalent Fractions

KEYWORDS

equivalent fractions – fractions that name the same amount, such as $\frac{1}{2}$ and $\frac{3}{6}$

GET READY

Introduction to Fraction Equivalence (D)

Students will get a glimpse of what they will learn about in the lesson. They will also read the lesson goals and keywords. Have students select each keyword and preview its definition.

Dividing by 6 Math Facts Game

Students will practice dividing by 6.

LEARN   Using Number Lines to Find Equivalent Fractions

Students will learn to use number lines to find equivalent fractions.

TRY IT   Use Number Lines to Find Equivalent Fractions

Students will practice using number lines to find equivalent fractions. Support will be provided to help students overcome misconceptions.

TRY IT   Practice Using Number Lines to Find Equivalent Fractions

Students will complete online practice problems. Then they will complete Practice Using Number Lines to Find Equivalent Fractions from *Summit Math 3 Activity Book.*

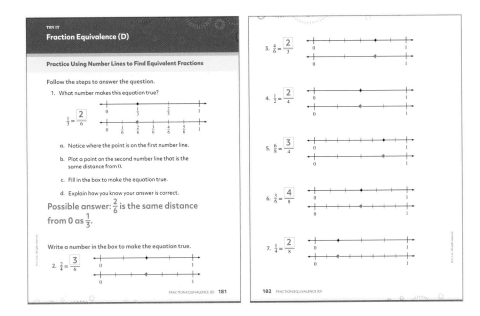

WRAP-UP

Using Number Lines to Find Equivalent Fractions

Students will solve a problem to show that they understand how to find an equivalent fraction using number lines.

Fraction Equivalence (E)

Lesson Overview

ACTIVITY	ACTIVITY TITLE	TIME	ONLINE/OFFLINE
GET READY	Introduction to Fraction Equivalence (E)	**2** minutes	📶
TRY IT	Review Fraction Equivalence	**18** minutes	📶
QUIZ	Fraction Equivalence	**25** minutes	📶
WRAP-UP	More Math Practice	**15** minutes	📶

Lesson Goals

- Review identifying and writing equivalent fractions using models.
- Take a quiz.

MATERIALS

There are no materials to gather for this lesson.

GET READY

Introduction to Fraction Equivalence (E)
Students will read the lesson goals.

TRY IT

Review Fraction Equivalence
Students will answer questions to review what they have learned about fraction equivalence.

QUIZ

Fraction Equivalence
Students will complete the Fraction Equivalence quiz.

More Math Practice

Students will practice skills according to their individual needs.

Fractions and Whole Numbers (A)

Lesson Overview

ACTIVITY	ACTIVITY TITLE	TIME	ONLINE/OFFLINE
GET READY	Introduction to Fractions and Whole Numbers (A)	**2** minutes	📶
	Look Back at Naming a Fraction of a Rectangle	**8** minutes	📶
LEARN AND **TRY IT**	Writing Whole Numbers as Fractions	**7** minutes	🖥
	Write Whole Numbers as Fractions	**7** minutes	📶
	Writing Mixed Numbers as Fractions	**7** minutes	📶
	Write Mixed Numbers as Fractions	**7** minutes	📶
	Practice Writing Whole and Mixed Numbers as Fractions	**20** minutes	📶 and 📄
WRAP-UP	Writing Whole and Mixed Numbers as Fractions	**2** minutes	📶

Content Background

Students will learn to represent whole numbers as fractions. For example, the fraction $\frac{0}{4}$ equals 0 because its numerator is 0. The fractions $\frac{4}{4}$ and $\frac{3}{3}$ both equal 1 because in each fraction the numerator and denominator are equal. Whole numbers greater than 1 are represented by a special type of fraction called an *improper fraction*. Shape models are used to demonstrate how to convert between whole numbers and improper fractions.

Students have developed an understanding of a fraction as a number between 0 and 1. When students have 3 slices of pizza out of 8 equal-sized slices in the whole pizza, they can write that comparison as $\frac{3}{8}$. When students have one whole pizza and 3 equal-sized slices out of 8 of another pizza of the same size, they can write that comparison as the mixed number $1\frac{3}{8}$ or the improper fraction $\frac{11}{8}$. Students will use shape models to help them represent mixed numbers and improper fractions.

Continue to emphasize that all the parts of a shape model must be the same size and shape and all the wholes must also be the same size and shape.

MATERIALS

Supplied
- *Summit Math 3 Activity Book:* Practice Writing Whole and Mixed Numbers as Fractions

KEYWORDS

improper fraction – a fraction whose numerator is greater than or equal to its denominator

mixed number – a whole number and a proper fraction that show a single amount

proper fraction – a fraction in which the numerator is less than the denominator

Lesson Goals

- Identify and name fractions that equal whole numbers.
- Identify and name improper fractions modeled by shapes.
- Identify and name mixed numbers modeled by shapes.

Introduction to Fractions and Whole Numbers (A)

Students will get a glimpse of what they will learn about in the lesson. They will also read the lesson goals and keywords. Have students select each keyword and preview its definition.

Look Back at Naming a Fraction of a Rectangle

Students will practice the prerequisite skill of naming a fraction of a rectangle.

LEARN AND TRY IT

LEARN   Writing Whole Numbers as Fractions

Students will learn to write whole numbers as fractions.

TRY IT   Write Whole Numbers as Fractions

Students will practice writing whole numbers as fractions. Support will be provided to help students overcome misconceptions.

LEARN   Writing Mixed Numbers as Fractions

Students will learn to write mixed numbers as fractions.

TRY IT   Write Mixed Numbers as Fractions

Students will practice writing mixed numbers as fractions. Support will be provided to help students overcome misconceptions.

TRY IT   Practice Writing Whole and Mixed Numbers as Fractions

Students will complete online practice problems. Then they will complete Practice Writing Whole and Mixed Numbers as Fractions from *Summit Math 3 Activity Book*.

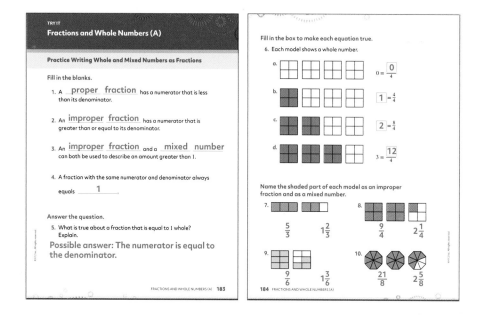

Writing Whole and Mixed Numbers as Fractions

Students will solve problems to show that they understand how to write whole numbers and mixed numbers as fractions.

Fractions and Whole Numbers (B)

Lesson Overview

ACTIVITY	ACTIVITY TITLE	TIME	ONLINE/OFFLINE
GET READY	Introduction to Fractions and Whole Numbers (B)	**2** minutes	🖥️
	Dividing by 9 Math Facts	**8** minutes	🖥️
LEARN AND TRY IT	Plotting Whole Numbers as Fractions on Number Lines	**7** minutes	🖥️
	Plot Whole Numbers as Fractions on Number Lines	**7** minutes	🖥️
	Plotting Mixed Numbers as Fractions on Number Lines	**7** minutes	🖥️
	Plot Mixed Numbers as Fractions on Number Lines	**7** minutes	🖥️
	Practice Plotting Whole and Mixed Numbers on Number Lines	**20** minutes	🖥️ and 📄
WRAP-UP	Plot Whole and Mixed Numbers on Number Lines	**2** minutes	🖥️

Content Background

Students will learn to represent improper fractions and mixed numbers as locations on a number line. Students understand how to locate fractions between 0 and 1 on a number line. Similarly, numbers can be located between other whole numbers greater than 1. For example, $\frac{3}{4}$ is located at the point exactly $\frac{3}{4}$ of the distance from 0 to 1 on the number line, and $5\frac{3}{8}$ is located at the point exactly $\frac{3}{8}$ of the distance from 5 to 6. Students will be given number lines that are already divided into the correct number of equal parts.

MATERIALS

Supplied

- *Summit Math 3 Activity Book:* Practice Plotting Whole and Mixed Numbers on Number Lines

Lesson Goals

- Identify and plot improper fractions on a number line.
- Identify and plot mixed numbers on a number line.
- Write whole numbers as improper fractions.

Introduction to Fractions and Whole Numbers (B)

Students will get a glimpse of what they will learn about in the lesson. They will also read the lesson goals.

Dividing by 9 Math Facts

Students will practice dividing by 9.

LEARN AND TRY IT

LEARN   Plotting Whole Numbers as Fractions on Number Lines

Students will learn to plot whole numbers as fractions on number lines.

TRY IT   Plot Whole Numbers as Fractions on Number Lines

Students will practice plotting whole numbers as fractions on number lines. Support will be provided to help students overcome misconceptions.

LEARN   Plotting Mixed Numbers as Fractions on Number Lines

Students will learn to plot mixed numbers as fractions on number lines.

TRY IT   Plot Mixed Numbers as Fractions on Number Lines

Students will practice plotting mixed numbers as fractions on number lines. Support will be provided to help students overcome misconceptions.

TRY IT   Practice Plotting Whole and Mixed Numbers on Number Lines

Students will complete online practice problems. Then they will complete Practice Plotting Whole and Mixed Numbers on Number Lines from *Summit Math 3 Activity Book*.

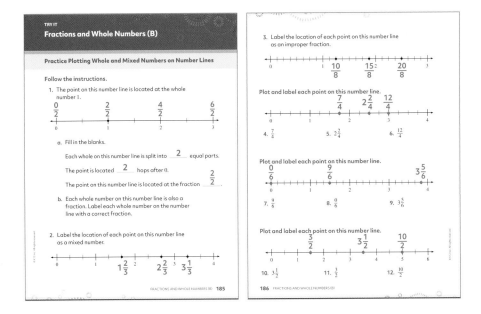

Plotting Whole and Mixed Numbers on Number Lines

Students will solve problems to show that they understand how to plot whole and mixed numbers on number lines.

Fractions and Whole Numbers (C)

Lesson Overview

ACTIVITY	ACTIVITY TITLE	TIME	ONLINE/OFFLINE
GET READY	Introduction to Fractions and Whole Numbers (C)	**2** minutes	🖥️
TRY IT	Review Fractions and Whole Numbers	**18** minutes	🖥️
QUIZ	Fractions and Whole Numbers	**25** minutes	🖥️
WRAP-UP	More Math Practice	**15** minutes	🖥️

Lesson Goals

- Review identifying, naming, and plotting improper fractions and mixed numbers.

- Take a quiz.

MATERIALS

There are no materials to gather for this lesson.

GET READY

Introduction to Fractions and Whole Numbers (C)

Students will read the lesson goals.

TRY IT

Review Fractions and Whole Numbers

Students will answer questions to review what they have learned about fractions and whole numbers.

QUIZ

Fractions and Whole Numbers

Students will complete the Fractions and Whole Numbers quiz.

More Math Practice

Students will practice skills according to their individual needs.

Compare Fractions (A)

Lesson Overview

ACTIVITY	ACTIVITY TITLE	TIME	ONLINE/OFFLINE
GET READY	Introduction to Compare Fractions (A)	**2** minutes	📶
	Look Back at Comparing Whole Numbers	**8** minutes	📶
LEARN AND **TRY IT**	Deciding When to Compare Fractions	**7** minutes	🖥️
	Decide When to Compare Fractions	**7** minutes	🖥️
	Comparing Fractions with the Same Denominator	**7** minutes	🖥️
	Compare Fractions with the Same Denominator	**7** minutes	🖥️
	Practice Comparing Fractions with the Same Denominator	**20** minutes	🖥️ and 📄
WRAP-UP	Comparing Fractions with the Same Denominator	**2** minutes	📶

Content Background

Students will first learn that fractions can only be compared when they describe the same whole. If the wholes are different sizes, fractions cannot be compared. Students will then use the comparison symbols <, >, and = to compare fractions with the same denominator. When comparing fractions with the same denominator, the comparison is determined by the numerator. The larger the numerator, the larger the value of the fraction.

MATERIALS

Supplied

- *Summit Math 3 Activity Book:* Practice Comparing Fractions with the Same Denominator

Lesson Goals

- Understand that fractions can only be compared when they describe the same whole.

- Compare fractions that have the same denominator.

KEYWORDS

denominator – the number in a fraction that is below the fraction bar

numerator – the number in a fraction that is above the fraction bar

GET READY

Introduction to Compare Fractions (A)

Students will get a glimpse of what they will learn about in the lesson. They will also read the lesson goals and keywords. Have students select each keyword and preview its definition.

Look Back at Comparing Whole Numbers

Students will practice the prerequisite skill of comparing whole numbers.

LEARN   Deciding When to Compare Fractions

Students will learn to decide when to compare fractions.

TRY IT   Decide When to Compare Fractions

Students will practice deciding when to compare fractions. Support will be provided to help students overcome misconceptions.

LEARN   Comparing Fractions with the Same Denominator

Students will learn to compare fractions with the same denominator.

TRY IT   Compare Fractions with the Same Denominator

Students will practice comparing fractions with the same denominator. Support will be provided to help students overcome misconceptions.

TRY IT   Practice Comparing Fractions with the Same Denominator

Students will complete online practice problems. Then they will complete Practice Comparing Fractions with the Same Denominator from *Summit Math 3 Activity Book*.

TRY IT
Compare Fractions (A)

Practice Comparing Fractions with the Same Denominator

Answer the question.

1. A fraction of each shape is shaded. Can these fractions be compared? Explain.

$\frac{1}{8}$

$\frac{1}{8}$

No. The wholes are not the same size.

Follow the instructions to answer the question.

2. A fraction of each shape is shaded. How do these fractions compare?

$\frac{1}{8}$

$\frac{1}{8}$ $\frac{1}{8}$ $\frac{1}{8}$

a. Fill in the blanks: The wholes are the same size and each whole has __8__ equal parts. Compare the __numerators__.

COMPARE FRACTIONS (A)   **187**

---

b. Fill in the boxes with <, >, or = to make the sentence true:

1 $\boxed{<}$ 3, so $\frac{1}{8}$ $\boxed{<}$ $\frac{3}{8}$.

Compare the fractions. Use <, >, or =.

3. $\frac{1}{4}$ $\boxed{<}$ $\frac{3}{4}$

4. $\frac{5}{6}$ $\boxed{>}$ $\frac{3}{6}$

5. $\frac{2}{3}$ $\boxed{=}$ $\frac{2}{3}$

6. $\frac{7}{8}$ $\boxed{>}$ $\frac{5}{8}$

7. $\frac{1}{6}$ $\boxed{<}$ $\frac{2}{6}$

8. $\frac{1}{2}$ $\boxed{=}$ $\frac{1}{2}$

9. $\frac{3}{4}$ $\boxed{>}$ $\frac{2}{4}$

10. $\frac{4}{8}$ $\boxed{>}$ $\frac{3}{8}$

11. $\frac{1}{3}$ $\boxed{<}$ $\frac{2}{3}$

188   COMPARE FRACTIONS (A)

Comparing Fractions with the Same Denominator

Students will solve problems to show that they understand how to compare fractions with the same denominator.

Compare Fractions (B)

Lesson Overview

ACTIVITY	ACTIVITY TITLE	TIME	ONLINE/OFFLINE
GET READY	Introduction to Compare Fractions (B)	**2** minutes	🖥️
	Dividing by 9 with Instant Recall	**8** minutes	🖥️
LEARN AND **TRY IT**	Comparing Fractions with the Same Numerator	**15** minutes	🖥️
	Compare Fractions with the Same Numerator	**10** minutes	🖥️
	Practice Comparing Fractions with the Same Numerator	**20** minutes	🖥️ and 📄
WRAP-UP	Comparing Fractions with the Same Numerator	**5** minutes	🖥️

Content Background

Students will use the comparison symbols <, >, and = to compare fractions with the same numerator. Throughout this lesson it will again be important to stress that comparisons are only valid when the fractions being compared describe the same whole. The denominator, or the number below the fraction line, of a fraction shows how many equal pieces the whole has been divided into. It is important for students to understand that as the denominator increases, the size of each piece decreases. These models represent fractions with a numerator of 1.

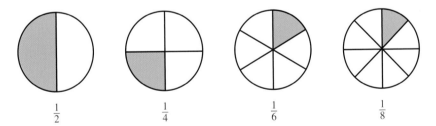

$$\frac{1}{2} \qquad \frac{1}{4} \qquad \frac{1}{6} \qquad \frac{1}{8}$$

Notice that the size of each part decreases as the numbers in the denominator increase. When the numerators are equal, the larger the denominator, the *smaller* the fraction pieces.

Lesson Goals

- Compare fractions that have the same numerator.

Introduction to Compare Fractions (B)

Students will get a glimpse of what they will learn about in the lesson. They will also read the lesson goals and keywords. Have students select each keyword and preview its definition.

Dividing by 9 with Instant Recall

Students will practice dividing by 9.

LEARN AND TRY IT

LEARN   Comparing Fractions with the Same Numerator

Students will learn to compare fractions with the same numerator.

TRY IT   Compare Fractions with the Same Numerator

Students will practice comparing fractions with the same numerator. Support will be provided to help students overcome misconceptions.

TRY IT   Practice Comparing Fractions with the Same Numerator

Students will complete online practice problems. Then they will complete Practice Comparing Fractions with the Same Numerator from *Summit Math 3 Activity Book*.

TRY IT
Compare Fractions (B)

Practice Comparing Fractions with the Same Numerator

Answer the questions.

1. A fraction of each shape is shaded. Can the fractions be compared? Explain.

$\frac{1}{6}$

$\frac{1}{4}$

No. The wholes are not the same size.

2. A fraction of each shape is shaded. Can the fractions be compared? Explain.

$\frac{1}{8}$

$\frac{1}{4}$

Yes. The wholes are the same size.

COMPARE FRACTIONS (B) **189**

Compare the fractions. Use <, >, or =.

3. $\frac{1}{2}$ > $\frac{1}{4}$

Fractions are fabulous!

4. $\frac{2}{6}$ < $\frac{2}{3}$

5. $\frac{3}{8}$ < $\frac{3}{4}$

6. $\frac{5}{6}$ > $\frac{5}{8}$ 7. $\frac{1}{4}$ = $\frac{1}{4}$

8. $\frac{4}{6}$ < $\frac{4}{4}$ 9. $\frac{2}{6}$ < $\frac{2}{4}$

10. $\frac{3}{4}$ > $\frac{3}{8}$ 11. $\frac{1}{4}$ < $\frac{1}{3}$

190   COMPARE FRACTIONS (B)

Comparing Fractions with the Same Numerator

Students will solve a problem to show that they understand how to compare fractions with the same numerator.

Compare Fractions (C)

Lesson Overview

ACTIVITY	ACTIVITY TITLE	TIME	ONLINE/OFFLINE
GET READY	Introduction to Compare Fractions (C)	**2** minutes	🖥️
TRY IT	Review Compare Fractions	**18** minutes	🖥️
QUIZ	Compare Fractions	**25** minutes	🖥️
WRAP-UP	More Math Practice	**15** minutes	🖥️

Lesson Goals

- Review comparing fractions with the same denominator or the same numerator.

- Take a quiz.

MATERIALS

There are no materials to gather for this lesson.

GET READY

Introduction to Compare Fractions (C)

Students will read the lesson goals.

TRY IT

Review Compare Fractions

Students will answer questions to review what they have learned about comparing fractions.

QUIZ

Compare Fractions

Students will complete the Compare Fractions quiz.

More Math Practice

Students will practice skills according to their individual needs.

Big Ideas: Extended Problems

Lesson Overview

Big Ideas lessons provide students the opportunity to further apply the knowledge and skills acquired throughout previous units. Each Big Ideas lesson consists of two types of activities:

1. **Cumulative Review:** Students keep their skills fresh by reviewing prior content.

2. **Synthesis:** Students complete an assignment that allows them to interweave and apply what they've learned. These synthesis assignments will vary throughout the course.

   In the Synthesis portion of this Big Ideas lesson, students will complete multistep problems that go beyond the short answer and multiple choice problems they encounter in their regular lessons. These problems give students an opportunity to demonstrate problem solving, reasoning, communication, and modeling skills. Students will need to use pencil and paper and/or technology to show their work.

   LEARNING COACH CHECK-IN   This is a graded assessment. Make sure students complete, review, and submit the assignment to their teacher.

All materials needed for this lesson are linked online. The materials are not provided in this Lesson Guide or in the Activity Book.

Measurement: Time and Length

Clock Time and Units of Time (A)

Lesson Overview

ACTIVITY	ACTIVITY TITLE	TIME	ONLINE/OFFLINE
GET READY	Introduction to Clock Time and Units of Time (A)	**2** minutes	🖥️
	Look Back at Telling Time	**8** minutes	🖥️
LEARN AND **TRY IT**	Expressing Time to the Minute	**7** minutes	🖥️
	Express Time to the Minute	**7** minutes	🖥️
	Expressing Time to the Quarter Hour	**7** minutes	🖥️
	Express Time to the Quarter Hour	**7** minutes	🖥️
	Practice Expressing Time	**20** minutes	🖥️ and 📄
WRAP-UP	Expressing Time	**2** minutes	🖥️

Content Background

Students will learn to tell time to the nearest minute or quarter hour. They will show and tell time on an analog clock (one with a face and hands) as well as a digital clock.

> **TIP**   For more practice, ask your students what time it is throughout the day, and have them tell you the time using an analog clock.

It is important to connect the idea of quarter hours to fractions of a circle. This will help students visualize the foundational clock concepts of quarter past and quarter to.

> **TIP**   Encourage your student to say the time in more than one way.

MATERIALS

Supplied

- *Summit Math 3 Activity Book:* Practice Expressing Time

Lesson Goals

- Use a clock to tell time to the nearest minute.

- Understand and use the terms *quarter hour* and *half hour*.

Introduction to Clock Time and Units of Time (A)

After a quick introductory activity, students will read the lesson goals and keywords. Have students select each keyword and preview its definition.

Look Back at Telling Time

Students will practice the prerequisite skill of telling time to the nearest 5 minutes.

LEARN AND TRY IT

LEARN Expressing Time to the Minute

Students will learn to express time to the nearest minute.

TRY IT Express Time to the Minute

Students will practice expressing time to the nearest minute. Support will be provided to help students overcome misconceptions.

LEARN Expressing Time to the Quarter Hour

Students will learn to express time to the nearest quarter hour.

TRY IT Express Time to the Quarter Hour

Students will practice expressing time to the nearest quarter hour. Support will be provided to help students overcome misconceptions.

KEYWORDS

analog clock – a clock that displays the time with an hour and a minute hand

digital clock – a clock that uses numerals to display time, with hours and minutes separated by a colon

half hour – a fraction of an hour, equal to 30 minutes

hour (h) – the unit for measuring time that equals 60 minutes

minute – the amount of time it takes for the minute hand on an analog clock to move one tick mark

quarter hour – a fraction of an hour, equal to 15 minutes

TRY IT   Practice Expressing Time

Students will complete online practice problems. Then they will complete Practice Expressing Time from *Summit Math 3 Activity Book*.

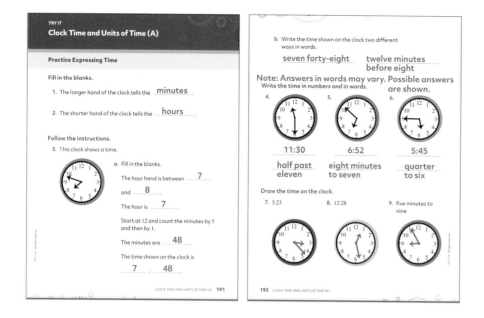

WRAP-UP

Expressing Time

Students will solve problems to show that they understand how to express time to the nearest minute or quarter hour.

Clock Time and Units of Time (B)

Lesson Overview

ACTIVITY	ACTIVITY TITLE	TIME	ONLINE/OFFLINE
GET READY	Introduction to Clock Time and Units of Time (B)	**2** minutes	🖥️
	Dividing by 9 Math Facts Game	**8** minutes	🖥️
LEARN AND **TRY IT**	Understanding A.M. and P.M.	**7** minutes	🖥️
	Understand A.M. and P.M.	**7** minutes	🖥️
	Finding Elapsed Time	**7** minutes	🖥️
	Find Elapsed Time	**7** minutes	🖥️
	Practice A.M. and P.M. and Elapsed Time	**20** minutes	🖥️ and 📄
WRAP-UP	A.M. and P.M. and Elapsed Time	**2** minutes	🖥️

Content Background

Students will learn to tell time using the labels a.m. and p.m. Students will also learn to determine elapsed time. Elapsed time is the amount of time that passes between a starting time and an ending time. Additionally, students will learn to find the end time of an activity given the start time and the elapsed time.

Elapsed time can include elapsed hours, elapsed days, elapsed months, or other time periods. This lesson focuses on finding elapsed time to the nearest hour, quarter hour, and minute. Students need to understand that when counting to determine elapsed time, such as hours, they count beginning with the hour after the starting time. For example, if students are counting how many hours there are between 2:00 p.m. and 7:00 p.m., they begin counting at 3:00—that is, 3:00, 4:00, 5:00, 6:00, 7:00—to find that there are 5 hours between 2:00 p.m. and 7:00 p.m. Students should use this counting principle in any type of counting-on situation, either from a number or from another starting point such as a time.

MATERIALS

Supplied
- *Summit Math 3 Activity Book:* Practice A.M. and P.M. and Elapsed Time

KEYWORDS

a.m. – a label for times between midnight and noon; stands for *ante meridiem*

elapsed time – the amount of time between a beginning time and an ending time

midnight – another name for 12:00 at night

noon – another name for 12:00 during the day

p.m. – a label for times between noon and midnight; stands for *post meridiem*

Lesson Goals

- Understand the difference between a.m. and p.m.
- Tell time using a.m. and p.m.
- Know the difference between midnight and noon.
- Determine how much time has elapsed between two times.

Introduction to Clock Time and Units of Time (B)

Students will get a glimpse of what they will learn about in the lesson. They will also read the lesson goals and keywords. Have students select each keyword and preview its definition.

Dividing by 9 Math Facts Game

Students will practice dividing by 9.

LEARN AND TRY IT

LEARN   Understanding A.M. and P.M.

Students will learn to use a.m. and p.m. when expressing time.

TRY IT   Understand A.M. and P.M.

Students will practice using a.m. and p.m. when expressing time. Support will be provided to help students overcome misconceptions.

LEARN   Finding Elapsed Time

Students will learn to find elapsed time.

TRY IT   Find Elapsed Time

Students will practice finding elapsed time. Support will be provided to help students overcome misconceptions.

TRY IT   Practice A.M. and P.M. and Elapsed Time

Students will complete online practice problems. Then they will complete Practice A.M. and P.M. and Elapsed Time from *Summit Math 3 Activity Book*.

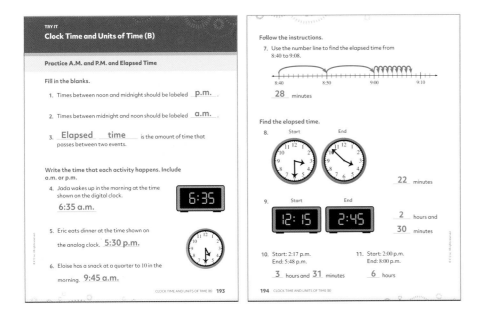

Practice A.M. and P.M. and Elapsed Time

Fill in the blanks.

1. Times between noon and midnight should be labeled __p.m.__

2. Times between midnight and noon should be labeled __a.m.__

3. __Elapsed time__ is the amount of time that passes between two events.

Write the time that each activity happens. Include a.m. or p.m.

4. Jada wakes up in the morning at the time shown on the digital clock.
   6:35
   6:35 a.m.

5. Eric eats dinner at the time shown on the analog clock. 5:30 p.m.

6. Eloise has a snack at a quarter to 10 in the morning. 9:45 a.m.

CLOCK TIME AND UNITS OF TIME (B) 193

Follow the instructions.

7. Use the number line to find the elapsed time from 8:40 to 9:08.

   8:40   8:50   9:00   9:10

   __28__ minutes

Find the elapsed time.

8. Start   End

   __22__ minutes

9. Start   End
   12:15   **2:45**

   __2__ hours and
   __30__ minutes

10. Start: 2:17 p.m.
    End: 5:48 p.m.
    __3__ hours and __31__ minutes

11. Start: 2:00 p.m.
    End: 8:00 p.m.
    __6__ hours

194 CLOCK TIME AND UNITS OF TIME (B)

WRAP-UP

A.M. and P.M. and Elapsed Time

Students will solve problems to show that they understand how to use a.m. and p.m. and find elapsed time.

Clock Time and Units of Time (C)

Lesson Overview

ACTIVITY	ACTIVITY TITLE	TIME	ONLINE/OFFLINE
GET READY	Introduction to Clock Time and Units of Time (C)	**2** minutes	📶
	Dividing by 7 Math Facts	**8** minutes	📶
LEARN AND **TRY IT**	Solving Time Problems Using Addition	**15** minutes	📶
	Solve Time Problems Using Addition	**10** minutes	📶
	Practice Solving Time Problems Using Addition	**20** minutes	📶 and 📄
WRAP-UP	Solving Time Problems Using Addition	**5** minutes	📶

Content Background

Students will build on previous knowledge of number line addition to solve problems involving the addition of time intervals. Students will solve some problems with the help of models or number lines and some problems without.

TIP Be sure students pay close attention when moving from morning times (a.m.) to afternoon times (p.m.).

Lesson Goals

- Solve time problems using addition.

> ### MATERIALS
>
> **Supplied**
> - *Summit Math 3 Activity Book:* Practice Solving Time Problems Using Addition

GET READY

Introduction to Clock Time and Units of Time (C)
Students will get a glimpse of what they will learn about in the lesson. They will also read the lesson goals.

Dividing by 7 Math Facts
Students will practice dividing by 7.

LEARN Solving Time Problems Using Addition

Students will learn to solve time problems using addition.

TRY IT Solve Time Problems Using Addition

Students will practice solving time problems using addition. Support will be provided to help students overcome misconceptions.

TRY IT Practice Solving Time Problems Using Addition

Students will complete online practice problems. Then they will complete Practice Solving Time Problems Using Addition from *Summit Math 3 Activity Book*.

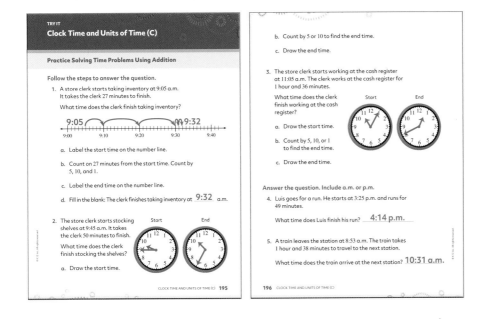

Solving Time Problems Using Addition

Students will solve a problem to show that they understand how to solve time problems using addition.

Clock Time and Units of Time (D)

Lesson Overview

ACTIVITY	ACTIVITY TITLE	TIME	ONLINE/OFFLINE
GET READY	Introduction to Clock Time and Units of Time (D)	**2** minutes	🖥️
	Dividing by 7 with Instant Recall	**8** minutes	🖥️
LEARN AND **TRY IT**	Solving Time Problems Using Subtraction	**15** minutes	🖥️
	Solve Time Problems Using Subtraction	**10** minutes	🖥️
	Practice Solving Time Problems Using Subtraction	**20** minutes	🖥️ and 📄
WRAP-UP	Solving Time Problems Using Subtraction	**5** minutes	🖥️

Content Background

Students will build on previous knowledge of number line subtraction to solve problems involving the subtraction of time intervals. Students will solve some problems with the help of models or number lines and some problems without.

TIP When students subtract time intervals, emphasize that they should begin at the ending time and work backward through the time intervals, moving left on the number line.

Lesson Goals

- Solve time problems using subtraction.

GET READY

Introduction to Clock Time and Units of Time (D)
Students will get a glimpse of what they will learn about in the lesson. They will also read the lesson goals.

Dividing by 7 with Instant Recall
Students will practice dividing by 7.

LEARN Solving Time Problems Using Subtraction

Students will learn to solve time problems using subtraction.

TRY IT Solve Time Problems Using Subtraction

Students will practice solving time problems using subtraction. Support will be provided to help students overcome misconceptions.

TRY IT Practice Solving Time Problems Using Subtraction

Students will complete online practice problems. Then they will complete Practice Solving Time Problems Using Subtraction from *Summit Math 3 Activity Book*.

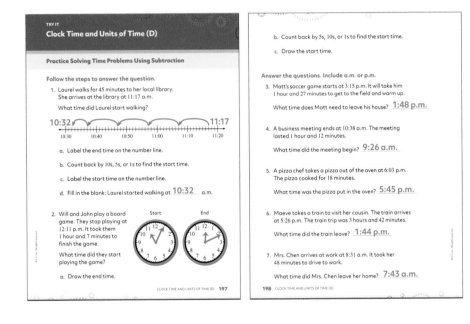

Solving Time Problems Using Subtraction

Students will solve a problem to show that they understand how to solve time problems using subtraction.

Clock Time and Units of Time (E)

Lesson Overview

ACTIVITY	ACTIVITY TITLE	TIME	ONLINE/OFFLINE
GET READY	Introduction to Clock Time and Units of Time (E)	**2** minutes	🖥️
TRY IT	Review Clock Time and Units of Time	**18** minutes	🖥️
QUIZ	Clock Time and Units of Time	**25** minutes	🖥️
WRAP-UP	More Math Practice	**15** minutes	🖥️

Lesson Goals

- Review telling time, finding elapsed time, and solving problems about time.

- Take a quiz.

MATERIALS

There are no materials to gather for this lesson.

GET READY

Introduction to Clock Time and Units of Time (E)

Students will read the lesson goals.

TRY IT

Review Clock Time and Units of Time

Students will answer questions to review what they have learned about clock time and units of time.

QUIZ

Clock Time and Units of Time

Students will complete the Clock Time and Units of Time quiz.

More Math Practice

Students will practice skills according to their individual needs.

Measuring Length (A)

Lesson Overview

ACTIVITY	ACTIVITY TITLE	TIME	ONLINE/OFFLINE
GET READY	Introduction to Measuring Length (A)	**2** minutes	🖥️
	Look Back at Estimating Length in Inches	**8** minutes	🖥️
LEARN AND **TRY IT**	Measuring Length	**7** minutes	🖥️
	Measure Length	**7** minutes	🖥️
	Estimating Length	**7** minutes	🖥️
	Estimate Length	**7** minutes	🖥️
	Practice Measuring and Estimating Length	**20** minutes	🖥️ and 📄
WRAP-UP	Measuring and Estimating Length	**2** minutes	🖥️

Content Background

Students will learn to estimate and measure the length of an object in inches. They will estimate to the nearest half inch and measure to the nearest quarter inch. Estimating and measuring objects is an important skill. When judging whether an object will fit in a given space, students estimate its length, width, and height. Then they compare the estimates to the given space to determine if the object will fit. Students often use familiar benchmark measurements when estimating and measuring. For instance, they may be familiar with $8\frac{1}{2} \times 11$ inch notebook paper. Students may use an object, like a piece of paper, to estimate the length of an object or judge whether it will fit in a given space.

At this level, students are not expected to know that the abbreviation *in.* stands for *inch*. A note is always included about what the abbreviation *in.* stands for when the abbreviation is used. Note that when measurements are abbreviated (cm, m, km, in., ft, yd, and mi), only the abbreviation for inch has a period. The period is added to avoid confusion with the word *in*.

MATERIALS

Supplied
- *Summit Math 3 Activity Book:* Practice Measuring and Estimating Length

KEYWORDS

half inch – one-half of the distance between the zero mark and the one-inch mark on a ruler

inch (in.) – the basic English, or customary, unit for measuring length

quarter inch – one-fourth of the distance between the zero mark and the one-inch mark on a ruler

Lesson Goals
- Measure the length of an object.
- Estimate the length of an object.

Introduction to Measuring Length (A)

Students will get a glimpse of what they will learn about in the lesson. They will also read the lesson goals and keywords. Have students select each keyword and preview its definition.

Look Back at Estimating Length in Inches

Students will practice the prerequisite skill of estimating length.

LEARN AND TRY IT

LEARN Measuring Length

Students will to learn to measure length.

TRY IT Measure Length

Students will practice measuring length. Support will be provided to help students overcome misconceptions.

LEARN Estimating Length

Students will learn to estimate length.

TRY IT Estimate Length

Students will practice estimating length. Support will be provided to help students overcome misconceptions.

TRY IT Practice Measuring and Estimating Length

Students will complete online practice problems. Then they will complete Practice Measuring and Estimating Length from *Summit Math 3 Activity Book*.

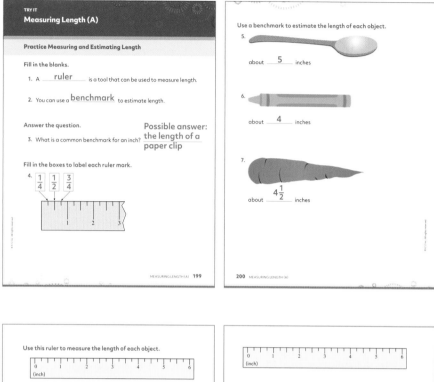

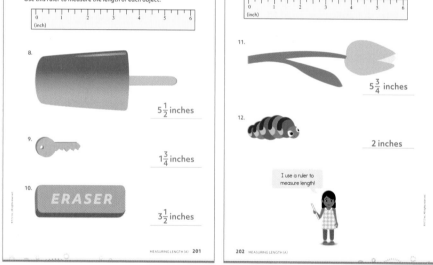

WRAP-UP

Measuring and Estimating Length

Students will solve a problem to show that they understand how to measure length.

Measuring Length (B)

Lesson Overview

ACTIVITY	ACTIVITY TITLE	TIME	ONLINE/OFFLINE
GET READY	Introduction to Measuring Length (B)	**2** minutes	🖥️
	Dividing by 7 Math Facts Game	**8** minutes	🖥️
LEARN AND **TRY IT**	Solving Length Word Problems with Multiplication	**15** minutes	🖥️
	Solve Length Word Problems with Multiplication	**10** minutes	🖥️
	Practice Solving Length Word Problems with Multiplication	**20** minutes	🖥️ and 📄
WRAP-UP	Solving Length Word Problems with Multiplication	**5** minutes	🖥️

Content Background

Students will learn how to solve real-world problems involving equal measures. In an equal-measure problem, several equal-sized measures, or parts, combine to make a total measurement amount. To solve problems involving equal measures, students can multiply or divide. When they know the number of parts and the measure of each part, they multiply to find the total measurement.

MATERIALS

Supplied
- *Summit Math 3 Activity Book:* Practice Solving Length Word Problems with Multiplication

Lesson Goals
- Use multiplication to solve real-world length problems.

GET READY

Introduction to Measuring Length (B)

Students will get a glimpse of what they will learn about in the lesson. They will also read the lesson goals.

Dividing by 7 Math Facts Game

Students will practice dividing by 7.

LEARN   Solving Length Word Problems with Multiplication

Students will learn to solve length problems using multiplication.

TRY IT   Solve Length Word Problems with Multiplication

Students will practice solving length problems using multiplication. Support will be provided to help students overcome misconceptions.

TRY IT   Practice Solving Length Word Problems with Multiplication

Students will complete online practice problems. Then they will complete Practice Solving Length Word Problems with Multiplication from *Summit Math 3 Activity Book.*

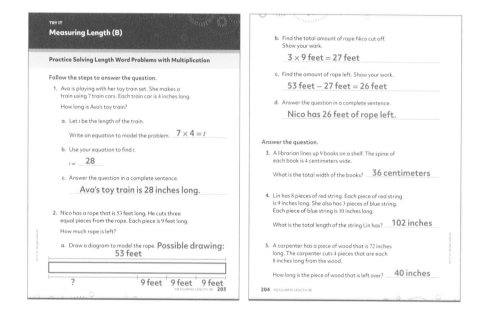

Solving Length Word Problems with Multiplication

Students will solve a problem to show that they understand how to solve length problems using multiplication.

Measuring Length (C)

Lesson Overview

ACTIVITY	ACTIVITY TITLE	TIME	ONLINE/OFFLINE
GET READY	Introduction to Measuring Length (C)	**2** minutes	🖥️
	Dividing by 8 Math Facts	**8** minutes	🖥️
LEARN AND **TRY IT**	Solving Length Word Problems with Division	**15** minutes	🖥️
	Solve Length Word Problems with Division	**10** minutes	🖥️
	Practice Solving Length Word Problems with Division	**20** minutes	🖥️ and 📄
WRAP-UP	Solving Length Word Problems with Division	**5** minutes	🖥️

Content Background

Students will learn how to solve story problems involving equal measures. In an equal-measure story problem, several equal-sized measures, or parts, combine to make a total measurement amount. To solve problems involving equal measures, students can multiply or divide. When students know the total measurement and the measure of one part, they divide to find the number of parts. When students know the total measurement and the number of parts, they can use division to find the measure of each part.

MATERIALS

Supplied
- *Summit Math 3 Activity Book:* Practice Solving Length Word Problems with Division

Lesson Goals
- Use division to solve real-world length problems.

GET READY

Introduction to Measuring Length (C)
Students will get a glimpse of what they will learn about in the lesson. They will also read the lesson goals.

Dividing by 8 Math Facts
Students will practice dividing by 8.

LEARN   Solving Length Word Problems with Division

Students will learn to solve length problems using division.

TRY IT   Solve Length Word Problems with Division

Students will practice solving length problems using division. Support will be provided to help students overcome misconceptions.

TRY IT   Practice Solving Length Word Problems with Division

Students will complete online practice problems. Then they will complete Practice Solving Length Word Problems with Division from *Summit Math 3 Activity Book.*

TRY IT
Measuring Length (C)

Practice Solving Length Word Problems with Division

Follow the steps to answer the question.

1. A store has a chain that is 63 inches long. The store separates the chain into 7 equal pieces.

   How long is each piece?

   a. Let p be the length of each piece of chain.

   Write a division equation to model the problem. $63 \div 7 = p$

   b. Use your equation to find p.

   $p =$ ___9___

   c. Answer the question in a complete sentence.

   Each piece is 9 inches long.

2. Rey puts ribbon along 4 sides of a box that is shaped like a pentagon. Each side of the pentagon is the same length, and the perimeter of the pentagon is 20 feet.

   What is the total length of ribbon Rey uses?

   a. Draw a diagram to model the problem.

   Possible drawing: ? feet   ? feet   ? feet   ? feet   ? feet

MEASURING LENGTH (C)   **205**

---

b. Find the length of each side of the pentagon. Show your work.

   $20 \text{ feet} \div 5 = 4 \text{ feet}$

c. Find the amount of ribbon Rey uses. Show your work.

   $4 \text{ feet} \times 4 = 16 \text{ feet}$

d. Answer the question in a complete sentence.

   Rey uses 16 feet of ribbon.

Answer the questions.

3. Mila runs a total of 54 miles. She runs the same distance each day for 9 days.

   How far does Mila run each day?   6 miles

4. An electrician places wire around 3 sides of a square window. The perimeter of the window is 24 feet.

   How long is the wire the electrician uses?   18 feet

5. Luis walks a nature trail 4 times. He walks a total distance of 28 miles.

   How long is the nature trail?   7 miles

206   MEASURING LENGTH (C)

Solving Length Word Problems with Division

Students will solve a problem to show that they understand how to solve length problems using division.

Measuring Length (D)

Lesson Overview

ACTIVITY	ACTIVITY TITLE	TIME	ONLINE/OFFLINE
GET READY	Introduction to Measuring Length (D)	**2** minutes	🖥️
TRY IT	Review Measuring Length	**18** minutes	🖥️
QUIZ	Measuring Length	**25** minutes	🖥️
WRAP-UP	More Math Practice	**15** minutes	🖥️

Lesson Goals

- Review measuring lengths, estimating lengths, and solving real-world length problems.
- Take a quiz.

MATERIALS

There are no materials to gather for this lesson.

GET READY

Introduction to Measuring Length (D)

Students will read the lesson goals.

TRY IT

Review Measuring Length

Students will answer questions to review what they have learned about measuring length.

QUIZ

Measuring Length

Students will complete the Measuring Length quiz.

More Math Practice

Students will practice skills according to their individual needs.

Big Ideas: Mini-Project

Lesson Overview

Big Ideas lessons provide students the opportunity to further apply the knowledge and skills acquired throughout previous units. Each Big Ideas lesson consists of two types of activities:

1. **Cumulative Review:** Students keep their skills fresh by reviewing prior content.

2. **Synthesis:** Students complete an assignment that allows them to interweave and apply what they've learned. These synthesis assignments will vary throughout the course.

   In the Synthesis portion of this Big Ideas lesson, students will complete a small, creative project designed to tie together concepts and skills that students have encountered across units. These small projects are designed to emphasize a real-world application that connects mathematics to other subjects, including science, technology, engineering, art, and history. Students will need to use pencil and paper and/or technology to show their work.

   LEARNING COACH CHECK-IN Make sure students complete, review, and submit the assignment to their teacher.

All materials needed for this lesson are linked online. The materials are not provided in this Lesson Guide or in the Activity Book.

Measurement: Liquid Volume and Mass

Liquid Volume (A)

Lesson Overview

ACTIVITY	ACTIVITY TITLE	TIME	ONLINE/OFFLINE
GET READY	Introduction to Liquid Volume (A)	**2** minutes	🖥️
	Look Back at Measuring an Object in Inches	**8** minutes	🖥️
LEARN AND **TRY IT**	Measuring Liquid Volume	**15** minutes	🖥️
	Measure Liquid Volume	**10** minutes	🖥️
	OPTIONAL Measuring with Milliliters	**7** minutes	🖥️
	OPTIONAL Measure with Milliliters	**7** minutes	🖥️
	OPTIONAL Practice Measuring with Milliliters	**10** minutes	🖥️
	Practice Measuring Liquid Volume	**20** minutes	🖥️ and 📄
WRAP-UP	Measuring Liquid Volume	**5** minutes	🖥️

Content Background

Students will learn to measure liquid volume to the nearest liter. Students will also learn to estimate the capacity of various containers in liters using common benchmarks. For example, a water bottle is a common benchmark for 1 liter.

Throughout their lives, students will have experiences measuring or estimating amounts of liquid volume, or capacity. Such experiences might include measuring in cooking, making lemonade, or drinking an adequate amount of water each day.

While many quantities must be measured precisely, some can simply be estimated. Estimation is an important skill for students, since it focuses them on which unit is being used in the measurement and it helps them develop a better feel for the size of that unit. Measuring precisely is a key skill as well; not doing so can lead to undesirable results, such as a fallen cake, a salty stew, or a watery milkshake.

When finding actual measures, students need to take special care to both use and read the measuring instrument accurately. They should understand that all measures that the average person makes are only close approximations, because of both the lack of precision of the tools used in daily life and of human error.

MATERIALS

Supplied
- *Summit Math 3 Activity Book:* Practice Measuring Liquid Volume

KEYWORDS

liquid volume – the amount of liquid a container will hold; the measure of liquid capacity

liter (L) – the basic metric unit for measuring capacity

OPTIONAL   Have students estimate the liquid volume of a bowl, vase, or other container. Then have them use a liter measuring cup or other benchmark from the pantry, refrigerator, or recycling bin to measure the actual liquid volume of the container.

Lesson Goals

- Measure liquid volume to the nearest liter.
- Estimate liquid volume to the nearest liter.

GET READY

Introduction to Liquid Volume (A)

After a quick introductory activity, students will read the lesson goals and keywords. Have students select each keyword and preview its definition.

Look Back at Measuring an Object in Inches

Students will practice the prerequisite skill of measuring an object in inches.

LEARN AND TRY IT

LEARN   Measuring Liquid Volume

Students will learn how to measure liquid volume.

TRY IT   Measure Liquid Volume

Students will practice measuring liquid volume. Support will be provided to help students overcome misconceptions.

LEARN   OPTIONAL   Measuring with Milliliters

Students will learn how to measure and estimate liquid volume with milliliters. Students will be directed to complete or skip this activity by their teacher.

TRY IT   OPTIONAL   Measure with Milliliters

Students will practice measuring and estimating liquid volume with milliliters. Support will be provided to help students overcome misconceptions. Students will be directed to complete or skip this activity by their teacher.

TRY IT   OPTIONAL   Practice Measuring with Milliliters

Students will complete online practice problems. Students will be directed to complete or skip this activity by their teacher.

TRY IT   Practice Measuring Liquid Volume

Students will complete online practice problems. Then they will complete Practice Measuring Liquid Volume from *Summit Math 3 Activity Book*.

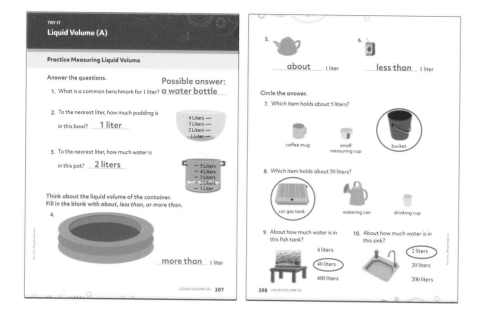

WRAP-UP

Measuring Liquid Volume

Students will solve problems to show that they understand how to measure liquid volume.

Liquid Volume (B)

Lesson Overview

ACTIVITY	ACTIVITY TITLE	TIME	ONLINE/OFFLINE
GET READY	Introduction to Liquid Volume (B)	**2** minutes	🖥️
	Dividing by 8 with Instant Recall	**8** minutes	🖥️
LEARN AND **TRY IT**	Adding and Subtracting with Liquid Volume	**15** minutes	🖥️
	Add and Subtract with Liquid Volume	**10** minutes	🖥️
	OPTIONAL Practice Adding and Subtracting with Milliliters	**10** minutes	🖥️
	Practice Adding and Subtracting with Liquid Volume	**20** minutes	🖥️ and 📄
WRAP-UP	Adding and Subtracting with Liquid Volume	**5** minutes	🖥️

Content Background

Students will use their knowledge of metric liquid volume to solve one-step problems using addition or subtraction.

Throughout their lives, students will have experiences that involve combining or separating amounts of liquid volume. As adults, they might mix paints, make homemade cleaning solutions with vinegar and baking soda, and possibly mix chemicals.

Students will have opportunities to learn and practice common problem-solving strategies like drawing a picture, working backwards, or solving a simpler problem. Encourage students to think about which problem-solving strategy will help them solve each problem they encounter.

> ### Lesson Goals
> - Solve liquid volume problems using addition.
> - Solve liquid volume problems using subtraction.

MATERIALS

Supplied
- *Summit Math 3 Activity Book:* Practice Adding and Subtracting with Liquid Volume

GET READY

Introduction to Liquid Volume (B)

Students will get a glimpse of what they will learn about in the lesson. They will also read the lesson goals.

Dividing by 8 with Instant Recall
Students will practice dividing by 8.

LEARN   Adding and Subtracting with Liquid Volume
Students will learn how to add and subtract to solve liquid volume problems.

TRY IT   Add and Subtract with Liquid Volume
Students will practice adding and subtracting to solve liquid volume problems. Support will be provided to help students overcome misconceptions.

TRY IT   OPTIONAL   Practice Adding and Subtracting with Milliliters
Students will complete online practice problems. Students will be directed to complete or skip this activity by their teacher.

TRY IT   Practice Adding and Subtracting with Liquid Volume
Students will complete online practice problems. Then they will complete Practice Adding and Subtracting with Liquid Volume from *Summit Math 3 Activity Book*.

TRY IT
Liquid Volume (B)

Practice Adding and Subtracting with Liquid Volume

Follow the steps to answer the question.

1. Debra is making batches of fruit punch for a dance. She buys 18 liters of grape juice, 22 liters of cranberry juice, and 17 liters of apple juice.

   How many liters of juice does Debra buy in all?

   a. Use the information in the problem to fill in the parts and symbols in this chart.

Part	+ or −	Part	+ or −	Part	=	Whole
18	+	22	+	17	=	57

   b. Use your answer from part **a** to find the whole. Fill in the whole in the chart.

   c. Answer the question using a complete sentence.

      Debra buys 57 liters of juice in all.

2. A tank has 389 liters of water. Water is drained out of the tank to fill a pool that holds 226 liters of water.

   How much water is left in the tank?

---

a. Use the information in the problem to fill in the start, change, and symbol in this chart.

Start	+ or −	Change	=	Result
389	−	226	=	163

b. Use your answer from part **a** to find the result. Fill in the result in the chart.

c. Answer the question using a complete sentence.

   The tank has 163 liters of water left.

Answer the question using a complete sentence. Show your work.

3. A doctor's office has two fish tanks. The larger tank holds 208 liters of water. The smaller tank holds 151 liters of water.

   How much more water does the larger tank hold than the smaller tank?

   $$\begin{array}{r} 208 \\ -151 \\ \hline 57 \end{array}$$

   The larger tank holds 57 more liters of water than the smaller tank.

4. A bathtub has 129 liters of water in it. Then, 107 liters of water are added to the tub.

   How many liters of water are in the tub now?

   $$\begin{array}{r} 129 \\ +107 \\ \hline 236 \end{array}$$

   There are now 236 liters of water in the tub.

LIQUID VOLUME (B) **209**

210 LIQUID VOLUME (B)

Adding and Subtracting with Liquid Volume
Students will solve a problem to show that they understand how to add or subtract to solve a liquid volume problem.

Liquid Volume (C)

Lesson Overview

ACTIVITY	ACTIVITY TITLE	TIME	ONLINE/OFFLINE
GET READY	Introduction to Liquid Volume (C)	**2** minutes	🖥️
	Dividing by 8 Math Facts Game	**8** minutes	🖥️
LEARN AND **TRY IT**	Multiplying and Dividing with Liquid Volume	**15** minutes	🖥️
	Multiply and Divide with Liquid Volume	**10** minutes	🖥️
	OPTIONAL Practice Multiplying and Dividing with Milliliters	**10** minutes	🖥️
	Practice Multiplying and Dividing with Liquid Volume	**20** minutes	🖥️ and 📄
WRAP-UP	Multiplying and Dividing with Liquid Volume	**5** minutes	🖥️

Content Background

Students will use their knowledge of metric liquid volume to solve one-step problems using multiplication or division.

Throughout their lives, students will have experiences working with equal amounts of liquid volume. Such experiences might include measuring in cooking, drinking an adequate amount of water each day, equally sharing a bottle of water with a friend, and deciding how much juice to buy for a large group.

Students will have opportunities to learn and practice common problem-solving strategies like drawing a picture, working backwards, or solving a simpler problem. Encourage students to think about which problem-solving strategy will help them solve each problem they encounter.

Lesson Goals

- Solve liquid volume problems using multiplication.
- Solve liquid volume problems using division.

Introduction to Liquid Volume (C)

Students will get a glimpse of what they will learn about in the lesson. They will also read the lesson goals.

Dividing by 8 Math Facts Game

Students will practice dividing by 8.

LEARN AND TRY IT

LEARN   Multiplying and Dividing with Liquid Volume

Students will learn to multiply and divide to solve liquid volume problems.

TRY IT   Multiply and Divide with Liquid Volume

Students will practice multiplying and dividing to solve liquid volume problems. Support will be provided to help students overcome misconceptions.

TRY IT   OPTIONAL   Practice Multiplying and Dividing with Milliliters

Students will complete online practice problems. Students will be directed to complete or skip this activity by their teacher.

TRY IT   Practice Multiplying and Dividing with Liquid Volume

Students will complete online practice problems. Then they will complete Practice Multiplying and Dividing with Liquid Volume from *Summit Math 3 Activity Book*.

TRY IT
Liquid Volume (C)

Practice Multiplying and Dividing with Liquid Volume

Follow the steps to answer the question.

1. Jan buys a large bottle of cleaning solution. The bottle has 10 liters of cleaning solution. Jan splits the solution equally among 5 small bottles.

   How much cleaning solution is in each small bottle?

   a. Write an equation to solve the problem.
      Possible answer: $10 \div 5 = c$

   b. Solve the problem. $2 = c$

   c. Answer the question using a complete sentence.
      Each small bottle has 2 liters of cleaning solution.

2. Julio makes 5 batches of soup. Each batch is 3 liters of soup.

   How much soup does Julio make in all?

   a. Write an equation to solve the problem.
      Possible answer: $5 \times 3 = s$

   b. Solve the problem. $15 = s$

LIQUID VOLUME (C) **211**

---

   c. Answer the question using a complete sentence.
      Julio makes 15 liters of soup in all.

Answer the question using a complete sentence. Show your work.

3. Maria is having a party. She needs 3 liters of iced tea for each table of guests. There are 6 tables.

   How many liters of iced tea does Maria need in all?

   $3 \times 6 = 18$; Maria needs 18 liters of iced tea.

4. Marco has 24 liters of water. He pours the same amount of water into each of 8 bottles.

   How much water is in each bottle?

   $24 \div 8 = 3$; Each bottle has 3 liters of water.

5. Ann's aquarium holds 45 liters of water. She uses a 5-liter container to fill the aquarium.

   How many times does Ann fill the container in order to fill her aquarium?

   $45 \div 5 = 9$; Ann fills the container 9 times in order to fill her aquarium.

212 LIQUID VOLUME (C)

Multiplying and Dividing with Liquid Volume

Students will solve a problem to show that they understand how to multiply or divide to solve a liquid volume problem.

Liquid Volume (D)

Lesson Overview

ACTIVITY	ACTIVITY TITLE	TIME	ONLINE/OFFLINE
GET READY	Introduction to Liquid Volume (D)	**2** minutes	🖥️
TRY IT	Review Liquid Volume	**18** minutes	🖥️
QUIZ	Liquid Volume	**25** minutes	🖥️
WRAP-UP	More Math Practice	**15** minutes	🖥️

Lesson Goals

- Review measuring liquid volume and solving liquid volume problems.
- Take a quiz.

MATERIALS

There are no materials to gather for this lesson.

GET READY

Introduction to Liquid Volume (D)

Students will read the lesson goals.

TRY IT

Review Liquid Volume

Students will answer questions to review what they have learned about liquid volume.

QUIZ

Liquid Volume

Students will complete the Liquid Volume quiz.

More Math Practice

Students will practice skills according to their individual needs.

Mass (A)

Lesson Overview

ACTIVITY	ACTIVITY TITLE		TIME	ONLINE/OFFLINE
GET READY	Introduction to Mass (A)		**2** minutes	🖥️
	Look Back at Measuring Liquid Volume in Liters		**8** minutes	📶
LEARN AND **TRY IT**	Measuring Mass		**15** minutes	📶
	Measure Mass		**10** minutes	📶
	OPTIONAL	Measuring with Milligrams	**7** minutes	📶
	OPTIONAL	Measure with Milligrams	**7** minutes	📶
	OPTIONAL	Practice Measuring with Milligrams	**10** minutes	📶
	Practice Measuring Mass		**20** minutes	📶 and 📄
WRAP-UP	Measuring Mass		**5** minutes	📶

Content Background

Students will learn to measure the mass of an object to the nearest gram and kilogram. Students will also learn to estimate the mass of various objects in grams or kilograms, using common benchmarks. For example, a small paper clip has a mass of about 1 gram and a textbook or a pineapple each has a mass of about 1 kilogram.

Throughout their lives, students will have experiences measuring or estimating how much objects weigh. Some examples include weighing themselves or a pet, measuring in cooking, and knowing how long to bake something by its weight. As adults they might need to weigh items to be mailed for proper postage, estimate how much potato salad to buy when serving a meal to a large group of people, and weigh luggage before flying.

Weight is the measurement of the pull of gravity on an object and *mass* is a measurement of the amount of matter something contains. The mass of an object doesn't change when an object's location changes. Weight, on the other hand, does change with location. For example, a baseball on the earth has one mass. On the moon, it has the same mass. On the earth, it has one weight; on the moon, it weighs less. The difference between weight and mass will be introduced later in students' math education. For now, make sure students are aware that the units to measure mass include grams and kilograms.

MATERIALS

Supplied
- *Summit Math 3 Activity Book:* Practice Measuring Mass

KEYWORDS

gram (g) – the basic metric unit of mass

kilogram (kg) – the metric unit for measuring mass that equals 1,000 grams

mass – the amount of matter in an object

Lesson Goals

- Measure mass to the nearest gram or kilogram.
- Estimate mass to the nearest gram or kilogram.

GET READY

Introduction to Mass (A)

Students will get a glimpse of what they will learn about in the lesson. They will also read the lesson goals and keywords. Have students select each keyword and preview its definition.

Look Back at Measuring Liquid Volume in Liters

Students will practice the prerequisite skill of measuring liquid volume in liters.

LEARN AND TRY IT

LEARN   Measuring Mass

Students will learn how to measure mass.

TRY IT   Measure Mass

Students will practice measuring mass. Support will be provided to help students overcome misconceptions.

LEARN   OPTIONAL   Measuring with Milligrams

Students will learn how to measure and estimate mass with milligrams. Students will be directed to complete or skip this activity by their teacher.

TRY IT   OPTIONAL   Measure with Milligrams

Students will practice measuring and estimating mass with milligrams. Support will be provided to help students overcome misconceptions. Students will be directed to complete or skip this activity by their teacher.

TRY IT   OPTIONAL   Practice Measuring with Milligrams

Students will complete online practice problems. Students will be directed to complete or skip this activity by their teacher.

TRY IT   Practice Measuring Mass

Students will complete online practice problems. Then they will complete Practice Measuring Mass from *Summit Math 3 Activity Book*.

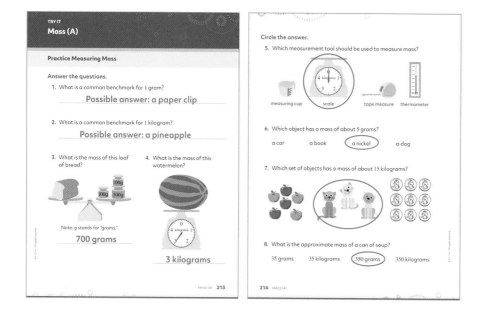

WRAP-UP

Measuring Mass

Students will solve problems to show that they understand how to measure and estimate mass.

Mass (B)

Lesson Overview

ACTIVITY	ACTIVITY TITLE	TIME	ONLINE/OFFLINE
GET READY	Introduction to Mass (B)	**2** minutes	🖥️
	Dividing Math Facts	**8** minutes	🖥️
LEARN AND **TRY IT**	Adding and Subtracting with Mass	**15** minutes	🖥️
	Add and Subtract with Mass	**10** minutes	🖥️
	OPTIONAL Practice Adding and Subtracting with Milligrams	**10** minutes	🖥️
	Practice Adding and Subtracting with Mass	**20** minutes	🖥️ and 📄
WRAP-UP	Adding and Subtracting with Mass	**5** minutes	🖥️

Content Background

Students will use their knowledge of metric mass to solve one-step problems using addition or subtraction. Problems will involve either grams or kilograms.

Students will have opportunities to learn and practice common problem-solving strategies like drawing a picture, working backwards, or solving a simpler problem. Encourage students to think about which problem-solving strategy will help them solve each problem they encounter.

Lesson Goals

- Solve mass problems using addition.
- Solve mass problems using subtraction.

> **MATERIALS**
>
> **Supplied**
> - *Summit Math 3 Activity Book:* Practice Adding and Subtracting with Mass

GET READY

Introduction to Mass (B)

Students will get a glimpse of what they will learn about in the lesson. They will also read the lesson goals.

Dividing Math Facts

Students will practice mixed division math facts.

LEARN   Adding and Subtracting with Mass

Students will learn how to add and subtract to solve mass problems.

TRY IT   Add and Subtract with Mass

Students will practice adding and subtracting to solve mass problems. Support will be provided to help students overcome misconceptions.

TRY IT   OPTIONAL   Practice Adding and Subtracting with Milligrams

Students will complete online practice problems. Students will be directed to complete or skip this activity by their teacher.

TRY IT   Practice Adding and Subtracting with Mass

Students will complete online practice problems. Then they will complete Practice Adding and Subtracting with Mass from *Summit Math 3 Activity Book.*

TRY IT
Mass (B)

Practice Adding and Subtracting with Mass

Follow the steps to answer the question.

1. Aisha and Alison each have a box. The mass of Aisha's box is 56 grams. The mass of Alison's box is 35 grams.

   How many more grams is Aisha's box than Alison's box?

   a. Describe a strategy you could use to solve the problem.
   Answers will vary. Possible answer: I can write an equation.

   b. Use your strategy to solve the problem. Show your work. **Answers will vary. Possible answer:**
   $$56 - 35 = b$$
   $$21 = b$$

   c. Answer the question using a complete sentence.
   The mass of Aisha's box is 21 more grams than the mass of Alison's box.

2. Mariah has 429 grams of grapes. Jordan has 223 fewer grams of grapes.

   How many grams of grapes does Jordan have?

   a. Describe a strategy you could use to solve the problem.
   Answers will vary. Possible answer: I could solve a simpler problem.

   MASS (B)   **215**

---

b. Use your strategy to solve the problem. Show your work. **Answers will vary. Possible answer:**

$$
\begin{array}{r} 429 \\ -223 \end{array} \longrightarrow
\begin{array}{r} 400 + 20 + 9 \\ -200 + 20 + 3 \\ \hline 200 + \ 0 + 6 = 206 \end{array}
$$

c. Answer the question using a complete sentence.
Jordan has 206 grams of grapes.

Answer the question using a complete sentence. Show your work.

3. An aquarium has 289 grams of sand in it. Kim pours 240 more grams of sand into the aquarium.

   After Kim pours in all his sand, how much sand is in the aquarium?

   $$\begin{array}{r} \overset{1}{2}40 \\ +289 \\ \hline 529 \end{array}$$ **; The aquarium has 529 grams of sand in it.**

4. A baker buys 23 kilograms of flour and 11 kilograms of sugar.

   a. How much flour and sugar does the baker buy in all?

   $$\begin{array}{r} 23 \\ +11 \\ \hline 34 \end{array}$$ **; The baker buys 34 kilograms of flour and sugar in all.**

   b. How much more flour than sugar does the baker buy?

   $$\begin{array}{r} 23 \\ -11 \\ \hline 12 \end{array}$$ **; The baker buys 12 more kilograms of flour than sugar.**

   216   MASS (B)

Adding and Subtracting with Mass

Students will solve a problem to show that they understand how to add or subtract to solve mass problems.

Mass (C)

Lesson Overview

ACTIVITY	ACTIVITY TITLE	TIME	ONLINE/OFFLINE
GET READY	Introduction to Mass (C)	**2** minutes	🖥️
	Dividing with Instant Recall	**8** minutes	🖥️
LEARN AND **TRY IT**	Multiplying and Dividing with Mass	**15** minutes	🖥️
	Multiply and Divide with Mass	**10** minutes	🖥️
	OPTIONAL Practice Multiplying and Dividing with Milligrams	**10** minutes	🖥️
	Practice Multiplying and Dividing with Mass	**20** minutes	🖥️ and 📄
WRAP-UP	Multiplying and Dividing with Mass	**5** minutes	🖥️

Content Background

Students will use their knowledge of metric mass to solve one-step problems using multiplication or division. Problems will involve either grams or kilograms.

Students will have opportunities to learn and practice common problem-solving strategies like drawing a picture, working backwards, or solving a simpler problem. Encourage students to think about which problem-solving strategy will help them solve each problem they encounter.

MATERIALS

Supplied
- *Summit Math 3 Activity Book:* Practice Multiplying and Dividing with Mass

Lesson Goals
- Solve mass problems using multiplication.
- Solve mass problems using division.

GET READY

Introduction to Mass (C)
Students will get a glimpse of what they will learn about in the lesson. They will also read the lesson goals.

Dividing with Instant Recall
Students will practice mixed division math facts.

LEARN   Multiplying and Dividing with Mass

Students will learn how to multiply and divide to solve mass problems.

TRY IT   Multiply and Divide with Mass

Students will practice multiplying and dividing to solve mass problems. Support will be provided to help students overcome misconceptions.

TRY IT   OPTIONAL   Practice Multiplying and Dividing with Milligrams

Students will complete online practice problems. Students will be directed to complete or skip this activity by their teacher.

TRY IT   Practice Multiplying and Dividing with Mass

Students will complete online practice problems. Then they will complete Practice Multiplying and Dividing with Mass from *Summit Math 3 Activity Book*.

TRY IT
Mass (C)

Practice Multiplying and Dividing with Mass

Follow the steps to answer the question.

1. Damian makes a stack of 8 bricks. The mass of each brick is 5 kilograms.

   What is the mass of Damian's stack of bricks?

   a. Write an equation to solve the problem. **Possible answer:** $8 \times 5 = m$

   b. Solve the problem. $40 = m$

   c. Answer the question using a complete sentence.
   The mass of the stack of bricks is 40 kilograms.

2. A garden store has 56 kilograms of potting soil. The store packages the soil in bags with a mass of 7 kilograms each.

   How many 7-kilogram bags of soil does the store have?

   a. Write an equation to solve the problem. **Possible answer:** $56 \div 7 = b$

   b. Solve the problem. $8 = b$

   c. Answer the question using a complete sentence.
   The store has 8 bags of soil with 7 kilograms each.

MASS (C)   **217**

Answer the question using a complete sentence. Show your work.

3. Otto buys a 36-kilogram package of horse pellets. He separates the pellets into 9-kilogram servings and pours each serving into its own plastic bin.

   How many plastic bins does Otto use?
   $36 \div 9 = 4$; Otto uses 4 plastic bins.

4. A pencil has a mass of 7 grams.

   What is the total mass of 5 pencils?
   $7 \times 5 = 35$; 5 pencils have a mass of 35 grams.

5. A bakery has 6 bags of flour. Each bag has a mass of 10 kilograms.

   How many kilograms of flour does the bakery have in all?
   $6 \times 10 = 60$; The bakery has 60 kilograms of flour in all.

6. Min has a stack of 7 graham crackers. The mass of each cracker is 6 grams.

   What is the total mass of Min's stack of graham crackers?
   $7 \times 6 = 42$; The mass of Min's stack of graham crackers is 42 grams.

218   MASS (C)

Multiplying and Dividing with Mass

Students will solve problems to show that they understand how to multiply or divide to solve mass problems.

Mass (D)

Lesson Overview

ACTIVITY	ACTIVITY TITLE	TIME	ONLINE/OFFLINE
GET READY	Introduction to Mass (D)	**2** minutes	🖥️
TRY IT	Review Mass	**18** minutes	🖥️
QUIZ	Mass	**25** minutes	🖥️
WRAP-UP	More Math Practice	**15** minutes	🖥️

Lesson Goals

- Review measuring mass and solving mass problems.
- Take a quiz.

MATERIALS

There are no materials to gather for this lesson.

GET READY

Introduction to Mass (D)

Students will read the lesson goals.

TRY IT

Review Mass

Students will answer questions to review what they have learned about mass.

QUIZ

Mass

Students will complete the Mass quiz.

WRAP-UP

More Math Practice

Students will practice skills according to their individual needs.

Big Ideas: Mini-Project

Lesson Overview

Big Ideas lessons provide students the opportunity to further apply the knowledge and skills acquired throughout previous units. Each Big Ideas lesson consists of two types of activities:

1. **Cumulative Review:** Students keep their skills fresh by reviewing prior content.

2. **Synthesis:** Students complete an assignment that allows them to interweave and apply what they've learned. These synthesis assignments will vary throughout the course.

   In the Synthesis portion of this Big Ideas lesson, students will complete a small, creative project designed to tie together concepts and skills that students have encountered across units. These small projects are designed to emphasize a real-world application that connects mathematics to other subjects, including science, technology, engineering, art, and history. Students will need to use pencil and paper and/or technology to show their work.

   LEARNING COACH CHECK-IN Make sure students complete, review, and submit the assignment to their teacher.

All materials needed for this lesson are linked online. The materials are not provided in this Lesson Guide or in the Activity Book.

MATERIALS

Supplied
- Mini-Project Instructions (printout)

Data Displays

Picture and Bar Graphs (A)

Lesson Overview

ACTIVITY	ACTIVITY TITLE	TIME	ONLINE/OFFLINE
GET READY	Introduction to Picture and Bar Graphs (A)	**2** minutes	🖥️
	Look Back at Skip Counting by 2s	**8** minutes	🖥️
LEARN AND **TRY IT**	Recording Data in Frequency Tables	**7** minutes	🖥️
	Record Data in Frequency Tables	**7** minutes	🖥️
	Interpreting Frequency Tables	**7** minutes	🖥️
	Interpret Frequency Tables	**7** minutes	🖥️
	Practice Working with Frequency Tables	**20** minutes	🖥️ and 📄
WRAP-UP	Working with Frequency Tables	**2** minutes	🖥️

Content Background

Data is numerical information that has been gathered through counting or measuring. Data can be organized and displayed in many ways. Students may have experience recording data in a tally chart. In this lesson, students will learn to record data in a frequency table. Data may be presented in a tally chart, as a collection of objects, or as a description in words. Students will also use a frequency table to interpret data, solve problems, and predict future events.

Lesson Goals

- Record data in frequency tables.
- Interpret frequency tables.
- Use frequency tables to solve problems.
- Use frequency tables to make predictions.

MATERIALS

Supplied
- *Summit Math 3 Activity Book:* Practice Working with Frequency Tables

KEYWORDS

data – numerical information that has been gathered

frequency table – a table that shows the number of times pieces of data occur

GET READY

Introduction to Picture and Bar Graphs (A)

After a quick introductory activity, students will read the lesson goals and keywords. Have students select each keyword and preview its definition.

Look Back at Skip Counting by 2s

Students will practice the prerequisite skill of skip counting by 2.

LEARN   Recording Data in Frequency Tables

Students will learn how to record data in frequency tables.

TRY IT   Record Data in Frequency Tables

Students will practice recording data in frequency tables. Support will be provided to help students overcome misconceptions.

LEARN   Interpreting Frequency Tables

Students will learn how to interpret a frequency table.

TRY IT   Interpret Frequency Tables

Students will practice interpreting frequency tables. Support will be provided to help students overcome misconceptions.

TRY IT   Practice Working with Frequency Tables

Students will complete online practice problems. Then they will complete Practice Working with Frequency Tables from *Summit Math 3 Activity Book*.

TRY IT
Picture and Bar Graphs (A)

Practice Working with Frequency Tables

Follow the steps to answer the question.

1. Raj counts the marbles in his collection. The tallies in this frequency table show his results.

   How many marbles of each color does Raj have?

   a. Count the tally marks in each row.

   b. Record the total for each row in the Frequency column.

Raj's Marble Collection

Color	Tally	Frequency
green	𝍷𝍷𝍷 IIII	14
red	𝍷 I	6
blue	𝍷 III	8
yellow	𝍷𝍷 I	11
orange	𝍷𝍷𝍷	15

Answer the questions.

2. Amy keeps track of the number of sit-ups she completes each day for four days. This frequency table shows her results.

   a. How many sit-ups does Amy complete on Friday and Saturday combined?

   33 sit-ups

Amy's Sit-Ups

Day	Frequency
Friday	15
Saturday	18
Sunday	21
Monday	24

b. This frequency table shows a pattern. How many more sit-ups does Amy complete from one day to the next?   **3 sit-ups**

c. The pattern continues for 3 more days. How many sit-ups does Amy complete on Tuesday, Wednesday, and Thursday?

27 sit-ups on Tuesday   30 sit-ups on Wednesday   33 sit-ups on Thursday

3. A group of people choose their favorite type of bagel. This frequency table shows the results.

   a. What is the most popular bagel flavor?

   plain

Favorite Bagels

Flavor	Frequency
plain	24
whole wheat	19
everything	16
cinnamon raisin	22

b. What is the least popular bagel flavor?   **everything**

c. How many people choose whole wheat or everything as their favorite bagel?   **35 people**

d. How many fewer people choose plain as their favorite bagel than whole wheat or everything combined?   **11 people**

Working with Frequency Tables

Students will solve problems to show that they understand how to interpret and record data in a frequency table.

Picture and Bar Graphs (B)

Lesson Overview

ACTIVITY	ACTIVITY TITLE	TIME	ONLINE/OFFLINE
GET READY	Introduction to Picture and Bar Graphs (B)	**2** minutes	🖥️
	Dividing Math Facts Game	**8** minutes	🖥️
LEARN AND **TRY IT**	Interpreting Scaled Picture Graphs	**7** minutes	🖥️
	Interpret Scaled Picture Graphs	**7** minutes	🖥️
	Drawing Scaled Picture Graphs	**7** minutes	🖥️
	Draw Scaled Picture Graphs	**7** minutes	🖥️
	Practice Working with Scaled Picture Graphs	**20** minutes	🖥️ and 📄
WRAP-UP	Working with Scaled Picture Graphs	**2** minutes	🖥️

Content Background

A picture graph is also called a pictograph. Students may have experience with picture graphs in which each symbol represents 1 object. Students will build on their previous knowledge to create and interpret scaled picture graphs with several categories. A scaled picture graph is one in which each symbol represents more than 1 object. As a result, half symbols are often needed.

In this picture graph, each symbol represents 2 people, so each half symbol represents 1 person. This data shows that 6 people study the clarinet, 12 people study the drums, 7 people study the flute, and 9 people study the trumpet.

MATERIALS

Supplied
- *Summit Math 3 Activity Book:* Practice Working with Scaled Picture Graphs

KEYWORDS

pictograph – a picture graph that shows information using picture symbols

picture graph – a graph that shows information using picture symbols

People Who Study Instruments	
Instrument	**Amount**
clarinet	🧍🧍🧍
drums	🧍🧍🧍🧍🧍🧍
flute	🧍🧍🧍🧍
trumpet	🧍🧍🧍🧍

Key: Each 🧍 = 2 people.

Students will interpret a scaled picture graph by answering questions, solving problems, and predicting future events. Students will create a scaled picture graph using data presented in a frequency table, a tally chart, or a description in words.

Lesson Goals

- Interpret picture graphs.
- Use picture graphs to solve problems.
- Use picture graphs to make predictions.
- Draw picture graphs.

GET READY

Introduction to Picture and Bar Graphs (B)

Students will get a glimpse of what they will learn about in the lesson. They will also read the lesson goals and keywords. Have students select each keyword and preview its definition.

Dividing Math Facts Game

Students will practice mixed division math facts.

LEARN AND TRY IT

LEARN   Interpreting Scaled Picture Graphs

Students will learn how to interpret scaled picture graphs.

TRY IT   Interpret Scaled Picture Graphs

Students will practice interpreting scaled picture graphs. Support will be provided to help students overcome misconceptions.

LEARN   Drawing Scaled Picture Graphs

Students will learn how to draw scaled picture graphs.

TRY IT   Draw Scaled Picture Graphs

Students will practice drawing scaled picture graphs. Support will be provided to help students overcome misconceptions.

TRY IT Practice Working with Scaled Picture Graphs

Students will complete online practice problems. Then they will complete Practice Working with Scaled Picture Graphs from *Summit Math 3 Activity Book*.

WRAP-UP

Working with Scaled Picture Graphs

Students will solve problems to show that they understand how to interpret and draw a scaled picture graph.

Picture and Bar Graphs (C)

Lesson Overview

ACTIVITY	ACTIVITY TITLE	TIME	ONLINE/OFFLINE
GET READY	Introduction to Picture and Bar Graphs (C)	**2** minutes	🖥️
	Multiplying and Dividing Math Facts	**8** minutes	🖥️
LEARN AND **TRY IT**	Interpreting Scaled Bar Graphs	**7** minutes	🖥️
	Interpret Scaled Bar Graphs	**7** minutes	🖥️
	Using Scaled Bar Graphs to Solve Problems	**7** minutes	🖥️
	Use Scaled Bar Graphs to Solve Problems	**7** minutes	🖥️
	Practice Working with Scaled Bar Graphs	**20** minutes	🖥️ and 📄
WRAP-UP	Working with Scaled Bar Graphs	**2** minutes	🖥️

Content Background

Students may have experience with bar graphs in which the scale counts by 1. In other words, where the distance from each grid line to the next is 1 unit. Students will build on their previous knowledge to interpret scaled bar graphs with several categories. A scaled bar graph has a scale greater than 1 unit. As a result, a bar sometimes reaches halfway between 2 grid lines.

In this bar graph, the distance from one grid line to the next is 4. The Tuesday bar reaches the line for 24 tickets. Notice that the Wednesday bar reaches halfway between the lines for 20 and 24. Since $4 \div 2 = 2$, half the distance from one line to the next is 2. The Wednesday bar reaches to 22 because $20 + 2 = 22$.

MATERIALS

Supplied
- *Summit Math 3 Activity Book:* Practice Working with Scaled Bar Graphs

KEYWORDS

bar graph – a graph that uses bars to show how much of a given category is in the data

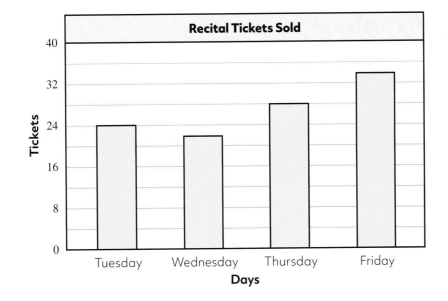

Recital Tickets Sold

Students will encounter some bar graphs with vertical bars and others with horizontal bars. Students will interpret a scaled bar graph by answering questions and predicting future events. Students will also answer "how many more" or "how many fewer" questions by solving problems with one or two steps using data from a scaled bar graph.

Lesson Goals

- Interpret bar graphs.
- Solve problems with one or two steps using bar graphs.
- Make predictions using scaled bar graphs.

GET READY

Introduction to Picture and Bar Graphs (C)
Students will get a glimpse of what they will learn about in the lesson. They will also read the lesson goals and keywords. Have students select each keyword and preview its definition.

Multiplying and Dividing Math Facts
Students will practice mixed multiplication and division math facts.

LEARN AND TRY IT

LEARN   Interpreting Scaled Bar Graphs
Students will learn how to interpret scaled bar graphs.

TRY IT   Interpret Scaled Bar Graphs

Students will practice interpreting scaled bar graphs. Support will be provided to help students overcome misconceptions.

LEARN   Using Scaled Bar Graphs to Solve Problems

Students will learn how to use scaled bar graphs to solve problems with one or two steps.

TRY IT   Use Scaled Bar Graphs to Solve Problems

Students will practice using scaled bar graphs to solve problems with one or two steps. Support will be provided to help students overcome misconceptions.

TRY IT   Practice Working with Scaled Bar Graphs

Students will complete online practice problems. Then they will complete Practice Working with Scaled Bar Graphs from *Summit Math 3 Activity Book*.

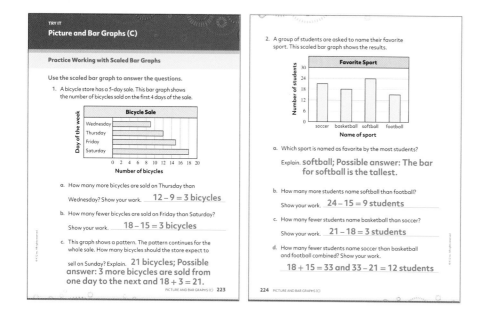

Working with Scaled Bar Graphs

Students will solve problems to show that they understand how to interpret and solve problems with a scaled bar graph.

Picture and Bar Graphs (D)

Lesson Overview

ACTIVITY	ACTIVITY TITLE	TIME	ONLINE/OFFLINE
GET READY	Introduction to Picture and Bar Graphs (D)	**2** minutes	🖥️
	Multiplying and Dividing with Instant Recall	**8** minutes	🖥️
LEARN AND **TRY IT**	Drawing Scaled Bar Graphs	**15** minutes	🖥️
	Draw Scaled Bar Graphs	**10** minutes	🖥️
	Practice Drawing Scaled Bar Graphs	**20** minutes	🖥️ and 📄
WRAP-UP	Drawing Scaled Bar Graphs	**5** minutes	🖥️

Content Background

Students will create scaled bar graphs using data presented in a scaled picture graph, a frequency table, a tally chart, or a description in words. Remind students that sometimes a bar reaches between two lines on a bar graph.

Lesson Goals

- Draw bar graphs.

GET READY

Introduction to Picture and Bar Graphs (D)

Students will get a glimpse of what they will learn about in the lesson. They will also read the lesson goals and keywords. Have students select each keyword and preview its definition.

Multiplying and Dividing with Instant Recall

Students will practice mixed multiplication and division math facts.

LEARN   Drawing Scaled Bar Graphs

Students will learn how to draw scaled bar graphs.

TRY IT   Draw Scaled Bar Graphs

Students will practice drawing scaled bar graphs. Support will be provided to help students overcome misconceptions.

TRY IT   Practice Drawing Scaled Bar Graphs

Students will complete online practice problems. Then they will complete Practice Drawing Scaled Bar Graphs from *Summit Math 3 Activity Book*.

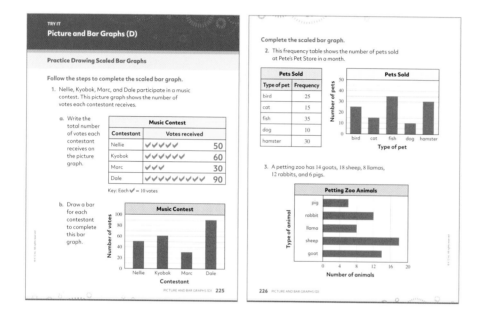

Drawing Scaled Bar Graphs

Students will solve a problem to show that they understand how to draw a scaled bar graph.

Picture and Bar Graphs (E)

Lesson Overview

ACTIVITY	ACTIVITY TITLE	TIME	ONLINE/OFFLINE
GET READY	Introduction to Picture and Bar Graphs (E)	**2** minutes	🖥️
TRY IT	Review Picture and Bar Graphs	**18** minutes	🖥️
QUIZ	Picture and Bar Graphs	**25** minutes	🖥️
WRAP-UP	More Math Practice	**15** minutes	🖥️

Lesson Goals

- Review working with frequency tables, picture graphs, and bar graphs.
- Take a quiz.

MATERIALS

There are no materials to gather for this lesson.

GET READY

Introduction to Picture and Bar Graphs (E)

Students will read the lesson goals.

TRY IT

Review Picture and Bar Graphs

Students will answer questions to review what they have learned about picture and bar graphs.

QUIZ

Picture and Bar Graphs

Students will complete the Picture and Bar Graphs quiz.

More Math Practice

Students will practice skills according to their individual needs.

Line Plots (A)

Lesson Overview

ACTIVITY	ACTIVITY TITLE	TIME	ONLINE/OFFLINE
GET READY	Introduction to Line Plots (A)	**2** minutes	🖥️
	Look Back at Plotting a Number on a Number Line	**8** minutes	🖥️
LEARN AND **TRY IT**	Interpreting Line Plots	**15** minutes	🖥️
	Interpret Line Plots	**10** minutes	🖥️
	Practice Interpreting Line Plots	**20** minutes	🖥️ and 📄
WRAP-UP	Interpreting Line Plots	**5** minutes	🖥️

Content Background

Students may have experience displaying measurement data in line plots in which the scale is marked in whole-number units. Students will build on their previous knowledge to interpret line plots where the scale is marked in halves and quarters. Students will interpret line plots by answering questions and solving problems with one or two steps.

MATERIALS

Supplied
- *Summit Math 3 Activity Book:* Practice Interpreting Line Plots

Lesson Goals

- Interpret data in line plots.

- Solve problems using line plots.

KEYWORDS

line plot – a number line that shows all the pieces of data with a mark or marks above each piece of data to show how many times that piece of data occurred

maximum – the greatest value for a data set

minimum – the least value for a data set

GET READY

Introduction to Line Plots (A)

Students will get a glimpse of what they will learn about in the lesson. They will also read the lesson goals and keywords. Have students select each keyword and preview its definition.

Look Back at Plotting a Number on a Number Line

Students will practice the prerequisite skill of plotting a number on a number line.

LEARN   Interpreting Line Plots

Students will learn how to interpret line plots.

TRY IT   Interpret Line Plots

Students will practice interpreting line plots. Support will be provided to help students overcome misconceptions.

TRY IT   Practice Interpreting Line Plots

Students will complete online practice problems. Then they will complete Practice Interpreting Line Plots from *Summit Math 3 Activity Book*.

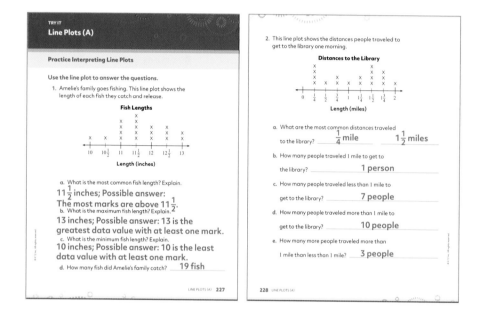

Interpreting Line Plots

Students will solve a problem to show that they understand how to interpret a line plot.

Line Plots (B)

Lesson Overview

ACTIVITY	ACTIVITY TITLE	TIME	ONLINE/OFFLINE
GET READY	Introduction to Line Plots (B)	**2** minutes	🖥️
	Multiplying and Dividing Math Facts Game	**8** minutes	🖥️
LEARN AND **TRY IT**	Drawing Line Plots Involving Whole Numbers	**15** minutes	🖥️
	Draw Line Plots Involving Whole Numbers	**10** minutes	🖥️
	Practice Drawing Line Plots Involving Whole Numbers	**20** minutes	🖥️ and 📄
WRAP-UP	Drawing Line Plots Involving Whole Numbers	**5** minutes	🖥️

Content Background

Students will create line plots to represent measurement data. In this lesson, all data represents measurements to the nearest whole number. As a result, the scale of each line plot will be marked off in whole-number units. Some data will be presented in a frequency table, while other data may be simply given as a list of numbers.

Lesson Goals

- Draw line plots with whole number scales.

MATERIALS

Supplied
- *Summit Math 3 Activity Book:* Practice Drawing Line Plots Involving Whole Numbers

KEYWORDS

line plot – a number line that shows all the pieces of data with a mark or marks above each piece of data to show how many times that piece of data occurred

GET READY

Introduction to Line Plots (B)

Students will get a glimpse of what they will learn about in the lesson. They will also read the lesson goals and keywords. Have students select each keyword and preview its definition.

Multiplying and Dividing Math Facts Game

Students will practice mixed multiplication and division math facts.

LEARN   Drawing Line Plots Involving Whole Numbers

Students will learn how to draw line plots with whole number scales.

TRY IT   Draw Line Plots Involving Whole Numbers

Students will practice drawing line plots with whole number scales. Support will be provided to help students overcome misconceptions.

TRY IT   Practice Drawing Line Plots Involving Whole Numbers

Students will complete online practice problems. Then they will complete Practice Drawing Line Plots Involving Whole Numbers from *Summit Math 3 Activity Book*.

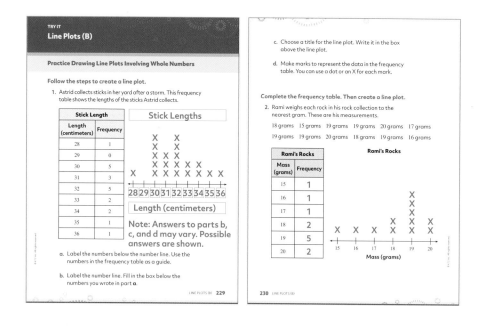

WRAP-UP

Drawing Line Plots Involving Whole Numbers

Students will solve a problem to show that they understand how to draw a line plot with a whole number scale.

Line Plots (C)

Lesson Overview

ACTIVITY	ACTIVITY TITLE	TIME	ONLINE/OFFLINE
GET READY	Introduction to Line Plots (C)	**2** minutes	🖥
	Dividing and Multiplying Math Facts Game	**8** minutes	🖥
LEARN AND **TRY IT**	Drawing Line Plots Involving Halves and Quarters	**15** minutes	🖥
	Draw Line Plots Involving Halves and Quarters	**10** minutes	🖥
	Practice Drawing Line Plots Involving Halves and Quarters	**20** minutes	🖥 and 📄
WRAP-UP	Drawing Line Plots Involving Halves and Quarters	**5** minutes	🖥

Content Background

Students will create line plots to represent measurement data. In this lesson, all data represents measurements to the nearest half or quarter unit. As a result, the scale of each line plot will be marked off in half or quarter units. Some data will be presented in a frequency table, while other data may be simply given as list of numbers.

Lesson Goals

- Draw line plots with scales that go by halves and quarters.

MATERIALS

Supplied
- *Summit Math 3 Activity Book:* Practice Drawing Line Plots Involving Halves and Quarters

KEYWORDS

line plot – a number line that shows all the pieces of data with a mark or marks above each piece of data to show how many times that piece of data occurred

---

GET READY

Introduction to Line Plots (C)

Students will get a glimpse of what they will learn about in the lesson. They will also read the lesson goals and keywords. Have students select each keyword and preview its definition.

Dividing and Multiplying Math Facts Game

Students will practice mixed division and multiplication math facts.

LEARN   Drawing Line Plots Involving Halves and Quarters

Students will learn how to draw line plots with scales that go by halves and quarters.

TRY IT   Draw Line Plots Involving Halves and Quarters

Students will practice drawing line plots with scales that go by halves and quarters. Support will be provided to help students overcome misconceptions.

TRY IT   Practice Drawing Line Plots Involving Halves and Quarters

Students will complete online practice problems. Then they will complete Practice Drawing Line Plots Involving Halves and Quarters from *Summit Math 3 Activity Book*.

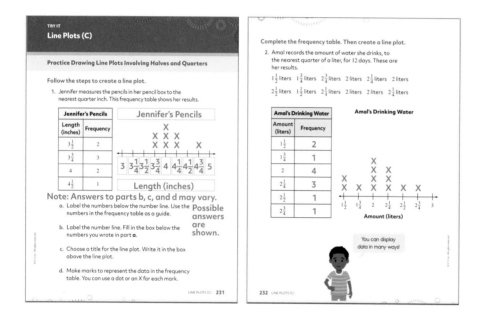

WRAP-UP

Drawing Line Plots Involving Halves and Quarters

Students will solve a problem to show that they understand how to draw line plots that go by halves and quarters.

Line Plots (D)

Lesson Overview

ACTIVITY	ACTIVITY TITLE	TIME	ONLINE/OFFLINE
GET READY	Introduction to Line Plots (D)	**2** minutes	🖥
TRY IT	Review Line Plots	**18** minutes	🖥
QUIZ	Line Plots	**25** minutes	🖥
WRAP-UP	More Math Practice	**15** minutes	🖥

Lesson Goals

- Review interpreting and drawing line plots.
- Take a quiz.

MATERIALS

There are no materials to gather for this lesson.

GET READY

Introduction to Line Plots (D)

Students will read the lesson goals.

TRY IT

Review Line Plots

Students will answer questions to review what they have learned about line plots.

QUIZ

Line Plots

Students will complete the Line Plots quiz.

WRAP-UP

More Math Practice

Students will practice skills according to their individual needs.

Big Ideas: Extended Problems

Lesson Overview

Big Ideas lessons provide students the opportunity to further apply the knowledge and skills acquired throughout previous units. Each Big Ideas lesson consists of two types of activities:

1. **Cumulative Review:** Students keep their skills fresh by reviewing prior content.

2. **Synthesis:** Students complete an assignment that allows them to interweave and apply what they've learned. These synthesis assignments will vary throughout the course.

In the Synthesis portion of this Big Ideas lesson, students will complete multistep problems that go beyond the short answer and multiple choice problems they encounter in their regular lessons. These problems give students an opportunity to demonstrate problem solving, reasoning, communication, and modeling skills. Students will need to use pencil and paper and/or technology to show their work.

LEARNING COACH CHECK-IN This is a graded assessment. Make sure students complete, review, and submit the assignment to their teacher.

All materials needed for this lesson are linked online. The materials are not provided in this Lesson Guide or in the Activity Book.

MATERIALS

Supplied
- Extended Problems Instructions (printout)

End-of-Year Project

End-of-Year Project

Project Overview

The end-of-year project is an extended, inquiry-based activity that is designed to build a deeper understanding of mathematics. Students use critical thinking skills and creativity as they explore an authentic, real-world problem. The project cuts across curricular areas, showing the impact and relevance of math while building twenty-first-century skills.

The project is structured around a driving question that is both engaging and relevant to students and their community. To find answers to the question, students will apply the mathematics they already know and then expand their knowledge to fill in the gaps. They will create and submit a final product that demonstrates what they have learned.

To complete the project, students should

1. Download the project packet.

2. Read the instructions and complete the project.

3. Submit the project.

   LEARNING COACH CHECK-IN This is a graded assessment. Make sure students complete, review, and submit the end-of-year project to their teacher.

All materials needed for this project are linked online. The materials are not provided in this Lesson Guide or in the Activity Book.

Advance Preparation

Read the project packet. Gather any required materials.

MATERIALS

Supplied
- project packet (printout)